To Georges

Thx for all your help tonight!

Thx xxx

Phily

PHIL TAGGART'S SLACKER GUIDE TO THE MUSIC INDUSTRY

Phil Taggart gave me this, but now it's all yours!

Keep your head up bro!

Phil Taggart's Slacker Guide to The Music Industry

Written By: Phil Taggart + Steven Rainey

All Illustrations by Chris Coll @hauntedboystuf

Published By Slacker Night Ltd

This book has been produced with support from Help Musicians UK.
A percentage of profits will go to Help Musicians UK.

ISBN 978-1-9160376-0-1
E Book ISBN 978-1-9160376-1-8

This first edition published in Great Britain in 2019
Printed by Akcent Media

PHIL
TAGGART'S
SLACKER
GUIDE
TO THE
MUSIC
INDUSTRY

In Memory of (Aunty) Mary Monaghan
1949 - 2018

Contents

Getting Started 21
The First Steps in Making Music 37
The First Gig 55
Music Videos 73
Building a Fanbase 89
Management 109
Image 127
Funding 143
Record Label 165
Publishing 183
D.I.Y 195
Recording The EP/Album 209
Distribution + Streaming 227
Radio 243
Online + Print Media PR 259
Booking Agents 277
Touring + Festivals 295
Merchandise 315
How to Make Money 335
Self-Care in Music 341

Thank You's

I have a lot of people to be thankful to... so stand by.

I thank my mum for being my guiding light in life and allowing me the freedom to get to where I am. She deserves many medals. I am thankful to my wife for the love, support, and endless levels of understanding. My God ... the understanding: I haven't shut up about this book for two years. I am thankful to my Aunty Mary for her affection and endless encouragement which I miss dearly. I am thankful to my sister for being a total rock. I am thankful to all of the strong women in my family. I am a very lucky man.

Thank you to Steven Rainey who has co-written/edited this book with me. He has the patience of a saint and is almost as talented as an editor/writer as he is at Warhammer or whatever nerdy game he plays. Thank you to Darach MacDonald for proof-reading the book and keeping it in the family.

Thanks also to:

My Family, Micky McCullagh, Zoe Rainey, Sam Gregory, Nico Taylor (Formatter), Chris Coll (IIllustrator), Jack Smyth (Front Cover Design), Akcent Media, Sam Jennings, James Moodie, Becky Anderson, Hometown Records, Johnny Le-Van-Gilroy, Help Musicians UK, BBC Music Introducing, BBC Radio 1, Ben Cooper, Aled Hayden Jones, Bob Shennan, BBC Radio Ulster, Paul McClean, Rory McConnell, TOUTS, Dad, Omagh and its enduring legacy as a Music Town, Fergal Lindsay, Paul Mellon, Myles McCann's Bar, Huw Stephens, Top of the Town, All the bands who filled out questionnaires, Stuart Bailie, Rocky O'Reilly, Rigsy, Auntie Annies, 78 Melrose Street, Gerry Norman, Colenso Parade, Dennis Monaghan, all the

Monaghans, all the Taggarts, Sam MacDonald, India MacDonald, Theo MacDonald, All the McArdles, Barney Leigh, Rat Boy, all the bands I've Played on the radio, Jason Carter, Shane Daunt, Mick Roe, Ken Allen, Angela Dorgan, Tommy Davis, Phil Stocker, everyone at the Oh Yeah Music Centre, Joe Lindsay, Carolyn Mathers, producer Jacob, producer Jay, Joe Frankland, Milli Nuckchaddy, James Moodie, Ali Tant, CBS Omagh, St Colmcille's PS, my deceased grandparents (Margret, John, James, Bridget), Niall Fox, The Auld Shillelagh, 73 Forest Road Crew, The Slacker Podcast Team, Graham Smith, Tommy Davis, Robert Stainforth, Mark Gordon, Carolyn Mathers, Lyndon Stephens, John Thompson, Al + Iain + Martha at Machine Management, all collaborators.

Thanks to all the people I have forgotten anyone whose ear I've ever bent over the years about this book.

Thank you to every single band, artist and person in the music industry who featured in the book and gave up their time to do so.

To all musicians and songwriters everywhere!

adidas

Introduction to the Author

Phil Taggart was born in Derry, Northern Ireland. He grew up in Omagh, playing music and getting kicked out of classrooms at school. For nine years, he played bass in Colenso Parade in scuzzy venues all around the UK and Ireland, while supporting many touring bands (Richard Hawley, Dirty Pretty Things) coming through Ireland.

At university, Phil won the BBC Skillset Young Broadcaster of the Year Award for his documentary on 'The Representation of Women in the Music Industry'. He has been a DJ on BBC Radio 1 since 2012, breaking countless new bands and artists on his night-time shows. He was nominated for the 'Rising Star Award' at the Sony Awards (now ARIAS) during his first year at the station. He started Hometown Records in 2014 and is still actively releasing bands and artists in 2019.

The book was co-written and edited by Steven Rainey. He's had as much luck in bands as Phil had. The jury's still out on whose band was better.

Follow Phil on Twitter + Instagram:
@philytaggart

For Everything Slacker + Merchandise + Books:
www.philtaggartslacker.com

For speaking engagements, conferences, workshops
or consultation please contact:
Sam Gregory at **sam.gregory@bigredtalent.com**

Introduction to the Book

Welcome to the *Slacker Guide to the Music Industry*. This book is designed to help every single person who lives and breathes music. This is for the people that want the exposure their music deserves, and who want to make a career from their creativity and passion. It's not the easiest road to navigate and it's taken me over two years researching, interviewing, and writing to complete the piece you are reading right now. You might be thinking, "Who does this guy think he is? How can you claim to comprehensively know everything about the music industry?" The answer is, I don't: there's not a person alive that understands every single facet of this spaghetti junction industry. However I do have access to the artists who've already walked this path and gained their stripes, as well as the industry leaders forging the future in their own respective lanes.

I started playing in bands when I was 14 years old. All I ever wanted to do was play music with my best friends and in turn become the biggest rock and roll band in the history of mankind. Is that really too much to ask for? It turns out after 9 years in the band, that it wasn't on the cards for us. Every year in the band, this journey brought a whole rollercoaster of ups and downs. There were a million little things you need to be on top of, and when you don't have a manager or a record label to lean on, it can get massively confusing. I used to go to music industry seminars, one to ones, workshops, anything that looked like it might remotely help me figure this whole thing out. When I was 17, I'd travel the length of Ireland to go and sit in a room to play someone my demo only for them to 'not get it'. The rejection was tough to take, the near wins were even tougher, but for every wrong turn there was an incredible show to play, for every knock back there was a eureka moment in the studio. I wouldn't swap a second of it for any amount.

When the band called it a day, I got a job manning the helm of a night time new music show on BBC Radio 1. I started out to be in a band and I ended up on the radio breaking new music. It is a daily dream giving new bands and artists the exposure they deserve night in, night out. I love radio and it was the hustle I learned from being in a band that got me there.

After having nothing but negative experiences in my old band with record labels, I decided that I was going to start a label that was artist friendly, that was fair, and that wouldn't deal in the currency of bullshit. Hometown Records was born. I've learnt a huge amount from the label and the acts I've worked with, making mistakes and memories along the way. No matter how much you learn or how much you 'think you know', fuck ups are inevitable.

This book is all the shit you need to know in one place. It's something you can leaf into if you need a bit of guidance, or something I hope gives you a realistic look at what's to come. I tried to make this as true to life as possible, and hope that it will inspire some of you to become the artist you want to be. I wrote this so that you would have more time to spend writing music and less time scratching your head trying to figure out the rest of it. The better your music, the easier this whole process will be.

FEATURED CONTRIBUTORS

Ali Tant (Polydor Records), Alistair White (Machine Management), Annie Mac (BBC Radio 1, DJ), Aoife McArdle (Director), Bry, Bryony October (Tour Manager), Cal McRae (Promoter), Cam Blackwood (Record Producer), Charli XCX, Charlene Hegarty (Manager/Oh Yeah Belfast), Chris Price (BBC Radio 1 Head of Music), Cheylene Murphy (Honeymoon PR), Claire Coulton (Senior Entertainment Publicist), Claudia de Wolff (Vevo), Connie Meade (AMF Records/Virgin), Darcus Beese (Head of Island Records), Darren McSorley (Web Designer), Deborah Sheedy (Artist), Dream Wife, Enter Shikari, Frank Turner, George Ezra, Hinds, Iain Archer (Songwriter), Ian Watt (Machine Management), Izzy B Phillips (Black Honey), James Passmore (Radio Plugger/National Anthem Records), James Spankie (Soundman), Jamie Oborne (Manager: The 1975), Joe Frankland (PRS Foundation), Julie McLarnon (Record Producer), Jungle, Kendal Calling, Kevin Baird (Two Door Cinema Club), Little Simz, Frank Turner, Loyle Carner, Lucy Rose, Lyndon Stephens (Manager), Martha Kinn (Machine Management), Matt Bates (Primary Talent), Matt Riley (Kobalt/Awal), Mike Smith (Warner/Chappell Publishing), Music Glue, Nao, Nialler 9 (Blogger/Journalist), Ollie Hodges (A + R Polydor Records), Phoebe Fox (Photographer), Rachel Holmberg (Former BBC Music Introducing/Current: Decca Records), Ray BLK, Rory Friers (ASIWYFA), Roisin O'Connor (Journalist), Run the Jewels, Ryan Bassil (Noisey), Soak, Shura, Simon Pursehouse (Sentric Music), Slaves, Simon Bush (Social Media Manager), Simon Neil

(Biffy Clyro), Stephen Agnew (Music Video Director), Steven Taverner (Manager), Steve Tilly (Killimanjiro), Tara Richardson (Manager), Terrible Merch, The Hunna, Tom + Joe (Blossoms), Twin B (BBC 1Xtra + Atlantic Records), Wolf Alice

C'MON KID, WANNA BE WORLD CHAMPION?
SHUT THE FUCK UP!!
EXIT
THAT G'S A LITTLE OFF..
I ♥ KILMARNOCK
ADELE'S FANCY FISH
RECIPE
3oz SALT
4oz BUTTER
10'000 FISH
TWAT
DEREK
PAPA'S ASHES
ASS SLAPPIN TECHNO
DEMOS #2
DEMOS #1
PRACTICE 1997
BAND MIX #2
JAM '03
RUN THE JEWELS
VINO

Getting Started

FEATURING ADVICE FROM:
Charli XCX
Hinds
Lyndon Stephens (Manager)
Simon Neill - Biffy Clyro
Run the Jewels
Wolf Alice

'It's not too late to turn back; there's still time.'

That would be my advice to anyone half-hearted or on the fence when considering a life's work making music.

On the other hand, if the notion of rock stars falling from coconut trees on private islands, revolving drum risers, and a litter of overzealous fans is what you live for, you may be better suited to finding an alternative, because those days are gone. At least, I think they are.

Creating and writing music is an incredibly rewarding and satisfying vocation. It has been the pastime and cultural signifier of humans since Derek the Caveman realised slapping his ass (and his neighbour Clive's) at regular intervals made for quite an enjoyable sound. Which is, coincidentally, how techno was invented.

Much of this process is private – laying out your joys, fears, anxieties and love through sonic creation and lyricism. This is not what this book is designed to help with. It's the public side of things I hope to help, getting your music from the brain to the practice room, studio, and beyond.

The entry-level moment of any project can be a real clusterfuck of emotions; you've got the flurry of excitement but on the flip side, absolutely no idea what to do or how to build a career out of your music. Everyone in music has faced this. I'm sure when Adele worked in that fish and chip shop as a teenager, she was plagued with doubts, wondering, 'How do I become one of the world's most well known voices?' while battering a piece of hake rapidly approaching its 'use by' date.

It's a long and winding road from the start to the end goal, and your parameters of what it means to be successful will most likely change many times along the way. The main thing at this stage is to go for it! I've always believed enthusiasm – if done right – can trounce experience. You just have to get stuck in, make mistakes, make more mistakes, and plough ahead with resilience, knowing that your music needs to be heard by the world.

Most bands at the beginning won't have a clue what to do, and that's kind of the fun of it. When starting off at the bottom, your progress will be incremental, fast and noticeable, not least to your tortured neighbours or rehearsal space pals. If a baby can learn to talk and walk in 18 months, you can learn to play 'Seven Nation Army' with a band in the same amount of time, right?

Getting the band or act together can be one of the most frustrating things for any furtive music-maker. I was fairly lucky: I made music with three of my best friends, with no prior knowledge of how to play an instrument, so we all sucked together at the same pace for the first few years. However, for many, finding the perfect bassist, a drummer that's not a total monster, or a guitarist without a messiah complex, can be an abject nightmare.

There's no real definitive answer on how you put a band together, as it can be done in so many ways. One of the best methods, I've discovered in my years spent in and around bands, is also the most obvious – friends. People you already get on with, people you can be yourself around, create with, and most importantly, people you can enjoy spending time with. That's a big one, especially when it comes to touring. If Big Matey McMaterson is one of your favourite people in the whole world, and loves music, then fire a bass at him/her and tell them to learn it. Alternatively you can go down the twisted dictator route, and rule everything with an iron fist, draft in keen musicians from your area, or like-minded souls online. Or just go full Bob Dylan, and brave it alone. The only person who can make this decision is you; you know your needs and how much you want to share and create with other people.

One word of warning: lazy people are a waste of space in a band. It doesn't matter if you have the world's greatest guitarist. If they won't bother their ass to turn up to practice, and put the hours in, they will slow you down way more in the long run. It's better to have a band of average musicians eager and willing to learn and improve, than a band full of loafers who have pots of potential, and quarries of excuses.

'You can choose your friends, but you sho' can't choose your family.'

So wrote Harper Lee in her classic novel, To Kill a Mockingbird. And y'know, she was right. That's one of the benefits of having friends – you get to pick which ones you want.

And when you look at Biffy Clyro as they lay assault to stages across the world, it's hard to imagine Simon Neill, James Johnston, and Ben Johnston as anything other than the last gang in town. But that relationship has to start somewhere, and for Biffy, it was in the Scottish town of Kilmarnock.

'I played violin from an early age, so I had music in my bones,' explains Simon Neil. But, given that he's not getting a crowd fired up with a particularly energetic fiddle solo, something happened that knocked this potential classical prodigy off his musical course. 'It was a Nirvana music video that made me pick up the guitar. When I saw Nirvana, I saw three guys that wanted to make music with no aspirations to make something pretty.'

That musical union between Neil and the Johnston twins, plus original guitarist Boyan Chowdury, earned the band a following locally, allowing them to cut their teeth, and develop as a band.

'It was really just to create something for us in our world

that I could play to my friends, and impress my family with, and say, "Hey, we've got a band." It was just a will to join this world I knew existed.'

And even though it was all tentative at this stage, once you're in that world, you've got to know that there are people around you that you can rely on.

'The joy was in playing together, getting drunk together, having a smoke together, and just being a nuisance. When you're a teenager, you want to be a nuisance. My friends and family didn't like our music. They thought it was way too abrasive. At that age we had a chip on our shoulder; we had a crazy band name, and we wanted to make crazy music that annoyed people. There'd be a rap on the door, and we'd get told to "Shut the fuck up!" That emboldened us, and we would think, "Yes we're not accepted, we're doing something right"'.

Even still, it took a few years before the rest of the world caught up with this self-confidence, and Chowdury left the band, joining up with The Zutons in Liverpool, leaving Biffy Clyro as a three-piece, just like their heroes Nirvana.

For Wolf Alice bassist Theo Ellis, hero worship also provided that kick-start to get involved with music but, in this case, it was an act a little closer to home.

'I remember the first time seeing The Horrors play when I was fifteen, and seeing all these different people who were the coolest people on earth, and this whole energy and scene. It made me instantly want to be a part of something like that, and to bring loads of like-minded people together. Music was such an exciting thing for me.'

From that seed, he embarked on his own musical journey, picking up the bass. And right from the start, you have to put the time in, or it isn't going to go anywhere.

'Practising an instrument is the foundation of everything you're going to do. You can talk the talk, and have a cool jacket and a pair of shoes, but if you can't play, you can't play.'

For drummer Joel Amey there was something about the band that just clicked.

'I did have this youthful determination when I was in my first band to put a record out and tour the world. We were kind of naïve and hyper-excited all the time. Then when I joined Wolf Alice, I wanted to do it because it was so much fun. That's when I stopped trying so hard, and started enjoying gigs and music for the right reason, which is really for the love of it. It was weird how things started happening more. We see a lot of bands that are deadly serious, and very on the nose from day one. It can put people off.'

That sense of enjoyment is palpable. And since the release of that first single in 2012, Wolf Alice have continued a steady rise to the forefront of contemporary indie music. But even though success is something that most bands aim for, they haven't let it get in the way of why they got involved with music in the first place, as Theo explains.

'I think if my thoughts were permeated with it being a career, I would have done things differently, and probably would be too careful and worried about it. The abandon and happiness and joy of playing together made it more attractive to watch our band, and that's why it now is a career. The most important thing is to love it.'

It's naïve to think that every single artist out there is truly in love with what they're doing. Just ask the dude who sang 'Blurred Lines'. Nobody could, presumably, love that song. It's going to help a lot in the long term if you actually have passion and really care for your music.

'I was just such a fan of music that I wanted to create it eventually,' says El-P, producer and rapper, and one half of hip hop Lords Run the Jewels.

'I was lucky my dad had a piano and a drum set and big vinyl collection. Music was always around in that early phase of my life. I got lucky because when I went from hobbyist to making my own music, it was an easy transition for me, because I didn't have that wall, thinking, "This is an impossible feat." I saw that it wasn't that hard, you just have to get obsessed with it.'

That obsession has helped Run the Jewels become one of the most critically acclaimed hip hop acts of the 2010s. Their third self-titled album scored a top 20 placing in the US charts and brought El-P and his partner, Killer Mike from Kings of the Underground, into the mainstream. And for Killer Mike, even though the record sales and acclaim seem to just keep building and building, there's still plenty of basic work that needs to be done, a lot of which takes place in the rehearsal room.

'We leave our sister cities (Atlanta and New York) and we go to Nashville, Tennessee, and we stay between one and three weeks to rehearse until necessary, to give you the best show possible. Before you can do cool shit and improvise and chat shit to the audience, you need to know your show.'

This commitment to working things out in the rehearsal room is something El-P echoes.

'Don't worry about being good yet. Don't run out and try and get criticism and feedback until you really have had that time alone to have fun with it, and to stumble around. Treat it as a craft. Wait, let yourself be your audience for a long time, until you're seeing progression in what you're doing. When you get to a point when you objectively like the song, not just, "I am psyched that I am making a song," then ok, yeah, start the process of sharing.'

Once you have it nailed down, or once you think you have it nailed down, then you can get on with the all-important work of putting your music out there in the world. And given the world we live in now, sometimes the difference between the real world and the digital world can get a little obscured.

'I got booked for shows via Myspace because that's where my music was,' says Charli XCX, one of those rare artists that makes straddling the commercial and the critical arena look easy. Her albums and mixtapes have picked up plaudits from across the critical spectrum, something which hasn't stopped her from being a genuinely 'popular' pop artist.

And while any number of earnest young musicians with guitars were making a racket in practice rooms up and down the country, she was taking a different route altogether.

'It was at these raves where I would basically turn up with an iPod with my songs on them and sing over them. I didn't have a band or anything like that.'

And while she didn't have a band, she did have something perhaps even more important – the support of her parents. Which is totally cool, right?

'I'd be playing at a rave at 3am when I was fourteen. None of my friends could go, and my parents were taking me to the rave. I wanted to die; I felt so uncool. I'm in such a cool place and my parents are fucking it up for me.'

A mum and dad's job is to fuck up a teenager's life, at least from their perspective.

'I was making music at my parents' house. I had a Yamaha Keyboard, you know the one you would hit a button and it would say "DJ" and two karaoke mics. I would just make beats on that and record it on an eight-track mini-box I had.'

And from such humble beginnings, something special emerged. However, it wasn't a straight journey from the bedroom to the charts, and with the benefit of hindsight, Charli XCX is able to see that rushing into things isn't always the best plan.

'Don't put everything on the internet. Think about the future. When you are making music, you have no hindsight and think it's great. Now, I listen to the stuff I put up when I was fourteen and think, "Oh no, it's so bad!" I'm at peace with it now.'

Most of the time, these things aren't as embarrassing as

you think they are, and no matter how half-baked something might seem in retrospect, there's a good chance whoever is listening has heard a lot worse. Unless, of course, your music is truly, truly awful, in which case maybe you should grow a thinner skin and start listening to criticism.

But for the rest of us, it's hard not to be a little sensitive, especially when you're also being judged by your peers, something that Wolf Alice's Joel Amey doesn't let concern him.

'Spend less time worrying about what other bands are doing and spend more time focusing on what you are doing. It's very easy to want to rush into every situation; it's exciting, and there's always that fear that if you say no to something, you won't get that again. You should trust your gut, trust your decision-making.'

But sometimes your gut is telling you that things are wrong, or at the very least, confusing. In which case, there's no shame in running away to regroup.

'There will probably be a point where there'll be a lot of internal factors telling you what to think. It can be really tough in that situation. If you are young, it's good to take a break and reconsider.'

After all, you don't have to do anything that you don't want to, and not everyone gets into the music business for the same reasons. And while it might sometimes seem like the whole industry is designed to chew you up and spit you out, Charli XCX has found the reality to be quite different.

'There's a real myth about the music industry, that it's hard to get into, and that there is only one aspect, and that's to be a huge musician. There are so many different roads you can take. You could be a touring artist and be successful and not be on the radio. You could be a songwriter, a producer, work at a management company. It's definitely a good career to get into, and when you get your foot through the door, the world is actually quite small and easy to navigate. As long as you're not a twat.'

Which is good advice for many things, not just wanting to be a musician. However, if you are a twat, please re-read the above statement.

Biffy Clyro aren't twats. But before they became Biffy Clyro, Biffy Clyro had to become Biffy Clyro. If you know what I mean.

This process takes years, not just for Biffy Clyro, but for all of us. And at the end, it's likely that we'll have learned something about each other along the way.

'When you are making music with people, don't worry about their technique levels,' states Simon Neil, someone who is no slouch on his instrument, it must be said. 'Make sure you like who you are playing music with, because then you can overcome anything.'

It sounds like a platitude, but in this case it seems to be true. The three-piece blazed a trail from their hometown across the UK, building up an incredibly strong grassroots following that took them to the very top of the music world. And in a world still dominated by hype and gimmicks, they did it the old-fashioned way, through sheer hard graft, something they seemed prepared to do, right from the beginning.

'I don't think you should ever start a band with a view to making money. That's when you paint yourself into a corner, or become something that you don't want to be. Whenever you start thinking about money, it's kind of the death knell. If you want to make money, go work for a bank. There are plenty of ways to make money. Financial ambition is the enemy of any kind of creativity.'

But in Biffy Clyro's case, that amount of talent didn't go unnoticed for long. And in a world where the music machine exists to make money, occasionally at the expense of art, it looked like their big break was destined to be a disaster.

'The day we got signed to Beggars Banquet, we played

one of the worst shows we ever played. I burst my finger on the guitar. I could barely strum, and Ben's drums broke. However the A+R guy, Roger, liked this. He saw the fight in us, the belief. Sometimes you can think you are having the worst show ever, but there can be something magical happening. It doesn't always compute in your mind why someone else likes what you do. That was a perfect example for me, because I thought we'd blown it and the opportunity was gone.'

And despite the burst finger and the broken drums, Biffy Clyro forged a relationship with Beggars Banquet. However, while there's a certain amount of financial freedom now to make more and more ambitious records, at the start, much like Charli XCX, it was a bit more low-rent.

'The limitations you have when you start give you strength when you grow. We made our first album on one amplifier each, one pedal, and one guitar. We didn't feel prohibited at all."

Obviously, the record-buying public agreed, and thus the unusually monikered Biffy Clyro began the slow climb to the top. And as the fans began to hitch a ride, Simon Neil has seen all manner of scenes come and go, and watched plenty of other bands fall by the wayside.

'You should feel like it's you against the world when you start as a band. Don't try and join scenes or cliques. Impress your friends, the people you're making music with. That's what it's all about. You should feel like you know something other people don't.'

So, whether it be slogging it out on the local gig circuit, becoming an online sensation, or just trying to create a cool scene around you, there are plenty of ways to make something happen. But there are also plenty of pitfalls.

If you care about what you do, then most of these things should take care of themselves. Which is not to say that there won't be a small amount of fine tuning. But if you've found the right combination of people, you're making the right sound, and you're excited by what you do, then perhaps the time has come to take things further, as Run the Jewels' El-P tells us.

'If the passion is there and the relationships are there with the musicians you're playing with, then you will come up with something. It just may take a minute. Enjoy the moment, enjoy the freedom and experimental time, figuring out who you are. Don't rush into it, have that moment for yourself, because when you put it out there, then you are in a career.'

TOP 10 TIPS TO STARTING A BAND

HINDS

Don't Choose a Joke Name

Make Merchandise Immediately

Go See Live Music In Your Town/City As Much As You Can

Believe in Your Shit

Bring On Tour More Underwear Than You Think You Need

6
Appear In Your First Music Video

7
Don't Kill Your Bandmates

8
Go to the Studio With the Purpose of Changing the World

9
Involve Your Friends in Your Project

10
Never Forget That the Role of the Artist is to
Make the Revolution Irresistible

Chimp-Shave Salon!
HOW'Z THAT, KID?
GEORGE EZRA
STAYING AT TAMARA'S
KFC
RECORD ALBUM
BUY MILK
FIND DRUMMER
REMEMBER, MY DADDY'S FUNDIN' THIS BAND, OK?
SET LIST
?
FRAGILE
RECORD ENGINEER
POWER: 10
AGILITY: 10
MEMORY: 9
SASS: 10
RAD RECORD CARDS!
VINO LUX
NASTY
CHEAPO BEER!
CAM BLACKWOOD'S BIG GUIDE TO RECORDING
IAIN ARCHER: THE SONGWRITING BIBLE

The First Steps In Making Music

FEATURING ADVICE FROM:
Cam Blackwood (George Ezra Producer)
Dream Wife
Frank Turner
Iain Archer
Jungle
Little Simz

So at this point, the dreams and the reality are at odds with each other. You've got the bare bones of your idea, and now you're dreaming of living life as a critically revered artist with caviar dripping from your jowls. However, either you've not actually got any recorded material, or the stuff you have recorded sounds like someone taped a dictaphone to the back wall of a dog pound.

Getting to that idyllic musical nirvana is going to take some serious work.

At this stage, the creative process is the most important thing in the world. It sounds like a basic and obvious concept, but while it's easy to get carried away with all the other tropes that come with music (gigs / image / branding / social media), nothing else in your career will fall into place without incredible tunes.

Recently, the manager of an act with two fairly average songs contacted me and was talking about the band's brand partnerships, clothing line, and own bespoke beer range. And all I could think was, "Who the fuck wants to buy merch from an average band at the start of their career?" They need to be in the practice room and in the studio, building the foundations for what's to come with their music. This is a time for finding out who you are sonically, and for making mistakes, and discovering the artist you intend to be by putting the hours in, not selling branded booze at a half-empty show.

From years of selecting music for my radio show on BBC Radio 1, I have found and spun music recorded in a myriad of ways, from artists that have recorded directly into their laptop, or had one microphone in the middle of a room, all the way through to having recorded with some of the world's elite producers.

Frankly, I couldn't give a shaved baboon bum about how it's recorded.

That's not to say you should just throw a microphone round a lampshade, hit 'record' and hope for the best. You have to identify the type of music you want to make and how best for it to be represented. For example, if you are a Pop Prince/Princess you are probably going to benefit better from a polished production. If strumming acoustic ballads is your sound, then lo-fi can work a charm. There is no definitive way to go about recording music. Just trust your gut and your ears.

Financing, or money in general, is the biggest hurdle for 99% of acts looking to record their music. Unless you are the son or daughter of KFC's finest Colonel Sanders, finding enough money to hire a recording studio, or buy the required equipment to record at home, is going to be hard. This is the first of many sacrifices you will face as a musician, and probably the most necessary of them all. Even if you are shit-hot live, the word of mouth will only go so far, and you'll need some ace recordings to represent the best 'you' possible. So in this chapter we will talk to recording engineers, artists, and producers alike to give you an insight into each of their worlds.

When my own band started out we pretty much tried everything, from recording on a rubbish digital eight-track in school, placing a microphone in the middle of my garage, to finally working up enough cash from gigs and pocket money to plant ourselves in a studio. It took a lot of binned recording sessions to finally get something we were happy with. Don't freak out or lose faith if it doesn't work first time. I know plenty of successful artists on their second record who, after fifty attempts, struggle to pour what's in their head onto a wav form. Persistence and love is key.

Recording engineers are a beautiful and odd breed. If they were Pokemon cards, they would be Shiny Charizards: fiery and rare. Try your best to find common ground with them on the first day, and they'll usually do the same with you. A happy relationship will mean a happy engineer, and that means – yep – better recordings. If that fails, bribe them with snacks.

If your engineer isn't playing ball, is in a mood, or is just not interested, and you're left staring at the back of their head wondering what's happening, just remind yourself that you are paying for this pleasure. Get firm and make sure they're helping you realise the sound you are after. It costs too much money to walk away with recordings you're deeply unhappy with. If this does happen, it's only a set-back.

Alternatively, get yourself the equipment and give it a go at home. To get the best results, you'll really want to have a love and fascination with recording music. It may take a long time to master the techniques of home recording, but it does mean you have the freedom to record at your leisure, without the albatross of expensive studio time leaking gold coins out of your already stretched purse.

If all else fails, then find an obscure artist nobody has heard of, assume their identity and pass their recordings off as your own. Although if you do this, I suggest you get a good lawyer and PR team.

'We started off with a laptop, a basic interface and one microphone,' explains T of neo-soul mystics Jungle. 'When we were making our first record in 2013, the laptop was full, and the fan didn't work. The summer was so hot that we had a huge metal fan pointing directly at the laptop to cool it down. The best ideas don't need technology.'

Technological hiccups or not, Jungle have shown that it's possible to overcome these kind of problems, and the band, led by J & T, took their first two albums into the UK top ten. Nobody saw Jungle coming. Their journey into music was unique. And as J outlines, the days of having to spend a small fortune just to demo your music, never mind record it for commercial release, appear to be over.

'We're at a stage now where people don't really go in and record anything anymore; it's all done at home. A lot of people have the technology to do it at home, and that's a massive change over the last ten years. That's where the heart and soul is - the things you make off-the-cuff.'

That playful experimentalism is a key aspect of Jungle's sound, and their creative process.

'All of our best ideas have come from things that have happened in five minutes. We worked on tracks for three or four months, and the one that was made in three or four minutes has often been better.'

But lest this seem like some kind of mantra you should adopt yourself, J is keen to point out that there aren't really any rules when it comes to the music Jungle makes.

'There is no right or wrong way to make music. Often the wrong way of doing it is the right way. Trying to follow the right way means you are following other people's guidelines in how to make and record music, and that can be quite corrosive. Trust your own ear; trust what you like instead of what other people like.'

Trusting in your own ear applies to more than just listening to your own music. And for Frank Turner, keeping abreast of other people's music is simply part of the writing process.

'I spend a lot of my time examining other people's songwriting. If there's a song that transports you either lyrically or logically to an interesting place, then I try and figure out why it did that.'

This analytical approach has paid dividends for Turner, who has probably played every tiny club or pub in the country after his exit from punk thrashers Million Dead. And over the course of a decade, he has steadily built up his audience, graduating to concert halls and stadiums, all the while maintaining an immaculately crafted goatee.

'A song is a simple but complex thing. The best songs in the world are the most simple songs, and they are the hardest to write. I've realised Abba and NOFX have more in common than what separates them, as they're engaged in the same artistic endeavour, and that is songwriting.'

While it's possible to imagine NOFX having a bash at 'Dancing Queen', it's somewhat harder to picture Abba giving 'Brain Constipation' a studio shakedown. But still, we know what Frank means, though perhaps his own earliest efforts had more of a foot in the 'punk' camp, than 'pop'.

'I started playing guitar when I was ten, and I started jamming with friends in my bedroom when I was eleven. Pretty early on, I started writing, bringing together four random chords and shouting lyrics I wrote in my school notebook. I wasn't any good for a very long time, but right from the beginning I wanted to participate.'

It all sounds a world away from the sophisticated troubadour he later became, but that's the thing about songwriting: for most people, the more you do, the better you get at it. And given how Turner's commercial prospects incrementally increased with each new release, he's proof that just because you start out doing one thing, it doesn't mean that you have to do that for the rest of your creative life.

'It's easy to get caught in certain habits and certain approaches, and I often try and find ways of tripping myself up and pushing myself out of my melodic and lyrical comfort zones. I try things like playing on piano rather than guitar, or changing the key to find ways not to repeat myself.'

This idea of testing yourself, of pushing your own boundaries can be one of the most satisfying parts of songwriting.

For some writers, the creative process is almost like an emotional exorcism, an opening of one's internal floodgates in an attempt to understand or cope with traumatic experiences. And while this has undoubtedly produced some incredibly powerful music, it's not always the easiest or most pleasant experience for the writer to go through. And when you're pouring your pain onto the page on a regular basis, it's sometimes easy to forget that this whole process is meant to be a positive experience.

'Enjoy it. It's meant to be fun, love it.'

Little Simz is inspiration incarnate. She is one of the most exciting MC's in the country releasing mixtapes and EPs to an ever-increasing audience, before crossing over to a bigger platform, releasing three highly-rated albums and collaborating with Gorillaz. And for her, it's easy to get wrapped up in her own writing, forgetting that not everything has to be the finished article right from the beginning.

'I wouldn't worry about making it perfect; that's going to come. You've got the time now and there's no pressure or no eyes on you waiting for your next move or next album. Take the time to learn the intricacies. Make mistakes, and learn from them. Challenge yourself.'

Part of that challenge can come from opening yourself up to the idea of letting other people's ideas filter into your own way of working.

'I would encourage people to work with as many people as they can early on. It's a great way to learn to see other people's creative process.'

But of course, this is something you can't really force. And plenty of writers have spoken at length of how they've found themselves staring at the blank page, awaiting inspiration, only for none to appear. But for Little Simz, you just have to let things take their own course.

'Everyone's writing process is different. The thing that helps me the most, is to leave it alone for a bit, and just go out and live. I always find the most inspiration when I'm not looking for it.'

Inspiration is a tricky beast. It's likely that if you have the makings of a songwriter inside you, once you open that door, you won't be able to stop what comes out. And this is especially true at the very beginning of your creative journey. Once you start writing and hit your groove, there's a good chance you'll just keep going, churning out songs at a frightening rate. Of course, that doesn't always mean they're good, but that's what the writing and demo process is for. It's up to you to sift through, looking for the gems. And as George Ezra explains, sometimes inexperience can actually be a really helpful creative tool.

'The beautiful thing when you start is that you're a kid, and kids are fearless, and they don't know the boundaries of what's cool, and what's not. That's what makes the coolest stuff. When you go into creativity without thinking about what's come before, or what's going to happen, it's so much more fluid.'

'Fluidity' is a concept that suits George Ezra. Effortlessly making music across several different platforms, his deceptively simple songs have brought him international recognition, and established him as one of the UK's leading songwriters. And when it comes to the song that put him on the world's stage, its origins are pretty straightforward.

'I had three chords under my belt – G, C, and D – which are the chords to 'Budapest'. I just loved it, and would write all sorts. Before you start, it feels like a members club; as if someone needs to tap you on the shoulder and say, "Come and do this thing we do." Then you realise that anyone can write music, and there's no right or wrong.'

That plainspoken approach to music took 'Budapest' to the Top Ten in more than twenty countries, proving the old saying that music truly is an international language. Either that, or it just had a catchy tune. Either way, it firmly established Ezra as a writer to be reckoned with, and he's continued to deliver the goods as his writing has developed.

However he's careful to not overcook things. And that's something that goes right to the core of the writing and rehearsal process.

'You play it once and you've got it. You play it again and you've got it. And then you play it ten or eleven times, and that's when you start to overthink it and you'll lose the spark.'

Ultimately, songwriting is a thing that can't really be taught; you either want to do it, or you don't. However, there are plenty of tips that can make it a little easier, and the important rule is that there is no one rule that works for everyone.

An idea can take root at any time. Something that provokes the idea for a hit song in one writer, might produce nothing more than total nonchalance in another. Q Tip, A Tribe Called Quest's leader, left his wallet in El Segundo and wrote a song about it. Had Slipknot's Corey Taylor done the same, it would probably have ended up a different song.

Regardless of any of the trials and tribulations that come with cooking up a recording, writing a really good song is the reason you're doing this in the first place. And when it all comes together, it can be the most satisfying part of the whole process. Just take your time, and let it happen, as Frank Turner explains.

'I know some writers who will slave away for two years, and come out with three songs. I know other people who can write a song a day. It's very much a personal thing. I write all the time, but don't necessarily finish songs. I have piles and piles of ideas, musical ones, lyrical ones, and chord changes. Then the process of turning those into finished songs is a much slower process. I wade through my collection of snippets and see what I can jam together to make a song.'

At the other side of the spectrum, sometimes you can just throw things together and see what happens, a method that's produced good results for T of Jungle.

'A lot of time being unprepared is the best way of being prepared. You don't go in with anything pre-prescribed. At the end of the day, you can't rush creativity, you have to be in recording every day.'

And when it comes to presenting that idea to the rest of the world, you can just let the music do the talking.

'As long as what you are trying to say is potent enough, it doesn't matter how you present it. You have Frank Ocean songs where it's just him and the guitar. His personality carriers it through. Doesn't matter at the end of the day, if the story is there.'

And beyond all else, you have to want to do it, or even better, need to do it.

For some writers, like Little Simz, this isn't a choice, this is what they have to do.

'The easiest way for me to communicate my thoughts and feelings, was to be creative, to write about it, and that's what I found in music. It always felt natural, like something I was born to do.'

TOP 10 TIPS TO GET CREATIVE AND WRITE MUSIC

DREAM WIFE

1 Make Things With People You Trust

To make music with other people is to do with trust. To really communicate and explore ideas together, you have to trust each other.

2 Remember to Have Fun

As a band we are serious about music, but don't take ourselves too seriously. This gives you room to be playful in the creative process. Making music is meant to be fun.

3 It's About the Process Rather Than the Product

Smash your own expectations, it's ok to figure it out as you go.

4 Believe in Yourself and Each other

Set your own standard, believe in each other, support each other, be each other's role models.

5 Challenge Yourself

Feel the fear but do it anyway.

Playing Songs Live

For us this has been such an important part of exploring song writing. When you play a song at a show it becomes a conversation with everyone else in that room, you can feel what is working, which bits are connecting with people, which bits feel like moments. You can get a unique perspective of a song when you experience it live.

Don't Rush to Define Yourself

Having too fixed an idea of who you are and what you want to make can be stifling. Feel it out and allow yourself to figure out why you did something after you did it.

Don't Let Anyone Else Define You

No one else knows what you've got to contribute, but people have a tendency to want to tell you what you should be doing. Don't let them. Stay true to you.

Look to the Creative Community

Go to local shows, meet people, support the things those people are making, make things with those people and if there is nothing happening where you live start something.

Always be Open to Grow and Learn

No matter how much you know or how proficient you are there is always limitless space to grow, stay curious and lean into it.

TOP 10 LISTS FOR RECORDING

CAM BLACKWOOD
RECORD PRODUCER + SONGWRITER

1 Be Open to the Ideas of the Producer

Don't necessarily say yes to everything, make sure you listen to what the recording engineer or producer has to say as they might have good ideas. Remember you're part of a team. Leave your ego at the door. Everyone has an opinion and it's all about collaborating to get the best thing you can and not just what works for you individually.

2 Drums

Make sure you have new skins on your drums and make sure you have the drums tuned. Practice everything to a metronome.

3 Guitars and Basses

Have new strings setup by someone in a guitar shop. Make sure your amps aren't buzzy or noisey. Buy some decent cables and bring batteries and pedals.

4 Demo

Bring the demo session with you as we might like to reference it in the studio.

5 Try Before You Deny

If someone in the studio, another musician or a producer, has an idea for a part don't break them down, hear them out. It might be that this triggers something exciting in you. You might spend an hour arguing over a part, just try it.

6 Support Your Other Band Mates/Musicians

Everyone gets nervous in the studio so try not to make them more nervous. If supporting them means taking the piss, then thats cool. Don't allow anyone to retreat into themselves. Have a laugh but don't make anyone feel like they aren't worth it. Normally it's the drummer or bassist who gets the brunt of it.

7 Be Professional

Don't turn up three hours late with a massive hangover. Be on time. Try and make a good impression especially on the first day.

8 Speak to the Producer Before Hand

Speak on the phone or email before hand. He/She might want you to bring certain equipment, they might want to know a bit about you, communicate with your producer or engineer. Best thing might be to go out with a pint with them beforehand.

9 Be Brave With Your Opinion

As soon as you feel it, say it. You don't want to get too far down the road where you're not happy and then you realise you've gone too far down that road. Don't be afraid to say 'let's try this part'.

10 Enjoy It

It should be a fun experience for everyone. It can be stressful but at the end of the day it's only music. Everyone should perform without fear and with love in their hearts. Perform it with joy even if its a sad song.

TOP TIPS TO SONGWRITERS

IAIN ARCHER

IVOR NOVELLO AWARD WINNING SONGWRITER

1

Practicing Your Songwriting

There's a sense with art that you either have it or you don't. You have the magic or you are a mogul. It actually takes a ton of hard work. When it comes to songwriting, the idea of practice is an alien concept and it shouldn't be, as it requires a lot of rewriting and scratching it all and starting again.

2

Playing That Song Live

You learn more about your song in the three and a half minutes of playing it live than you do in all the time of writing it or practicing it. You realise some things do work that you didn't think would and vice-versa. It shifts the axis of how you understand the song. As does recording it, it changes your take on the song.

Write About What You Know

A lot of the time when I write with younger writers, I will predominantly be saying 'write what you know' because it does make the framework. It also makes the performance stronger because you are performing something that you really feel. However that's a principle rather than a cast-iron rule.

Direct Influence

The great artists are the ones that are totally crap at copying other artists. A big percentage of what is going into their writing is a lot of themself sneaking through and from that you get originality and honesty.

Getting the Best Out of Young Artists

It's trying to get as much from the artist as they are willing to talk to you about. You are trying to highlight 'you have really interesting experiences where you've got a really unique take on the world' and it's sometimes as simple as that.

Fake Notion of Writer's Block

There's a fake notion of writer's block. People rely on free flowing expressive songwriting to be their one method. If you have multiple methods of approaches to songwriting you don't get blocked.

LIVE! FROM ISLINGTON PUB
MY BRAIN IS SPEWIN' OUT MY EARS! I CAN NO LONGER SPEAK COHERENTLY!!
...BUH...
Wolf Alice
LIQUID HELL
BIN BOOZE
9% PISS
JOY
PARTY ★ BLEACH
NEVERMIND THE BOLLOCKS... ...HERE'S THE SEX PISTOLS
DALLAS-HEATHROW
SEAT 4B
GROUP A - SEAT 4B

The First Gig

FEATURING ADVICE FROM:
Cal McCrae (Promoter)
James Spankie (Freelance Soundman)
Lucy Rose
Mikey Johns (This Feeling - Promoter)
Simon Neill (Biffy Clyro)
Wolf Alice

The 'first gig' is one of those stories that seems to surface time and time again with artists as a cringeworthy look back to their less professional days. It doesn't have to be like that, though, and with a little bit of preparation it might – shock horror! – go OK. However, if you think you will get through your first few gigs without any hiccups or drama, you are either:

A. The most organised and boring person in the world.

or

B. Deluded to the point of danger.
Being in a band can be an ordeal, but it's how you deal

with it and how you prepare for it that often dictates your longevity. One thing that all acts share at the beginning is a sense of naivety about what the journey has in store. Don't look at that as a bad thing, it's natural. When you're arriving to set up for your first show at the local Dog and Bone pub, it's completely reasonable not to know what the evening has in store for you. Will the equipment work? Does the Soundman hate us? What's a DI box? What happens if my brain melts out my ear holes and I can't remember how to speak, walk, sing, or cry?

Nobody just turns up and nails it first time around. If they say they did, well... they're either lying or full of cow manure.

Along with some insight into bands' experiences, we'll have the view from the other side.

The Promoter, that gnarly bastard who wouldn't spring to more than four cans of warm beer on your rider, has some handy tips on how to impress and not get yourself blacklisted from a venue before you've even started. We can't forget the Soundman, probably the most important non-band member at the show. You could have Foo Fighters, Radiohead or Kendrick Lamar up on stage, but with the wrong sound person, they're going to create a racket akin to someone kicking a whoopee cushion full of Bolognese sauce into a skip. They'll give us some tips on how to approach the first show, what gear you have to bring, and how to work efficiently with them.

My advice: Don't book your first show too early. I booked my band on to a Mid-Summer Carnival in my hometown of Omagh WAAAAAAY before we should have even contemplated playing live. It was an absolute horror show – forgotten parts, whole songs played on the wrong string, and depressed-looking relatives trying to keep us positive. But we learnt from it. I mean, how could we not? After all, the band came third in a talent show at an all-girls school a few months later. We won three Easter eggs.

There were four of us!

In so many respects, that first gig is totemic in the minds of all bands, successful or otherwise.

You might remember the second show and there'll be a few cloudy memories of the third one, but after that, it all fades into a rock and roll shaped blur of mis-steps, awkward glances, bad pay cheques, and the occasional all-conquering moment of total brilliance. The more gigs you play, the better you get (hopefully). But even for the most adventurous musical explorers, a routine sets in and you start to get the hang of what you're supposed to be doing. What once seemed magical, now appears fairly regular, and a lot of the tension ebbs away. It becomes less scary, and you can just get on with being in a band.

Of course, things don't always go according to plan. Or, more accurately, they rarely go according to plan. Like anything we do for the first time, we have no experience to draw upon, other than what we've seen others do. This can lead to some unrealistic expectations, some of which can be difficult to get over. For instance, when you sit in your bedroom or make the weekly trek to the practice space, it's easy to get lost in your own songs, to over-exaggerate their importance. In fact, if you're not doing that, then you should probably work on some new material!

But then you get on stage, start belting out your songs, and you start to realise that the crowd isn't hanging on your every word. They're not analysing your lyrics, or studying the chord changes like you have. In spite of what you're trying to do on stage, the crowd are likely talking, or drinking. Or talking and drinking.

And then you come off stage and – rather than the expected queue of people lining up to congratulate you, the record company guys brawling with each other over who gets to sign you first, and the legions of groupies who just want to get to know you – well, there's a wave of indifference. A few pats on the back, maybe someone wanting to get you a drink, your cousin Nora, who likes shit music, giving you the thumbs up, and always – always – someone hurrying you along to get your crap off the stage so the next band can get on.

Still, that doesn't always mean it went well!

Dreamboat indie band Wolf Alice may have gone on to have two albums at number two in the UK chart, but right back at the beginning, they learnt a lot of lessons at a predominantly folk-based music festival.

'We were on this mezzanine platform,' recalls bass player Theo, 'And I think we got to play about three very loud, abrasive songs of whatever we were doing at the time, before someone very politely, or impolitely, asked if we could do just one more... and then give it a rest.'

Appearing at a folk festival was probably the wrong choice. Far from creating a 'Dylan goes electric' vibe, it led to an early exit, and more than a few disgruntled punters. Knowing your market is always a good thing if you want to make it through the set.

But getting to the stage where you're standing in front of a load of people, playing your own music, is quite a journey. And sometimes, even if you're playing the kind of music they want to hear, it's hard not to get nervous. After all, it's so much easier in your head.

Wolf Alice's drummer Joel lays it down: 'I think adrenaline kicks in, and you know that you have to do something that you actually really want to do, even though parts of your body are telling you otherwise. But you have to tell yourself that you WANT to do this; it wouldn't be happening unless you wanted it to. Different instincts kick in, and you get on stage and you play everything too fast, and just smile your way through it.'

In those early days, the adrenaline and fear can still take hold, even for a band as successful as Wolf Alice. Every new experience is the first 'something', and what was true at that debut gig can still be true a little further down the line.

'We flew in from America to do Jools Holland (legendary BBC Music TV Show), and we landed from Dallas with jet lag, and we had a nap. But I don't think I've ever been more nervous than when we did that show. And I don't remember doing it. I just remember thinking, "I've always watched this programme, and I've always wanted to be on it, and I'm so fucking nervous, and I've played 'Mona Lisa Smile' more times than I'd care to remember, and I don't know how it goes." And we had John Lydon looking at us!'

In situations like that, where a Sex Pistol is scrutinising your every move, you just have to get on with it.

'You've got to remember that you're doing it because you want to be on that stage in front of maybe ten, maybe ten thousand people. And once you get up there, you're going to have the best time of your life. You just have to break through that barrier, and know that you know those songs. That's the only way that I ever really get through it.'

In practical terms, your first gig is more likely to be seen by ten than ten thousand people, but the principle is the same; you chose to do this, so deep down, you must really want to do it.

Biffy Clyro regularly play to crowds of ten thousand people, but like so many of us, their first steps were in front of a more manageable gathering.

'We skipped school. We skipped physical education, to play our first show in East Kilbride,' says Simon Neill, looking like someone who could afford to skip the occasional PE class. 'We played nine songs; five of them were our own, and four of them were covers, and we supported a band called Pink Cross, who had once supported Hole at the Glasgow Barrowlands. And we were like, "We are fucking playing the East Kilbride version of Live Aid, and no-one is ever going to take it away from us!"'

While Biffy Clyro's first gig might not be as well documented as Live Aid, the euphoria you can feel at just getting to the stage of doing a gig can carry you through some ropey songs, nerves, and dodgy equipment.

'Kids were coming to this show to see music, and we were playing the music. And that was the moment – even more so than getting signed by Beggars Banquet – where I thought, "I'm going to be doing this for the rest of my life." I was quite a shy kid, and it gave me this inner confidence that I didn't know I had.'

This can be the moment when you know if a life in music is really what you're looking for. Up on stage, making your way through your set, you could be struck by that flash of divine inspiration. Just like Simon Neill, you might realise that this is what you were put on the Earth to do.

Or, by the same token, you could come to feel that this isn't quite what you were expecting, and find yourself quietly clocking all the emergency exits.

'You've just got to accept that certain live shows – and even your first couple of records – are not going to sound like you hear in your head. And that's part of the addiction that keeps you coming back. You aspire to the live show and the album sounding perfect. But I don't even think we've reached that point yet!'

An important part of that journey to perfection is to get as much experience under your belt as possible. For Simon Neill, one of the big hurdles to doing that didn't exist when he was taking his first steps.

'I would always have said, "Play your first gig as soon as you can." These days it's tough, because there's going to be proof, people will film it. Nowadays it's more important to feel you're ready to present your music and let other people hear it. Because, sadly now, people can film you when you're not playing great. Whereas when we started, we were able to play a bunch of shows when we were rotten, and get good by doing that. But I do think the only way to get good at playing shows is to play shows. It's as simple as that.'

Seeing a video of yourself on stage, sounding totally different to how you imagined, can be utterly demoralising. But it's the nature of what you're doing; at least part of the band's life will be online. And that's a double-edged sword because, while it's not nice to see yourself looking like an idiot on YouTube, the careers of some bands have been made on the internet before they played a note.

But for Wolf Alice, there's still no substitute for good, old-fashioned experience.

'There's an idea that you can drop a song online and orchestrate a sensation around your band. Like before you play your first show, people will know about your band because of the hype on the internet. 'We very much did it in reverse. We played as many shows as we could, until someone knew about us. The live show would inform what was happening on the internet, and then we would put music out.'

So while a brilliant song can get people talking about you, if you have any ambition to play that song in front of people, then maybe it's better to get good at playing that song before you try to build a profile.

Thankfully, when Lucy Rose played her first gig in an Islington pub, no-one filmed it. There wasn't really anyone there to hear it, never mind film it.

'My first show was an open mic at a pub called the Queen Boadicea in London. It was the first time I'd ever used a microphone, so that was really tough for me. I had all these songs. I'd moved to London to pursue music, but had no idea how to sing into a microphone. I'd never even heard my voice amped. So that was really tricky, y'know?'

Festival dates, major tours, TV appearances and critical success must all have seemed pretty far-fetched when Lucy Rose was playing her first open mic night. But things can be very different when you first step out of your bedroom to showcase your music. And sometimes, a little family support doesn't go amiss.

'I was like, "I'm actually really doing it!" I had two songs I could play! The whole of the pub was empty, and the room I was in had both my sisters in it. And that really was it, just my two sisters! But I really felt like I was truly doing it. I felt great about it.'

For the singer/songwriter, open mic nights are normally the first port of call. Usually run by an eager local musician, they allow anyone the freedom to get up on a stage, and showcase what they've done... usually to very few people. But you have to start somewhere. And, unlike a band, you generally don't have to book the gig, you don't have to supply the equipment, and you don't have to promote it. You just turn up and perform. Of course, sometimes you need a bit of help getting up there, but once again, this is where a sister comes in handy.

'Me and my sisters, we all did a shot before my first gig. I wouldn't recommend that, because I never do the best performance if I've drank. But that little bit of Dutch courage helped me just get on like there wasn't even a stage, just get out on the mic and actually try it.'

Once you're up on the stage – Dutch courage or not – you've got a fairly open remit to do whatever you want, presumably until you either stop, or you are given the 'comedy hook' off stage. For a young performer like Lucy Rose, part of that freedom involved how to deal with making mistakes.

'I make mistakes all the time. Even for my headline gig last month, I had to stop the songs. I just did it wrong. When I was younger, I made a lot of mistakes at open mic nights. My friend asked, "Who's your favourite artist at the moment?" At that time it was Elliott Smith. My friend then went and found me a video of Elliott forgetting the lyrics to one of his songs, and said, "See? It happens to everybody." It's just part of it, isn't it? It's human nature.'

But once you've worked out the kinks of your live set, you'll hopefully have the hunger to take a bigger bite. It's unlikely you'll ever get through more than one or two songs at an open mic night, unless it's particularly dead. And after a while, you'll almost certainly want to do something more ambitious. It's time for you to point at the poorly made poster on the inside of the venue's toilet cubicles, and yell out 'That's my name, this is my gig.'

'Some promoters had these rules, like you can only play if you can guarantee thirty people are going to come. And I'd moved to London and I didn't have any friends there. The thought of trying to persuade thirty people to come to my very first proper gig was just really difficult. So it's really hard to get booked when you're first starting out.'

I can relate to Lucy's description of what is in essence a 'pay to play' scheme. So I'd encourage anyone not to do these, no matter how desperate you are to gig. They're a con! You are providing music and entertainment, they'll be picking up money from drinking punters and from the entrance fee.

If they aren't, well then maybe they shouldn't be promoting shows.

By using those DIY skills that you pick up at an open mic night – dealing with grassroots promoters or just getting up there and making something happen – you might then be able to take matters into your own hands. You could also open the door for some other people while you're at it.

'I started booking my own gigs and promoting my own shows in pubs," explains Lucy, "Getting friends and people to come along. The pubs were all still quite empty but there was no pressure for anyone to bring anyone.'

Thus far, promoters and venue managers haven't come out of this particularly well. They're the ogres that prevent you completing the quest, or that little negative voice in your head which tells you that you aren't good enough. This isn't particularly fair, because without them you'd be headlining the No Bands Tent at Mum's Shed Festival. Your debut gig might well be what your whole life has been building up to. But for them, it's just another night. Another night with the same problems they're going to face most days. Will a crowd turn up? Will the show run on time? Will the equipment work? It's all in a day's, or night's, work for a promoter or venue manager.

Cal McRae is a promoter and the brains behind some of London's most celebrated grassroots venues, places where thousands have cut their teeth in live performance, and continue to do so. This dude has likely seen it all.

'This headline band showed up,' he begins, and you know this is going to be a nasty one. 'They don't have any of their own equipment, and they can't really be trusted with anybody else's. So they just started stealing all of the support band's stuff! And then the drummer went over to the headline band's drummer, and was like, "What the fuck are you doing!" And he's going, "Chill out man! Chill out! Sniff some of this glue." And the other guy's like, "No I don't want any fucking glue;

I just want my drums!" They then proceeded to piss everywhere. Quite a lot of naughty stuff. It was one of the worst shows I think I've ever had my hand in dealing with.'

Thankfully, most shows don't go like that, and if your debut show involves using glue for anything other than gluing things, then you can't realistically expect to have a glittering future ahead of you. But you will have the utensils to make great glitter pictures.

But not all of Cal's experiences have been of that ilk. Over the years, he's developed a real knack for spotting talent. And when you're making an overture to a venue owner or promoter, it's always a good idea to consider who they are, and what they're looking for. After all, you might love your band, but that doesn't mean they're going to. And when it comes to making that all important first-contact, there's a few easy rules that can help you along the way.

'Don't copy and paste the same thing you sent out to everyone else. Don't call me "Carl" instead of "Cal". Try and stay away from being generic. You get so many things come through that you've seen a million times before.'

But coming up with an original hook can be difficult. And if you're struggling, you might want to – as a last resort, obviously – tell the truth.

'If somebody is honest, that might be all it takes. I got an email that said, "I'm really sorry to be filling your inbox with just another shitty band email, but we really like this band that you're putting on. Would you mind considering us to support it?" Just because of that... because he was honest, I put them on that support.'

On top of that, you might be worried as a new band, that your online profile isn't quite as hot as you'd like it to be. At the time, you thought having your mum 'like' your band page was sort of naff, but also encouraging. But that isn't going to put bums on seats for a gig, is it?

For an experienced promoter like Cal McRae, the online world can only tell you so much about a band, and while good numbers are… good, they're not all he's looking out for.

'I honestly wouldn't care if the social numbers are low. Or if they haven't got many Spotify plays, or anything like that. If I like the music, I'll try and find a support or headline position for them to play in. If it's just run-of-the-mill, and they've got a shit press release attached to some shit songs, then I'm not really that interested! But I think personality shines through, and if you're able to translate that digitally via email or Twitter, then I think that really helps you stand out from the rest of the crowd.'

So they're not ogres, after all. Most people who work behind the scenes are trying their best to put on a good show, one that creates a good night, makes a bit of money, and helps the band. And if the bands are easy to work with, then that's a bonus for them.

"There's a million bands I book on line-ups that I think are not that good,. But because they are the nicest people in the world, I'm more than happy to accommodate them as much as possible. And I think that stands true for quite a lot of independent promoters as well. Because it just makes our life so much easier to be dealing with people that are nice.'

Essentially, if you have a bit of charm and manners, this would be the ideal time to deploy them.

This lesson in etiquette isn't quite over yet because, once you've got the gig, the venue can be a social minefield. Essentially, it is a series of little kingdoms, each with its own ruler. And you're just an interloper, important for the night – if you're lucky. But you'll be gone long before the sun comes up, while they'll be beginning the whole process all over again.

So, yet again, being amenable to people can go a long way, especially if you want them to help you.

And one of the key people you'll want to be nice to is the

sound engineer. They're in charge of a lot of things. But most importantly, they're the person who handles the actual noise that paying punters get to hear.

'I always advise that a new band coming should always use our engineer,' explains Cal. 'At the end of the day, our venues are pretty small. They're 180 to 350-capacity and our engineers have been working here for ten to twelve years. They know the room better than anybody else, and they've done every single type of band that has played here. So by using your own engineer, it's probably more detrimental to you than using our own in-house one.'

Once you've got the sound sorted, and you're now involved with the seemingly inconsequential issue of playing the actual songs, this lesson in manners isn't quite over.

And while it might seem less like a sweaty rock and roll gig and more like a particularly restrained episode of 'Downton Abbey' where everyone is fretting about a slightly smudged handkerchief, treating people with respect is something that will go a long way towards encouraging people to bring you back to their venue. And that also works for the headline act that you're opening up for.

'It's good advice for opening bands to not play longer than 25 minutes as a support band,' Cal advises. 'I put on a band who are incredible, but they played the first set of a four-band bill on a Wednesday night for 45 minutes. It's completely out of order. Also, don't steal all of the headline band's beers.'

Depending on the venue, there's a good chance there'll be booze involved at some point. And, if the stars align, some of that can be yours.

The rider is a rock and roll tradition, with stories of outlandish demands, and brown M&Ms becoming the stuff of legend. But given that this is your first gig, you might want to hold off on requesting that the band will only play if the backstage requirements include a single olive floating in perfume contained in a bowler hat.

'A rider can be a crate of beers with some fruit, snacks, and sweets,' says Cal, 'Or it can go as far and wide as a pair of pants, alcohol and loads of food. A new band can expect four cans of Coors Light. That's about it, really! At a free show we'd always give away one crate of beers, and that's usually split between the two support bands. Sometimes the headline band will take the majority of that as well. It depends on what level the night is.'

It's not exactly a feast fit for a king. But if you manage your expectations, you might still enjoy yourself.

Ultimately, there's a lot going on at your first gig, and while some of these things are one-offs, plenty that you pick up will stand you in good stead for everything that happens afterwards. If they're done right, gigs should work like clockwork. And if you do your bit, they most likely will. On the other hand, if a venue or a sound engineer aren't pulling their weight, you'll know what should be happening and can compensate.

It gets easier, in some respects, though some things never change.

One thing that you might have to continually face is nerves. Some people get them, and some people don't. Those that don't are lucky, and can enjoy a performance for what it is. But it's more likely that you'll get that feeling – to a greater or lesser degree – every single time you get ready to strap on an instrument and take to the stage. But it's how you deal with it that counts.

'I find I have this inner turmoil with myself,' explains Lucy Rose. 'It's like: you're not any good, no one's going to come and watch you, and no one's going to enjoy it. Is anyone even going to clap? Am I going to play well? Is my voice going to sound good? That is just so constant. I just need it to stop. It can take all the enjoyment out of it, and I'm actually having a really great time, and I'm being able to play a gig and this is great! Can't you just stop worrying and just enjoy it?'

Sometimes, simply stopping worrying isn't an option. But as many seasoned performers know, those nerves can bring an edge to a show. They prevent you from taking it too easy, and they can feed into a gig to make it something special. It's just a case of how you stay on top of it.

'You know your music, and your band, inside out,' says Simon Neil of Biffy Clyro. 'The people that come to watch you don't notice the small things. Something that could be the biggest mistake you've ever made, no one else notices. And that still happens to me. It's part of growing, and they're always going to happen. That's what music is about.'

TOP 10 DO'S AND DON'TS FROM THE SOUNDMAN

JAMES SPANKIE

1

DO Know your Equipment as well as you Know your Song

Practice setting up just as you practice your playing. Make sure your power supplies are good quality and working properly, the same for your guitars, pedals, amps, laptops and sound cards.

2

DON'T use Ridiculously Over Complicated Setups

I get it. We all get it. You have this perfect, ambitious, theoretical hi-fi idea in your head about all the stuff your sound needs to have. Keep it simple.

3

DON'T use IEMs in Pubs

What the fuck are you doing? We're in a small venue. There's limited time to set up, and you're fucking around with wireless and in-ear monitors? You're playing to 20 people, all of whom you know personally. This isn't Brixton Academy, fuck off with ye!

4

DON'T Fuck around with Vocal Pedals

A lot of small venues are prone to feedback due to the small stage's proximity to the PA. One of our main tools to combat this is our ability to adjust the sensitivity of the vocal mics. If you put a pedal before our desk, we no longer have that control over how sensitive the mic is, the pedal has control.

If we say Tape/Deaden the Drum Kit, DON'T Get Arsey. Just Tape/Deaden your Fucking Drum Kit

It's your first gig. You're playing in a small room. Your singer will thank you, the people on the front row will thank you, everything will sound SO much better balanced. Same rule can be applied to guitar amps.

DO Turn up on Time!

There are a lot of variables in a live situation that need properly addressing. Sound checks are for our benefit just as much as yours, so it's fully in your best interests to turn up at the right time so we can iron out any problems and just generally get everything as solid as possible, so you can concentrate on giving your best performance.

7

If you Can't Hear Yourself DO Tell Us! We Can Fix it!

But don't instantly give off in soundcheck about not being able to hear yourself. We're not mind readers man, and we're over the other side of the room. We can't tell what you're hearing too much/little of!

Please DON'T Kick Off in Soundcheck if it Doesn't Instantly Sound Perfect

Newbie managers, read this too. If there are problems with the sound, I've already noticed them. Along with several other things you haven't even considered yet. You carry on playing and let me fix it. That's why it's called a sound check.

DO not Move Stuff Around Without Telling Me

Fuck sake man, I put those DI boxes there for a reason. I hadn't got round to marking them or the cables yet because I'm fucking busy. I have a lot to think about and I put everything in a place for a reason.

Please DON'T Take your Nerves out on us. We're Here to Help

I know engineers have a bit of a rep for being miserable c****. My sweary tirade probably isn't helping the impression, but honestly, it's mainly for comic effect. Truth is, I love my job. You're doing your first gigs. We understand. You're nervous. You're not in the context of your bedroom/garage anymore. Almost all of us are musicians and producers too. WE GET IT.

HEY GUYS! I'M A DIRECTOR! COULD I FILM YOUR BAND?
HULK
DRESS-UP KIT!
IT'S ME, HULK!
ZERO BUDJET ViDS!
NAO
BRAIN WASH
DEATH SHOTS
MUSIC ViDEO iDEAS!
VOL.46
WONDER BOOZE
OUR ViD TAKE #9

Music Videos

FEATURING ADVICE FROM:
Aoife McArdle (Director)
Blossoms
Claudia DeWolfe (VEVO)
Jamie Obourne (Manager)
Martha Kinn (Manager)
Nao
Slaves
Stephen Agnew (Director)

My band did not give a twisted nipple about music videos at the very beginning. Whatever meagre funds we had pooled from dinner money and general jiggery-pokery, would go directly into recording the music. Surely that's the most important part? Music videos were a luxury for bands that had record deals and millions of fans. We had neither but we were on our way... at least to making a music video, one day. It just wasn't something on the radar for an act of our standing or our penniless budget in the mid-noughties.

In hindsight, we were foolish. The benefits of expressing a whole other side of the band's identity was lost on us. We missed out on the ability to get creative and add another layer to the musical narrative. I could finally have played out my twisted fantasy of painting myself green, ripping my shirt off, and harassing innocent bystanders as the Hulk at PC World, all in the name of the artistic process. However, let my mistakes with music videos be the fuel to your fire. If you want to don green make-up and throw cordless speakers around, be my guest! You just have to get off your ass and film it.

If you've got something that points and shoots (not a gun), then you can make a music video. It mightn't be up to Spike Jones' level, but having visuals to accompany your music is more important now than ever in this never-ending quest for social media content. Even the shittest smart phone has a decent camera, and most laptops have editing software that's free and pretty user friendly. So let me begin this chapter by saying there are 'No Excuses'.

It's all about creating a vignette that says something about you, or your group, something that can help you connect to your audience and give them a bit more understanding as to where you're coming from artistically. Play to your character strengths: if you're a conglomerate of grumpy goths whose idea of a nice evening is burning ancient literature, then maybe going down the bubblegum pop video route won't be for you... unless your flipping the form on its head. Try and stay true to who you are as people and then embellish that truth.

Please promise me one thing. Don't make a video with the following:

1. A rented sports car you can't afford.

2. A half-naked woman lying on said sports car.

Those videos are fucking dreadful. A lot of my favourite artists have made them and it eats me up inside that they have done so.

One of the biggest hurdles to jump-with-music videos is the expense. If I take the cost for an average release by a new band on my label Hometown Records, the music video will cost around a quarter of the entire budget. Not always but very often. And even then, the director/producer/cameraman are normally working for a lot less money than they usually earn.

If you don't have a music video, or something imaginative to complement your music, then it's going to make life harder in terms of spreading your message. It's pretty important to have your music on YouTube, Vevo or wherever people are consuming their music videos. These are the places people go to discover and binge-watch music videos. It might sound incredibly straightforward but if you don't have a music vid, then what are your fans or potential fans going to share? Sure they can share audio links but it is generally accepted that videos travel further.

I'm probably the worst when it comes to video concepts, however. I've got a real knack for either pitching something that's been done before, or pitching ideas that are so high budget that they'd make Star Wars look like a fairly pedestrian GCSE media project. This is where the brain pool comes into operation. If you have creative friends, get them on board. If not, then go looking. There will be people in your locality or online who are deeply creative and skilled, and who are looking for the same leg-up that you are. It's a 'you wash my back, I'll film it and put it online' vibe.

A young prospective director is going to need a portfolio. So if you need a video, then it would be rude not to offer up your music as a sonic easel for them to paint their masterpiece on, particularly if it won't cost a lot of money.

Ratboy, one of the artists I worked with on my label, was incredible at this part of the business. He was able to create incredibly exciting music videos that captured the fever and unhinged nature, not only of his live shows, but also of who he is as a person. He would dive into references of the Beastie Boys, Quentin Tarantino movies, skate culture and pranks, and then mobilise a young and engaged team of like-minded souls to create insanely thrilling visual postcards of his creativity. His hard work and vision is proof that great videos are possible on a tight budget.

There was a time when the music video was the territory of the mega rich, with the average pop promo costing more than the economic budget for a small country, featuring a cast of thousands and special effects that would put The Avengers to shame.

There had always been a steady stream of low-budget videos, made by indie bands on a shoestring. But next to the majors, they looked kind of pathetic on the likes of MTV. By the beginning of the 21st century, if you hadn't spent a lot of cash on your video, there were very few places you could expect it to be seen.

The Internet has changed all that. Now creativity is the real currency people deal with, so you can showcase a well-made and engaging video without resorting to signing up for medical testing.

Director and fellow Irishman Stephen Agnew has helmed videos for Royal Blood, Wolf Alice, and Drenge. For him, it's a great way to get creative, if you just remember to be realistic about it.

'The best advice I could ever give is to take something that's a limitation, and force it into a stylistic choice. If you've got no money, don't pretend you've got fuck-loads of money. Shoot a no-money video; buy a VHS camera for £20, and that's now a 'look'. If you shoot it on a webcam, try and make it look like it's on a webcam. Don't try and shoot No Country for Old Men on an iPhone. If you want to make a cool performance video, buy some old security videos. You buy shit cheap, and make it look class for fuck all.'

So if you happen to have a crazy old uncle who has a warehouse full of old, out-of-date surveillance equipment, then now is the time to make that paranoid, anti-government video, with a striking political message.

For the most part though, if you're hooking up with a talented director like Stephen, you can probably leave most of the logistics to him. Making that special connection can be crucial to making it all work in the first place, and when it comes to hooking up, a band isn't the only one with needs.

'I generally find that the best artists to work with are the ones that want to be open and collaborative. Music videos are such an important part of a band's identity. The bands that really care about that are the ones I enjoy working with, as we have a mutual respect of each other's craft,' says Stephen. 'Most of the things that I stand by, and am proud of, tend to feel like a collaboration, rather than an exercise in me being an auteur.'

Blossoms hail from Stockport in Greater Manchester. Despite breaking through in a climate when love for bands was pretty thin on the ground, they managed to steer themselves to the top of the UK charts with their debut album in 2016, helped in no small part, by some nifty videos. And it turns out, as lead vocalist and songwriter Tom Ogden explains, they weren't exactly new to the process of making videos.

'I was into making films before the band. That's what I was trying to do. We kept our first video simple, just lyrics, red and black colouring, very moody, with some dancers. And we did it for free.'

Cost-effective, and high impact … every band's dream.

But despite this familiarity with the process, when it came to the bigger picture, it was important for Blossoms that the visual aspect didn't overshadow what they were doing as musicians.

'At the beginning, you want people to think about your music, rather than just saying, "There's the band with the really cool music video." Our fans would like to see a bit of our character in it, of us just driving about on bikes and having fun (the 'Honey Sweet' video), instead of loads of shots of me cause I'm the singer.'

Getting something that complements who you are, is crucial. But if the video is getting all the attention, rather than the song, then you've probably missed the target.

When it all comes together in perfect harmony, a great video can actually do something that perhaps the music can't do all on its own. For Laurie Vincent of punk rock duo Slaves, there's been a palpable impact on their commercial fortunes from some of their videos.

'As time goes on, I've realised how important a video is. It gives people a talking point on a song, it gives it more of a life. 'Cheer Up London' was probably ten times more successful because the video was good.'

Slaves have made their videos into a crucial part of their identity as a band and over time, the two media have become absolutely complementary to each other.

'A music video is essentially something you want someone who has never heard you, to watch and get an understanding of what your band is like. So you've got to try and portray your band in three minutes as best you can. When you are starting out, it's important to have some live footage in there so people can see the setup. You should try to be very creatively involved, so people get to see what you want them to.'

Something as simple as seeing how a band operates on stage has been crucial to helping Slaves connect with a curious audience, and they were fortunate enough to get a real platform for their live performances when the BBC got involved.

'When we first did the Reading and Leeds festivals, BBC Music Introducing uploaded the footage from it. It changed everything.'

For the uninitiated, getting a glimpse of what you look like on stage, how you carry yourself, or even the kind of gear you use, could be the key to unlocking the elusive concept of fandom. Indeed, if you're hoping to go on tour, you'll likely be going places where people have never seen you perform before. Getting a taste, however brief, of what you're like on a stage can help curb any unrealistic expectations on the part of the audience. After all, if your whole deal is standing behind a laptop, noodling on a guitar and staring into the middle distance, it'll not be helpful when people come to your gigs expecting the zip wires, flamethrowers, and motorbike stunts that you put in your music video.

But even though a bit of live footage can go a long way, that shouldn't stop you from pushing the boat out a bit. East London-based singer NAO says you should run riot with a video, if you get the right idea. And sometimes, that idea will spring from the mind of someone outside your creative sphere.

'A director will send in a treatment, which is basically a plot. They listen to your song and their imagination runs wild, and then they send you in their treatment. You get it and you love it, hate it, or suggest some ideas. At that point, you start to collaborate and amalgamate an idea that works for both of you.'

And what works for NAO is something that will likely take you out of your comfort zone.

'My music videos aren't too conventional. I like weird stuff happening in them. I've got plants growing out of people's mouths in 'Bad Blood'. I like quirky things going on.'

But this kind of idiosyncratic weirdness isn't going to work if you get saddled with the wrong person. And after working on their own videos, Blossoms are weary of getting slotted into someone else's creative vision, as Tom Ogden reveals.

'When we became successful as a band, we'd get busier, and we wouldn't have time to make the videos ourselves. The label would get directors to pitch ideas, and then we would all agree on one. You can lose a bit of your soul doing this, as they look great, but they look like everybody else's.'

Looking the same as everyone else can be the kiss of death. And in that case, maybe it's time to fall back on either your own skills, or the skills of people who know you and get what you're about. And for Laurie from Slaves, it's never been easier to go down the DIY route.

'Technology is great and it's evolving at such a fast rate. Most people have Mac computers, or know someone with one, and it has iMovie on it. If you have that, you can even use your webcam to film a video. It's just about being creative.'

Years and Years manager Martha Kinn of Machine Management thinks it's usually best to be realistic about what you're trying to do at the beginning.

'So many people try and over-complicate things. The best thing you can do is to come up with a simple idea, and execute that well. If you can, come up with something unique, amazing... which you probably won't at the start. But whatever you do, don't make it complicated. My rule is you have to be able to describe the music video in one sentence. If you can't, you've over-complicated it.'

As well as making your video more relatable, keeping it simple can also make a big difference to your bank balance.

'Due to the limitations of a budget, you can end up doing something amazing. Sometimes money can complicate things, and you come out with a worse video. You just have to be resourceful. Years and Years first proper video was for the song Real. I used to waitress at a bar, and I got them to let us use the back room which was a strip club with an awesome light up dance floor. We put a bit of money in for food, and everyone else did us a favour and it's still one of their best music videos.'

Of course, no matter what way you spin it, money is going to come into the picture, even if it is just for getting food for the strip club. And for Jamie Oborne, manager of The 1975, regardless of the amount you put in, it's what you get out of it that matters.

'The first 1975 video cost £50. The second video ('Sex') cost £200, and people love that video. One thing you can't buy is a great idea. If you have an idea and energy and commitment and desire to create, then finance should never stop you.'

Once you get that great idea captured in the digital medium, the next trick is to put it somewhere that people can actually see it. For most of us, that's currently YouTube. But things can change, and as Jamie advises, it's always good practice to pay attention to which way the wind is blowing.

'For anyone who is looking to develop an artist or develop into an artist, they need to study what the market is doing. You don't want to be putting time and effort into things that are obsolete. You have to be culturally aware, because we're dealing with an ever-shifting pattern of cultural consumption.'

At the moment, a big part of that cultural consumption is Vevo, the video-hosting service made up of various input from the 'Big Three' record companies – Universal, Warners and Sony. They tie everything together, from advertising, distribution, original content, sales, and music.

It attracts a huge global audience. All the biggest artists in the world are under its umbrella and regardless of whether you're punk rock, an anti-capitalist culture warrior, or a dyed-in-the-wool pop kid, Vevo probably has what you're looking for.

For Martha Kinn of Machine Management, it has become a valuable tool.

'I find Vevo great, as they're quite transparent in what they can do for you. They give you a number of impressions, and they'll push the video, which is great. They'll work with any act as long as the video is good.'

You'd be forgiven for thinking that Vevo and YouTube are the same thing. After all, when you go on YouTube and start looking for music, you're almost guaranteed to encounter that now familiar Vevo logo. But there is a difference, as Claudia de Wolff, Vice President of Content and Programming at Vevo explains.

'We've got an in-house editorial team here. At Vevo we're very focused on artist development. The idea is, if you come to us as a new artist, we have original content formats that are there to support you at the early stage of your career. DSCVR is something we started in 2013 in the UK. We have worked with sixty to seventy artists each year, and we produce really beautifully shot sessions with great audio mixing for each of those artists that we promote on our DSCVR channel.'

And with literally hundreds of thousands of videos under its belt, it's safe to assume that the Vevo team knows a thing or two about how the worlds of music videos and marketing work. And while they frequently work with the most successful artists in the world, they're always on the lookout for the little guys, too. Because the next little guy to come along might just be the big guy of tomorrow.

'We're here to work with artists at every level, from an artist's first video, all the way through to their fiftieth. For artists that aren't coming through a major label, we would encourage them to look for a distribution partner (e.g. AWAL, Tunecore, The Orchard). We can work with them in uploading their video and once the video is ingested, look at where we can support the artist editorially.'

All this, however, depends on you being awesome in the first place. So don't get too far ahead of yourself. Video director Stephen Agnew knows that the 'getting good' process starts right at the beginning, and it shouldn't be overlooked.

'Get good first. Write good songs, practise and rehearse and know who you are as a band. Until you know that, you aren't going to be able to execute a good video. If you're still trying to find out what you sound like, or who you are, or what your tone of voice is, your videos are going to suck no matter what, as you won't know what you are trying to say.'

So if you're not ready for it, there's not likely to be a director in the world who can turn things around for you, no matter how talented they are.

By the same token, assuming you have a great idea, a great song, and a great creative team to make the video, it's still possible to muck things up. And that can come from the age old problem of just being a dick.

'Bands might have no respect for the process, or the amount of man hours it takes to create a music video. You hear horror stories of people coming in and being massive divas.'

And when this happens, you face the nightmare situation of doing all the hard work to produce something terrible.

'You can pay all the money you want to get a terrible piece of work on everyone's timeline. But nobody's going to watch it, because it's terrible. It needs to be good first, and then everything else will fall into place.'

If everything does fall into place, you're looking at something which could be the absolute making of you as an artist – part marketing tool, part creative expression, and something that has become absolutely essential in the current music world. It's certainly possible to still connect with an audience and not have a music video, but it's a hell of a lot easier if you do have one.

The right one will open doors for you, both within the industry, and with audiences. But audiences can be a fickle beast, and even if you make the best music video of all time, there's still going to be some fool who says something cruel about it, and you. That's the Law of the Internet.

And as Isaac Holman of Slaves says – in a tone that is clearly born from experience – you just have to face up to it.

'There are definitely times when you're feeling a bit shit, and you start reading through your comments. And it makes you feel even more shit.'

And in that case, you're advised to follow another Law of the Internet – Never read the comments.

That's just good advice for life, generally.

TOP 5 TIPS TO BUDDING DIRECTORS

AOIFE MCARDLE

DIRECTOR

Find Your Band/Artist

The best way to learn how to a make video is to just make one. Harass a local artist or band whose music you like.

D.I.Y

Learn how to shoot and edit yourself so you can make a living when the budgets are low.

Be Daring

Good videos are all about good, bold ideas so don't let lack of funds hold you back. Some great films have been shot on an iPhone.

Get into art

Read, get into photography, go to art galleries and watch as many films as you can. Be inspired.

Live your life

Live your life. Be open and curious about everything and everyone. Fresh ideas will come from your unique life experience.

Building a Fanbase

FEATURING ADVICE FROM:
Alistair White (Manager: Machine Management)
Bry
Izzy B Phillips (Black Honey)
Jamie Obourne (Manager - The 1975/Label Owner - Dirty Hit)
Nialler9 (Blogger and Journalist)
Simon Bush (Social Media Manager)
Slaves
The Hunna

Building a fanbase and creating a conversation around your band is probably the hardest thing to get right at the beginning. If anyone had the golden formula for this, they would presumably have been kidnapped by one of the major record labels and held in a windowless room, made to sprinkle their magical hype dust over a conveyor belt of musical hopefuls.

There's no 'one size fits all' science to it, but there are tried and tested paths. However, the music industry and technology are advancing at such a rate that a PR technique or whimsical flip of social media that worked for an artist's project last year might be completely defunct now. It's wise to stay savvy to how other acts are building their buzz, as you will start to understand what works and what doesn't.

Every act is different and you have to play to your strengths, you're better being honest at the very beginning with yourself. Do you enjoy being in the spotlight, or would you rather let the music do the talking? Fans and potential fans can see through a phony gimmick 140 characters off, so best start the way you mean to go on by being yourself. If you are a total freak and love using social media as a platform for your 'hilarious' musings, then tailor it to fit in around your music. If you are more shy and retiring, then maybe let the music and considered social media do the talking for you.

It's all about working out what you are comfortable with, and then exaggerating it. We all are transfixed when Kanye West goes on a tirade on twitter, but do you really care about what sort of milk he pours onto his cornflakes? My educated guess would be: yak milk. My point is, you are fighting to be heard against the whole of social media, so what makes you stand out from the crowd?

When my band got interviewed on the radio or for mags/blogs, we would just plainly lie about our origins, because saying we were 'four boys who met at school' is probably the most mind-numbingly boring origin story you can give. I'm not saying you should go out and fabricate, we did it because we were a conglomeration of dickheads trying to make each other laugh. Instead, you should take your traits and make them more interesting.

If you can't get people talking about you in your hometown, you're going to find it difficult getting wider notoriety. This really only applies to bands and acts that are out playing live. If bedroom producing is your flex, then we'll get to you in a minute. Building your audience locally and then spreading like a tidal wave from town to town is such an old school move, but it still works as well today as it did in 1066 when 'The Normans' were out hammering their unique blend of yodelling indie pop. Book yourself a local venue a few months in advance of the gig. Keep it small. Don't book any gigs around it. Make this gig the focal point and then hit the promo trail. Think of it like a political campaign without the backstabbing and treachery ... even though inter-band politics can often end up like that.

You've got to be telling everyone – from your friends, to their friends, to Big Daniel who works at the bakery, friendly dogs in the street, and whoever else you can to make sure the venue is heaving for your first show. And if that's a success, then pack your bags and travel twenty miles to the next town and start all over again.

However, before you go on this Genghis Khan-style takeover, there's a few things to take into consideration.

Are you ready? Are your songs sounding incredible? Are you tight enough live? Have you got the music online? Are your press shots looking sharp? Is your online and social media game tight?

When you step on stage and give the crowd that religious experience you were hoping for, you want them to be able to find all your music, and for them to be able to share it, engage with it and scream your name from the terraces. Seems simple, but there is nothing worse than a half-baked band going out too early. YOU ONLY GET ONE CHANCE

TO BE A NEW BAND. I could probably just copy and paste that until the back page – it's that important.

If you've ever cared about a band, then – on some level – you've been the target of a successful PR campaign.

That doesn't necessarily mean a multi-million dollar machine, and a team of thousands of people artificially generating hype – although it can mean that too. In essence, someone has made you care about something that you previously didn't, and you've become a fan.

Fans are the fuel that power all music. From the rabidly devoted, to the mildly interested, a person who is prepared to devote any kind of positive attention, and possibly even money, is a fan. And one of the benefits of social media is that you can occasionally engage with these people in a more direct fashion than ever before.

'I played in Dublin as much as possible, but that didn't get me anywhere. I don't know why people are content to play the same gigs in their hometown. It was about going different places for me.'

Bry O'Reilly is a 28 year old singer songwriter from Dublin, better known as Bry. And after slogging it out on the streets of his hometown, he came up with a different approach.

'I have a personality, so I started tweeting and putting things on YouTube and Facebook, which got me international numbers. After a year, I had 100,000 subscribers on YouTube and 30,000 followers on Twitter. And instead of just sitting at home in Dublin and thinking it was great having all of these international fans, I decided to ask them where they lived.'

When the fans responded, that led to a breakthrough for

Bry.

'I would go to their city, and I would essentially busk. About thirty to fifty kids would turn up. I would sell my t-shirts and my EPs and whatever. Then at the end, I would ask the people: "If I came back to do an actual show would you guys turn up, buy tickets and tell your friends?" And they did. Then a few months later I'd come back and do a 200-capacity show. I did an Australian tour in my first year of doing this full-time."

Since then, Bry has made it to sixty-two countries around the world (as of time of writing). Along the way, he's clocked up a self-titled album, a handful of EPs, and toured alongside platinum selling band Twenty One Pilots. Safe to say, remorselessly playing small pubs in his locality won't be an issue for the foreseeable future.

But all this didn't come overnight, and reaching out to your fans can be a tricky proposition if you haven't developed that relationship adequately. That was something Bry was very careful to do, occasionally flying in the face of accepted wisdom.

'I don't treat my social media like a business. Most people will use it to just announce shows and sell merchandise. I get criticised by managers, saying I don't promote my things enough. But it was always this thing where I would put up personal videos, or just silly videos of me doing stupid shit. When I went to Australia, instead of a tour diary or a live video, it would be me bungee jumping in New Zealand, or sky diving in Australia. Then at the end I'd mention the tour. I made it as little about the business as possible, and just said "Here's your new best friend!" essentially. And he has some decent songs.'

Avoiding that 'corporate' approach can be key to making this work. Over the years, big companies have jumped on social media as a way to connect with a young, engaged audience. And time and time again, they have utterly failed to connect with their target audience, while simultaneously using a platform that enables their failure to be easily shared amongst friends for a negative impact.

Ryan Bassil says 'Authenticity' has a currency in the world of social media, even if it's just the veneer of authenticity. And sometimes, the platform itself can be the problem.

'I think paid adverts don't work because of the way Facebook and Instagram work. The algorithms don't work if you don't already have a big fanbase.'

Ryan Bassil is the associate editor of Noisey, the incredibly popular music off-shoot of Vice. For the last few years, they've been making and breaking acts, taking over the role that traditional print media had in the UK since the Sixties. And for him, using cash to artificially build up your online profile doesn't always work out for the best, because... science.

'Paid adverts only work if a certain amount of people click on or like your post, and then more people see it. If you only have thirty fans, probably only three of those people are going to see the post and it's never going to go out to more people. You've got to ask yourself how often have you ever engaged with an advert on Facebook or an advert on Instagram. Probably never, so it's not really worth your money. Invest in doing creative stuff. Advertising isn't creative, but you can advertise yourself creatively by making cool videos or doing cool promotional stunts on your Instagram, and not paying for an advert.'

A case in point would be American band Brockhampton. Given that they formed in an online forum and have been dubbed by I.D. magazine as 'The Internet's First Boy band,' it's reasonable to expect that they'd be well suited to utilising the promotional opportunities provided by the online world.

'They were putting out videos for every single song, and everyone was really on point,' explains Ryan. 'The creative direction was amazing, the set design was amazing, and the ideas were amazing. It probably didn't cost them that much to make, maybe the same amount as it would to do two Facebook adverts. All they invested in was a camera, and I found out about them through videos, not through adverts.'

'Advertising' can really seem like a dirty word, but ultimately it just means the various ways you have to reach out and let people know what you're doing. And for manager Jamie Oborne, who steered Pale Waves and The 1975 to international success, the trick is to advertise without it ever feeling like 'advertising'.

'If you are advertising, who are you advertising to? If you're just pushing links into a vacuum, then you might as well not bother.'

For Jamie, one solution involves the delicate balance of making posts that offer something without the readers feeling necessarily that they need something back.

'Building an audience through passive, identity-led posts – they're not asking you to do anything, they're just beautiful in their own way. That's a good thing. Have a sense of identity in everything you do, so that you have a unique selling point. How you communicate is as much part of your identity as your music, or how you dress. So this is of paramount importance.'

Most of us, though, aren't quite that savvy, and frequently when you dip your toe in the online world, it can seem like everyone is better at it than you. Don't worry if you get freaked out, you are not alone.

Alistair White of Machine Management helped take Clean Bandit to the Number 1 spot in the UK charts. And for Alistair, one of the most important lessons to learn before you jump into the world of online promotion, is how to do it right. And in order to do that, you need to know what you're up against.

'With the younger generation, everyone creates content now. You need to think that when you are posting online, you are not only competing against other bands but you're competing against people who are experts in creating viral content, Buzzfeed and others. So how are you going to create content that is going to make people stop and look at it? You need to think very carefully about what you post, and what it says about you. What makes it interesting for an audience?'

And for Alistair, sometimes finding inspiration isn't that hard.

'You need a clear idea of who you are as an act, and the image you want to convey online. Try and think of the bands you like and what you understand about them simply from the imagery that is available. Is there a consistency of look on Instagram? On twitter, don't just put information out there, consider your identity and personality.'

It's a minefield, obviously, but if everything goes according to plan, the goal is to get something happening around the band, the elusive concept of 'buzz'.

Getting a buzz going is the Holy Grail when it comes to picking up fans. When you've got the buzz, people talk about you. They share links to your music. They slag you off, inevitably, but it's OK because you're a buzz band. And if you play your cards right, you can transform this buzz into something longer lasting and more concrete, fans who will actively support you through thick and thin, as long as you keep delivering the goods.

Niall Byrne is no stranger to buzz. He's been making it happen for bands for quite a few years now. Through his blog, Nialler9, he has single-handedly introduced thousands of people to their new favourite bands.

'I don't think there's any such thing as a bad buzz, as long as it's based around the music. You can't do enough to get yourself out there at the start. A buzz is a really good thing as it means people are paying attention.'

And frequently, an artist needs something to help them stand out from the crowd; a 'pre-buzz', in order to help secure the hype.

Once again, social media can be the best way to cut through all the noise out there, and a lot of that comes down to how you put yourself across. You might be the nicest bunch of people to have ever walked the face of the Earth, and your music could have what it takes to be studied by future generations, long after the planet has been burnt to a crisp. But if you have a bland or off-putting social media presence, there's a good chance that no-one is going to ever find out about you.

'I think your social media needs a bit of personality about what you're posting," explains Naill, "And Instagram is really good as it gets to show a little more personality than just saying "we've got a gig coming up".'

But Instagram isn't your only platform, and as Machine Management's Alistair White points out, they all have their strengths and weaknesses. What's good for someone else, might be disastrous for you.

'If an act is rubbish at taking pictures, don't put them on Instagram. I think you need a presence on all social media but you have to think about what works best for you to convey your message as an artist.

'Twitter is probably a bit of a dying format right now; so maybe focus more on Instagram and YouTube. With YouTube, you need to think of yourself more as a TV Broadcaster than a musician when creating your videos. Similarly looking at Instagram, you want a consistency of imagery on there, so when people look at the page they instantly get an idea of your identity as an act, as you can't put that much music on there.'

For Noisey's Ryan Bassil, the social media platform can actually come after hearing the music, laying more concrete foundations for a curious listener to become a fan.

'Twitter and Instagram are really important for just building a voice. If I like an artist, or I hear a cool song, I'll check them out on Instagram. If they have a fucking boring Instagram with nothing on it – or sincere but dry posts – then it puts me off them. If you look at Mac DeMarco's Instagram or his Twitter, it's really funny, and it's the same with Tyler the Creator. You're more interested in the artist.'

When you put all this together, you'll be a digital ninja, presenting your own YouTube show, winning awards for beautiful Instagram images, and cracking wise like a stand-up comedian on Twitter. And you'll probably be knackered, and not have made any music.

Keeping an online life can be draining, and can get in the way of your real life. And when it comes to making music, it's pretty easy to forget how important it is to actually still keep a foot in the real world, and connect with living, breathing fans, rather than their digital counterparts.

'Our band was just an expression of ourselves, and that ended up being successful because other people believed in it.'

Laurie Vincent and Isaac Holman were two kids from Kent who were already fed up with the life that looked set to unfold for them. They turned that anger and disaffection into music. They became Slaves, and released three Top 10 albums in the UK, the second of which was produced by Mike D of the Beastie Boys. While there's no doubting the inescapable importance of an online presence for them, there's still no substitute for the real thing.

'You've got to get out there and gig, and physically meet your fans and put faces to names. At an early stage, you need to know who's turning up at your shows, and you need to interact with them. Once we realised it was good, we took it to social media.'

The results weren't exactly instantaneous.

'Really, for us, it was a slow build. A hundred followers was a massive milestone. Then getting to three hundred was an even bigger one, and it just carried on doing that. It never really felt like, Bang! Here's ten thousand followers. But we interacted with our Facebook really well. We were quite personal and told stories. We weren't using it to get people on our side. We were just a bit silly on it and just speaking to people who were already our fans.'

Keeping that connection with budding fans can be really crucial to a band's development, in more ways than one.

The Hunna formed in 2015 and they've put a 'hunna' (sorry) percent into making the band work, and a large part of that has been maintaining those relationships with fans.

'We used to be in a post-hardcore band, quite different to this one,' explains lead singer Ryan Potter. 'We fitted in a bit, but we were a bit more indie than what was going on. We played gigs every weekend with Don Broco, Enter Shikari, Floods, and Friendly Fires. It was hard but we just showed up, did our thing and I think people respected that'

That respect stood them in good stead in their current incarnation as The Hunna, and the band continued to grow that connection to both other bands, and the people coming to see them.

'After our first tour supporting Coasts, we obviously spent a lot of time with their fans. After gigs we spoke with them and got to know them a bit. I think that resonated. And then they went online, on Facebook, and saw what we were doing. The social media marketing had a big part to play in getting it out to as many people as possible. We pretty much try to reply to everyone who comments on any of our posts. Facebook has been huge for us, and Instagram and Twitter as well. We try and focus on all of them.'

Ultimately, when it comes to building a buzz around a band, or picking up a fanbase, there's no definitive rule that applies to all acts, other than 'have awesome music'. That's not enough to do it on its own, but it's a good place to start. It's a mantra I hear so much, If your music is shit, you are fucked. It's horrible, but it's true.

But all these strategies have something in common – sincerity. You've got to believe in what you're doing, You've got to mean it, and you've got to enjoy it. Even when the last thing you want to be doing is replying to Facebook or Twitter comments after a packed gig, you still have to remember that these people care about your band, and if you care about them, that relationship can only become stronger.

And when it comes to platforms, it's a free-for-all. Watch which way the wind is blowing, see what's working for other people, and work out whether that sits well with your band. Not everything is going to fit you as well as you'd like, and while it's always good to diversify, there's a strength in focusing on what you're good at, and building upon that. Social media can be fickle, so be prepared to jump ship to a new platform. As long as you keep that genuine connection to your fans, they'll go where you go.

And maybe then, that buzz starts to happen. People take note, you get written about, interested parties start sniffing around. Just don't let that go to your head. Keep your wits about you, and work out the best course of action. What seems like the easy option isn't always the best, as Noisey's Ryan Bassil explains.

'There are people with good buzz behind them and they have the music to back it up, but I think so many people rush into things too quickly. They might only have had one or two songs out, and then labels are getting on to them and they sign a deal too quickly. I think the thing is, if you have buzz behind you, you could actually capitalise on that by not doing any record deals or not doing anything. Just focus on yourself and keep making cool music and cool videos.'

Beyond everything else, that's arguably the most important lesson here. If you aren't doing stuff you enjoy, making sounds you like, or videos you'd like to watch, how can you expect anyone else to?

For manager Jamie Oborne there are some things that stay the same.

'First and foremost, I will say to our artists when we're making a record, if at the end of the record process we're all proud of it, then we've already won. We'll break our necks trying to make it reach as many people as possible, but as long as we're proud of it, then I'm confident that things will happen.

And always – always! – remember to take your time. After all, you can't take your first steps more than once. YOU ARE ONLY A NEW BAND ONCE.

'Think of your favourite band," advises Jamie. "Go and listen to the first thing they put out. Then lock yourself in a rehearsal room until you're confident your first thing is as good, and only then release it on the world. Until you put in your 10,000 hours, you shouldn't be doing anything.'

TOP TIPS FOR MANAGING YOUR SOCIAL MEDIA

SIMON BUSH
SOCIAL MEDIA MANAGER

1

Do You Have an Objective?

Do you want to sell gig tickets? Increase your follower numbers to help radio and press take notice, push more video views? These will change as you go through your campaign, so re-evaluate this every few weeks to make sure you're focussing in the right place at the right time.

2

Stay Relevant to Your Fans

Think about what your fans want to see, candid pictures or videos of you? Interesting design and imagery? References to your musical tastes? Connections you have with other artists? You'll find this out by trying things out and analysing.

Get to Know Platforms and What they're used for..

•Instagram: This is where you should focus on what visually defines you. Stylistic photography does well on Instagram, as does live photography (Easy win - hit up the promoter after your show and ask them to link you with the venue photographer if there was one).

Use Instagram Stories too. It's becoming the most valuable place on the internet. Get filming everything and everything. Give people a behind-the-scenes look at your life and what you're up to.

•Twitter: It's a place to talk to your fans and listen to what they're saying. Talk about whatever interests you and whatever interests your fans. Use it like anyone else and engage with other accounts you're a fan of.

•Facebook :This is the home for all the important info and content. Emotional posts do really well here as well. So if you're thankful for people coming out to a show, tell them in a heartfelt message.

Use the same username, url, and profile picture across all your channels as well. People's attention spans are minuscule, so make it as easy as possible for people to know it's the real you.

Ready? Engage.

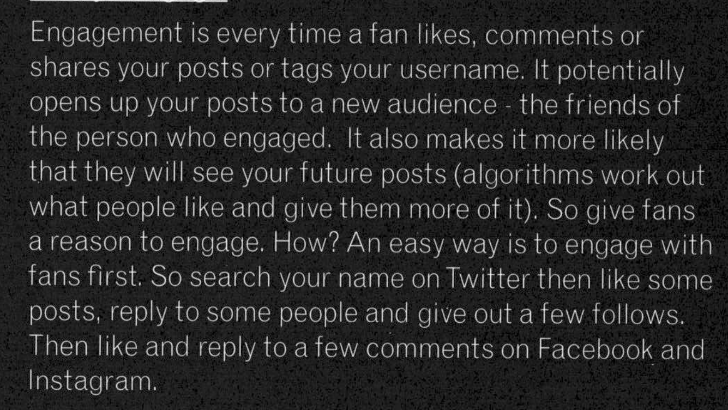

Engagement is every time a fan likes, comments or shares your posts or tags your username. It potentially opens up your posts to a new audience - the friends of the person who engaged. It also makes it more likely that they will see your future posts (algorithms work out what people like and give them more of it). So give fans a reason to engage. How? An easy way is to engage with fans first. So search your name on Twitter then like some posts, reply to some people and give out a few follows. Then like and reply to a few comments on Facebook and Instagram.

Engage with other artists as well. Be a user of Twitter in the same way you want your fans to use Twitter. Make conversation, support other artist's releases etc. In turn, hopefully they'll support you, which will connect you with their followers.

Give People Content They Want to Engage With

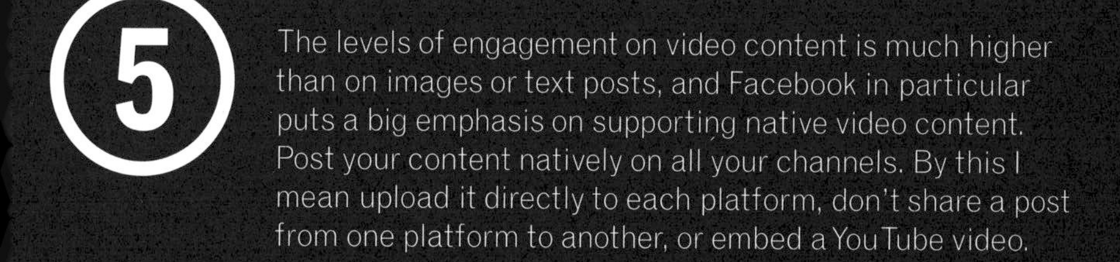

The levels of engagement on video content is much higher than on images or text posts, and Facebook in particular puts a big emphasis on supporting native video content. Post your content natively on all your channels. By this I mean upload it directly to each platform, don't share a post from one platform to another, or embed a YouTube video.

Be Active But Don't Over-Post

You want to keep your fans drip-fed with content so they continue to re-visit your page. This means thinking about what you can fill the gaps with in a quiet period. This is where #throwbackthursday, #mondaymotivation and so on come in useful. That being said, don't spam fans with things they aren't interested in. And don't force yourself to post things that aren't interesting when you don't have anything interesting to post.

Don't Buy Followers or Likes. You've got other shit to pay for.

People can usually tell they're fake if you've got 20k followers but only 2 likes on your post. If you've paid for comments, they'll usually be so general and unrelated to what you've posted, they'll stick out like a sore thumb - 'Cool pic!' 'LOVE this!' 'Awesome!'.

Plan and Analyse (Then Plan Again)

Once you've posted, use the free insights or analytics on your Facebook page and if you have access to it, Twitter and Instagram analytics (or just manually look at the number of likes and comments your posts have). See how well (or how badly) each post performs, and work out why. Do this regularly to see if there are any trends in the good stuff that you can stick with. Then start

TOP 10 TIPS FOR ARTISTS USING SOCIAL MEDIA

IZZY B PHILLIPS (BLACK HONEY)

1

Reply to Your Fans

They are are the most important part of what you are making. Replying is a really good way of reaching them personally. Chatting with them one to one will help you build a dedicated relationship with them. Putting in the leg work early helps you create something more solid and sustainable.

2

Check Your Analytics

The key ones are figuring out what time of day you should post and look at what posts did well then try and recreate them.

Ask People Questions

Replies boost your algorithm and will help you deepen your bond with fans.

Know Your Artistic Direction

Start by making mood boards on Pinterest with things that artistically speak to you. Try and think about art that visually represents the songs you are making. Then plan how you want to intersperse art with your more promo based posts. Also you can get cool apps to colour the photos to your art direction.

Tell a Story

A story bigger than "hey we are a band playing a show this month." Think open journal or if your not comfortable with that, talk about things that interest you or what is happening whilst you were in the van.

Do Fun Stories.

The shitter the better. Honesty is really important here. You wanna use stories to self unveil all the funny/stupid/gross behind the scenes moments.

Don't Get Bummed Out

For every high there's about 10 lows and if you go on your news feed feeling down and start comparing your project to all your mates headlining Glastonbury it will make you feel worse. Turn your phone off and write a song.

Make a Schedule

Treat your project like a business so once you know your high interaction times you can schedule the posts with a month plan. Then book the shoots in advance so you don't end up having to do a full shoot everyday.

The World Loves Faces

Especially Instagram. We are in a world of completely insane vanity where your face will get you more rewards on platforms than your music. It's shit but also you can use this to your advantage.

Concentrate on the Music

It starts and ends with good tunes, you could spend your whole career trying to make the perfect social media strategy and hope it works for you. But if you write a great song the fan base will find its way to you.

BUSINESS CARD!!
YOUR HIT SINGLE
£
I COULD BE A DREAM OR A NIGHTMARE...
CARE TO TAKE A RISK AND
SIGN ON THE DOTTED LINE?

Management

FEATURING ADVICE FROM:
Lyndon Stephens (Manager)
Jamie Obourne (Manager/Label Boss)
Kevin Baird - Two Door Cinema Club
Steven Taverner (Manager: Wolf Alice + Alt J)
Simon Neill - Biffy Clyro

'If we want to get anywhere as a band we are going to need a manager.'

Every time it was said, year after year, my voice would shudder with desperation, and my body language would droop. When my band started out, we did so under the presumption that getting a manager means you're getting there, and getting a record deal meant you've made it. 'I'm gonna buy a jet ski and live in a hollowed-out mountain with a string of supermodels!'

Times have changed, and to be fair, I don't even think those times even existed in my lifetime. One thing I did know was that we needed songs, support, vision, and to somehow acquire an embarrassment of riches.

Then we'll buy the jet ski!

At some point, most acts will want to have a manager involved in their project. Some bands revel in the DIY nature of it, and can forge their own career with 100% autonomy. But realistically, most want a helping hand to reach their full potential. The main problem is that there aren't enough managers to go around, and even with bands that have a modicum of success, there's barely enough 'good' managers to make it work. The majority of managers will have three or four acts.

So of course the big question is: how do we do this ourselves, OR how do we go about getting a manager on-side?

The role of a manager is constantly evolving and at the time of writing, it seems to be more of a full 360-degree role than what it used to be. Not content with just looking after the personalities within an act, the manager has to be versed in marketing the band, getting their music released across various platforms, and generally being more hands-on in all capacities than ever before. The music industry barely knows what it is right now, and a manager is like a weatherman trying to predict if it's going to rain by staring into the sky. Your potential manager needs to know a lot about a lot if you are to get the best experience. Of course, enthusiasm can win over experience when done right, but if your potential manager doesn't know what a distribution deal is, for example, they probably aren't worth working with.

Every industry has chancers, and music is no different. At some point, someone in the band has wandered in with that 'Eureka' glow, proclaiming that their cousin – or their friend from school, or Mary from the Post Office, or even Quarg from the planet Zutron (delete as applicable) – is a bit of a nifty geezer, has their head switched on, and therefore they will be the person to secure the legacy of your band.

Case closed, pass the doughnuts.

Truth is, unless they love your music, really want to make a difference, and consistently learn to better themselves at their job, then it's probably best to keep going on your own. Trust me, from my experience of having two absolutely rubbish band managers during my bass-fingering days, both of whom were more interested in the title than the graft, it will just waste time and cause heartache.

If you are one of the lucky ones that lands great representation, then nice work. It is astonishing how much easier your life can become with an extra pair of hands and some experienced guidance. However, remember they're only there to aid your career, and it's up to you to provide the groundbreaking music, the ideas, and the overall identity of your act. It's their job to work with that and make it as good as it can possibly be.

Take football managers, for example. They're as big a part of the media hype as the players. While they might not be as visible in music, they do much the same thing in essence. They motivate, organise, counsel, plot, and scheme to help the artist/band reach full potential. And they all do it out of the goodness of their heart. That, and because success is great for them as well as you.

Believe it or not, the music industry can still be quite lucrative if done in the right way. Ask the dude who manages Adele.

Back at the start of the 21st century, Matty Healy hooked up with some school friends in Wilmslow High School in Cheshire. Their aim: world domination.

It's not a bad place to start, but back in 2002, there were plenty of bands vying for that position, and getting to the top turned out to be a little harder than they first thought. After cutting their teeth on the local music scene playing covers, Healey and the rest of the band started crafting their own songs, going through a succession of band names, each more terrible than the last. Not convinced that 'Forever Enjoying Sex' was the name that would take them to the top of the charts, the guys eventually settled on The 1975, inspired by a line found scribbled on the back page of a book of poetry by Jack Kerouac.

Perhaps the lgendary Beat writer was smiling on them, as just over a decade later, the band had become one of the biggest bands in the UK, with Number 1 albums on both sides of the Atlantic, hit singles, and sold-out gigs under their belt. Would it have still happened if they were called 'Forever Enjoying Sex'?

Sadly, we will never know.

But one thing is for certain: much of their success is down to the tireless work of their manager, Jamie Oborne. Not content with just managing the band through his company All on Red, he is also one of the driving forces behind their record label, Dirty Hit, which has steered them towards phenomenal success.

But, like so many things, it didn't all happen overnight. Prior to The 1975, Oborne already had previous experience in the music industry. He was in a signed band when he was in his early twenties. It didn't go according to plan and after a period in university, he was lured back to music.

'The role of a manager is to help an artist form and execute the vision of their career,' he explains. 'Artists who have a vision.'

But in order to make that vision work, a certain kind of relationship has to be struck up between band and manager, and it's not one that's always going to be pleasant.

'It's imperative to have an honest and trusting relationship. Because you need your manager to be the person who can tell you anything, good and bad. And by the same token, I only want artists around me who feel like they can be really honest with me.'

Right from the very beginning, Oborne saw something within The 1975, and he saw a connection with the band that he knew could be built upon.

'I was told about them by a girl who was a fan of another band I worked with at the time. She sent me a song and she thought I'd like it. It was 'Robbers', and I loved it. I went to meet them in a rehearsal room that was this converted, weird, run-down outhouse in Matthew's parent's house. It was sort of a garage that they'd put egg-boxes on the wall. It was a hideous room! But we loved it. I sat down, and they just played. It was so emotionally laden and uncompromised, and they weren't following trends. They were just brilliant, and had obviously rehearsed for years. They were all good players, and were just totally uninformed by anyone other than each other. It was all about the pursuit of music, and the purity of that expression. And they didn't even know that at the time! They were just doing it because they loved playing music!'

For Oborne, the impact of what he'd just witnessed was immediate, and right then, he saw what the future could hold.

'Moments after they stopped playing, I said to them, "I want to manage you. I have to manage you! You are going to be one of the biggest bands in the world, I promise you. I will not fuck this up!"' Matthew's answer was, "We want you to manage us, but we don't have any money." I knew he'd be the biggest star in the world, because it was just about him creating, and how nothing would stop that.'

When you've just formed the band, it can seem like the whole world is sitting out there, just waiting for you to conquer it. So you get motivated, and start gigging. You take every gig that's coming, because, y'know, it might be the one that breaks you. And before long, you end up knackered, having played to dozens of uninterested people in tiny bars and clubs, singularly having failed to make the world pay attention.

And for a bunch of hopefuls in East Ayrshire, it was starting to look like they'd used up every ounce of rock and roll that their hometown of Kilmarnock could offer them.

"Playing every single show, playing every battle of the bands isn't always the best idea," explains Simon Neil, with a tone clearly born from experience. "Rather than playing in five different pubs, do one gig and try and get your friends to come to it. And take that one gig seriously, rather than taking five gigs as just a knees-up."

That good advice of picking your battles didn't just come to them in a flash of inspiration

'I think any manager that comes in and says, "We're gonna make you guys stars!" You have to take with a pinch of salt. No-one knows what the future holds for anyone. And I've had friends who've had those types of manager. And inevitably it falls apart.'

The band climbed the ladder one step at a time, winning over small towns and cities through sheer, hard graft. But as the years went by, each record went further than the last, and by the mid-noughties, the three-piece had cracked the mainstream.

The way Simon Neil tells it, you get the impression that it's unlikely they'll ever abandon their roots, even if those roots saw the band trying to manage itself.

'Being in a band can be hard work in itself. If you play a gig, then you have to talk to someone about numbers or contracts, that's hard work. And it becomes more of a job. I think you have to be prepared, that if you want to manage your band, it's hard work. I'd recommend you get someone from outside the band. It's a different perspective. Any perspective coming from inside the band is coloured by the personalities, the music, your ambitions together. Someone else can shed some light on what you want to do.'

But finding that special someone is no easy task. And while there are currently apps that can help those of us who are unlucky in love, at the minute, there's no equivalent for bands.

'It's such an abstract thing to look for a manager. It's the same as looking for a record company. Everything comes from what you exude as people, and as a band. Trying to look for a manager is really tough. Whenever you try chasing something, it tends to lead to disappointment.'

For Biffy Clyro, perseverance was the key. And when they met their manager, things seemed to click. But still, it took some time to hammer out the finer points of what a manager actually does.

'A good manager is someone who doesn't try to change who you are. The best reason to have a manager is that when you have someone phoning venues saying, "THIS BAND ARE GREAT!" It's a lot more convincing if that person isn't in the band. James (Johnston, bass & vocals) did that for us for years, and people can be dismissive of that. He almost managed our band for the first five or six years, and he spent a lot of time on the phone organising gigs. You want someone that can understand the creative side of it, and the music and personalities, rather than just the business side.'

If you're lucky enough to find someone outside of the band who's taken an interest, the next hurdle is knowing whether they're the right person for the job. Some people have great ideas, but can't articulate them. Some people only care about the money. And for Biffy Clyro, they learnt that they needed someone who understood them as a band, rather than just someone to handle their business interests.

'A manager is different to everyone else that you'll have a relationship with in the music industry, because a manager is in your team. They might not be in the band, but they're part of the band, whether you like it or not. You've got to be aware of managers that are trying to come in because they see you as one thing, but you want to be something completely different. I think it's really important if you meet a manager that's interested, to actually get down to what they want to do. Because if they're just about 'bottom-line' money, and you don't make money in a year or two, then they're going to end up dropping you, and moving on to the next big thing. Just make sure that they understand what you're about.'

Of course, you might just be lucky, and have all the pieces fall into place without much work. It doesn't happen all that often, but that doesn't mean it's a myth. However, when it seems too good to be true, that probably means it isn't true.

Take Two Door Cinema Club. The Northern Irish three-piece started out as an after-school project, even securing a place in a local BBC battle of the bands TV programme. They came last, of course. But undeterred, their nascent musical ambitions coalesced into something exciting and fresh, and the band carved out a strong reputation on the live circuit in Ireland and the UK. And this is when management got involved.

'Our progression wasn't as stereotypical as a lot of other people,' explains bassist, Kev Baird. 'We had a lawyer and an agent first. And then these two other guys started managing us really early on, and they were just full of it. To this day, I don't really understand what they got out of it. They'd tell us, "We've booked you this tour, and we've got you this van, and it'll be delivered on this day." And then the day before the tour, nothing happens. "We've got you a record deal for £10,000,000." I don't understand what they got out of it. So we were naturally sceptical of management after that. But it definitely made an impact, once we were willing to trust our current management.'

Surviving their phantom managers, Two Door Cinema Club ploughed ahead, with their debut album making an impact at home, as well as across Europe and America. And once you get to that level, a band has to become a well-oiled machine, frequently with an increasingly large cast list.

The days of three school-friends in the back of a van are over. You need someone to make it all work. And that person is the manager.

'These days, the manager does kind of everything. Essentially, it's the entire business of the band. They're the quarterback of the whole band. Especially in a scenario with an independent label, we ended up doing everything, just us and the management, directing people where we wanted them to go in terms of PR campaigns, marketing and tours.'

But despite that hands-on approach to management, it's not like the band can sit back and wait for someone to feed them grapes while they recline on a chaise-longue. Because, while it might be comforting to know that someone else is looking after your PR campaign, you still have to get on with the actual job of being in a band.

'They can definitely point you in the right direction. But at the end of the day, it's you who has to write the music, and it's you who has to get up there and play the show, and it's you who has to express yourself when you're talking to people. They can put the opportunities in front of you, or lay out the dinner, but it's you who has to eat it up!'

So evidently, once that issue of trust was conquered, the band picked the right people to work with. And when it came to picking the right people, they went with the tried and tested route of simply knowing who they wanted, and seeking them out.

Good things come to those who wait, but listening to Kev Baird, there's definitely something to be said for being pro-active.

'It seems totally pre-historic, going by how people are being discovered these days. We looked at bands we thought were doing well. Then, through lots of investigative work, found out who their management were. And then we sent them a cold email. It worked for us! You used to hear of mad things happening like people getting a cast made of their foot, and then sending it to someone, so they could get their "foot in the door!" But we just sent them an email, and they asked us for some music, and we were like, OK!'

For Kev, even with management in place, a big part was making sure everything happened at the correct time.

'The important point to having management is when you feel like they're going to add something. Or they're going to give you something that you can't get yourself. The most important thing is having the music in a place you want it to be. Don't put it out there unless you're really proud of it, and you're totally finished with it. Don't expect people to hear what you had in your head, or where it could potentially go.'

Getting established as an artist isn't an easy thing, and it's not unreasonable to hope for a few quick fixes when it comes to getting the breaks. After all, you've got a lot on your plate, right?

'There's no shortcuts. You have to spend a lot of time and effort building things the right way, if you want to have a band that's got a career. So, it's not easy at all.'

When you're a manager like Stephen Taverner, the trick is to make it look easy. And when pop-punk trio Ash found themselves plastered over every magazine cover, and on every television programme at the end of the '90s – despite still technically being at school – he made it look pretty damn easy.

Since those days, he's applied that knack of working with bands to look after the careers of Wolf Alice and Alt-J. And despite the industry changing in so many respects, the work has remained largely the same.

'Touring shitholes, essentially,' he says, with the good humour of a hardened road veteran. 'Just getting good music up online, and chipping away at small publications, specialist radio, and the smaller playlists.

'It's really important that you put that time in. Some record companies sign the band in January, put out three singles, and then the record comes out in September. And it needs to be Number 1 on the charts. This is the wrong way to do it; you need to spend a good couple of years building things.'

Finding the right person is always key, and for Stephen, there's a few tried and trusted ways to do it.

'The MMF (Music Managers Forum) is good. They've got a list of managers on their site. Word of mouth... if you know any other artists who are signed, they'll tell you who the good managers are. There's the Unsigned Guide, which is a Manchester publication which has a list of managers in it.'

A bit of leg work can go a long way. And if you're prepared to do the research, the information is all out there somewhere. Once you've checked people out, and are happy you've made the right choice, it's time to knuckle down and embrace the exciting world of making a business strategy. That's harder than it sounds, as well as less glamorous.

'A manager's role is to develop a campaign for the artist, and support the artist in all aspects of their career. In the beginning, it's helping them find gigs, and getting them on the right shows. And making sure their bookkeeping is up to scratch,' says Stephen. 'Keep your receipts. You'd be amazed how many people don't keep their receipts, and when it comes to a tax bill, they've got nothing to offset against their first bill. Usually, a lot of your receipts can be offset against your tax bill.'

It's hard to imagine Iggy Pop having a little wallet to keep all his receipts in (indeed, it's hard to imagine there being receipts for the kind of things he might have been after back in the '70s). But that's what a good manager is for. And whether or not you've got the best songs ever written, a big tax bill when you're skint and on the road could be the death blow that brings your dreams of success crashing to the ground.

But as well as balancing the books, the manager also has to help make the long-term strategy to get your songs recorded, and then finding a home for them online.

'Sometimes management companies fund recordings. Once you've got those, you've to put together a good online strategy in terms of streaming services, and putting a team around the release – a PR person, a radio plugger, and making sure the band has a booking agent. You build the team around the artist, and then roll the campaign out."

Alt-J became critical darlings when their debut album was released in 2012, and An Awesome Wave went on to win the Barclaycard Mercury Prize later that year. Since then, they've survived the increased visibility that the Mercury brought with it, overcome line-up changes, and released two more albums to critical acclaim. But like so many things, it all began with that original word-of-mouth connection.

'A friend of the keyboard player sent me the demos, and I went to see them in their rehearsal room up in Leeds. A lot of people send me stuff, and I listen to everything that comes into my inbox. We take on bands, literally from their bedrooms. And over the years, I've specialised in finding bands, rather than signing artists who are already established.'

With Alt-J under his wing, Stephen Taverner set out to help the band make an impact on an already incredibly overpopulated marketplace. And while their debut album would eventually win them a large following, there are steps to take before even thinking about releasing an album.

'We tend to focus on building a career, building a following. Generally what happens is record companies come to us. We don't like to go out there and shop deals without a following for the band, a definite fanbase. Otherwise, you're on the back foot in terms of negotiations. You're going to them, rather than them coming to you.'

Traditionally, bands made music, managers looked after the interests of the bands, and record labels released records, filtering the money back down that tree. But in recent years, the lines have become much more blurred and, for Taverner, that means having to redefine the role of the manager.

'We tend to do everything now. Even when the artist is signed to a label, we do a lot of the things that the label would be doing as well. Most of the product managers at the major labels have a lot of artists, and are really overworked. We find that it's better if we get involved, help pool our work together, put the strategy together with the product manager, and support and enhance what they're doing. And I think the labels like to see management that can be proactive.'

That role of manager and label boss is something that's also in flux. Since the band first met their manager in that makeshift rehearsal studio, the entire industry has changed multiple times, and running a label isn't quite what it used to be.

Jamie Oborne has seen the industry turn on its head.

'It's changed in the last 24 hours. All we've witnessed is that the business has mutated. It's actually a cultural change that's happened, not a business change. Twelve years ago, if I said "Download", you'd have said Limewire? Five years ago, you'd say iTunes. If I said "Download" to you today, you'd be fucking confused! You'd think of litter on your computer! It's all about streaming. That's the linear pathway of how the business has changed, but what we're actually talking about is a cultural shift. And I saw that ten years ago when I started the label.'

That foresight has paid off, and it made both The 1975 and Jamie Oborne very successful.

But even though there's a continual state of flux, the role that the manager plays for a band is still solid, like an anchor. Sure, there are different ways of doing it, but at its core, it's about connecting with an artist, and helping them articulate their vision, making it as successful as possible.

There's an art to management, but management isn't necessarily concerned with the business of making art. That's where the band come in.

For Kev Baird and Two Door Cinema Club, they get to do

what they want to do, because their manager does what's required to make that happen.

'It's that old cliché of them being the fourth or fifth member of the band, and for us, that's true. And they have such a pastoral care role in the band.

Especially for young musicians who are navigating the industry they're the first line of defence. They have their fingers in all the pies, and they know what's going on. They have such an important role in the business side of things, but also directing you, and helping you be as creative as you can be.'

For others, like Stephen Taverner, the manager is there to make the band work, but that still involves a lot of input from the band itself.

'The Rolling Stones manager has this quote, which is, "The best bands manage themselves." And he's right. The best bands are the ones that have got the vision, know exactly who they are, where they want to be, know how they want to sound, how they want the artwork to look. They're the best bands.'

Of course, not everyone can do that, but with the right help, and a whole lot of luck, maybe you'll find the right person, the personalities will click, and it'll be the start of a beautiful relationship. Or maybe not. After all, Rome wasn't built in a day, and sometimes you need to try on a few people for size to see what works best. The trick is to build up your armour, and carry on when things don't look too good, something that has always stood Biffy Clyro's Simon Neil in good stead.

'Almost everyone's favourite band has been turned down by a record label or a manager, and it doesn't negate one inch of the quality of their music.'

BIG P'S

LYNDON STEPHENS (MANAGER)

The Big P is a pretty philosophical question: what is the point of you existing and why should anyone care? If you can sum up your philosophical mission statement as a band and communicate it well in two lines, then this will stand you in good stead. The more interesting and truthful the better

Example of a bad one: 'We are a four-piece band who met at school and were inspired by Oasis/ Kasabian/Arctic Monkeys to form a band.' I have actually received this as a line in a hundred emails. It's probably one of the most uninspiring lines ever written.

Example of a good one: 'We're a two-piece band who want to destroy the music industry from within by having huge popular hits, utilising the secrets of chaos magic, whilst mapping out tours in the shape of a great old Norse rabbit god'

The next thing to think about is the product you are going to make and the three small Ps. These are: Positioning, Packaging and Pitch.

Positioning is what your project is and who it is for. Think about your audience, where can you reach them, where do they hang out, what online platforms do they use?

Packaging is what it looks like and what it is called. Make sure that the title is great. Make sure the art reflects the music and is coherent with the ethos of the band.

Pitch is the sell, how the project is described and what it offers to the audience. Your album will need a story, something about its creation. Otherwise it will get lost in the huge selection of albums that are released every week. Give people a reason to be curious, give the media a story to tell.

Your music is art and should be thought of as such, but there is no harm in thinking also about your art as a product for a short while and considering the principles above.

1.
2.
3.
ironic slogan
4.
5.
HOW
SHOULD
WE
LOOK?

Image

FEATURING ADVICE FROM:
Alistair White (Manager - Machine Management)
Annie Mac (Broadcaster - Radio 1)
Darren McSorley (Web Designer)
Deborah Sheedy (Artist)
Jungle
Phoebe Fox (Photographer)
Rou Reynolds (Enter Shikari)

The age old question: is it possible to polish a turd?

Technically it's not, and after much research and trial, we've realised it's an investigation best left to the professionals.

But is image something you need to consider deeply when it comes to presenting your musical statement to the public? To a certain degree, it's very important, but this all has to be based on a strong body of work, it's very much a 'cherry on top of the ice cream' scenario. If the music you are waiting to release is not as good as it needs to be, there's not much point creating art noir posts for Instagram, getting the perfect off-centre angle for your fringe, or raiding Granddad's wardrobe for clobber.

This running theme of 'get the music right first' will come up many times in this book; if the music isn't something you can triumphantly stand behind and be proud to ride into battle, then the rest is pointless. Get that step right and then all of the superfluous side feathers of releasing music will come into play.

Fashion and music have always gone hand in hand, and out of that is born an image, a style. Do you think The Sex Pistols tearing through 'Anarchy in the UK' or 'God Save the Queen' in the 1970s would have been as impactful if they were wearing baggy brown cords, milk-bottle glasses, and a flowing-tassel cowboy jacket? Possibly not, although it didn't do your dad any harm.

For some people, music is the pure pursuit of spinning webs of sound, dedicated and dependent on the sonic joy emitting from the chosen instrument, image will never come into play. For others it's a way of life, something that perfectly jigsaws with them, that fits hand in glove with their surroundings, their attitude and their world vision.

When it's the latter, there's very little thought needed about image, as usually it already exists. It's deep woven into the fabric of that person or group's core. If you grow up on an estate in East London, and you're forging a career in Grime, the look and the authenticity should come naturally. The same goes for a load of metal-head kids who live and die for post hardcore music. That look and that authenticity is going to flow freely.

It's when you're trying to be something you're not that

the problems arise. It's all about authenticity and what comes naturally to you. There's no problem in accentuating a few things, procuring some nice clothes, and putting a little spin on your social media, but when you stray too far out of that zone of who you are, that's when you are found out. And believe me, you will get found out. If people are good at one thing, both online and off, it's that they can spot a 'try hard' a mile away, and nobody wants to be a try hard.

The most successful bands will have an instantly recognisable aesthetic. If you take a minute and just think of your three favourite artists, you will instantly associate a certain look with them. Now think about yourself or your act: what do you guys look like? If the answer is a mumbling 'I don't know,' then you either haven't got one, or you are just one cool dude who does have one, but is just humble for the sake of it.

Either way, every great act has some sort of look. And even if you don't think that you do, you probably do. Who would have thought that the Arctic Monkeys exploding like a neutron star onto the scene in mismatching tracksuit tops would have become a look. But it was natural to who they were then, and that's why it worked.

Use what's at your disposal and if you need to ham it up to a comfortable level, feel free to do so. If not, don't. Image isn't a 'one size fits all'. What works for you won't for others and vice versa.

PRO TIP: Dressing like a 17-year-old when you're in your forties would be deemed as extremely worrying behaviour in any other profession. In music, the same holds true.

On the face of it, British heavy metal warriors Iron Maiden, and French electro-disco futurists Daft Punk have very little in common. Hell, Daft Punk are robots, so they're not even of the same species!

But beyond the differences, they're united by their striking band image, and their coherent visual package.

Maiden, with their band t-shirts, love of denim, heavy metal logo, and band mascot Eddie – the ultimate rock icon – display themselves as the complete package. Even if you'd never heard of them before, one look at them would tell you all you need to know. And that's at least partially how they continue to be one of the most successful bands on the planet after almost forty years of rocking.

Daft Punk, on the other hand, with their sleek logo, striking design, sharp outfits and robot heads, have done exactly the same thing. In a genre frequently categorised by anonymity, Daft Punk are bona-fide superstars with a brand image that connects pretty much everywhere on the planet.

But, of course, these visual packages didn't come about overnight, and a bit of research (Google images) will show you the evolution of both acts from clueless amateurs to corporate brand.

When you're first starting out, it is a good bet that your band image won't be the first thing on your mind. Stuff like songs, equipment, and lineup will likely occupy most of your time. But it's not a bad idea to get on it sooner, rather than later. No one is expecting you to get the band identity right first time, but the Internet has a long memory. And if you do manage to touch the Holy Grail of success, you better get ready for those early press shots of you in unflattering, figure-hugging spandex to come back and haunt you. Underworld became one of the biggest dance acts in history, but if you fancy a chuckle, look up Freur, their first musical incarnation.

But where do you start? For J of Jungle, it's pretty straightforward – don't go for anything that you wouldn't be comfortable with in your real life.

'You ultimately have to be yourself and embrace all the things in your personality. People can see through things that are fake and aren't real. In Jungle we found other things to create that image, we never really liked the idea of being in front of the camera, so we made things that looked cool and put it out for other people to enjoy, things that we liked to see.'

J and T don't particularly look like superstars, but they've developed a coherent band image, using their videos, artwork, and live shows to present themselves as a band. It's something that connects with them, and with their music, and has allowed them to cultivate a sizeable fanbase, as T explains.

'We just wanted to not be part of the image, because we felt like we said enough in our music, videos and artwork. You see so many bands who obsess about what their online presence is like, even before they record their first demo. What's the point?'

It worked for Jungle, but there are plenty of artists out there who do work hard on the band image right from the beginning. Sometimes that can actually pay dividends.

Alistair White is a manager at Machine Management, and has helped steer the careers of Clean Bandit and Rae Morris. For him, if a band has a strong image, it can be a plus point.

'When we're looking at acts we're potentially going to work with, image is a factor. You wouldn't say no to an act because the image is wrong, but if the artist has a clear idea of their image, it makes everything much easier.'

That doesn't mean that, alongside a drummer, a programmer, a vocalist, and whatever else you might need, you need to start scouting for an image consultant while you're still practising in your parents' garage. If it's not coming easy, there are ways to deal with that.

'If an artist has a clear vision about their identity that's great. If it comes from the artist, it's the best thing, but if it is something they struggle with, then being able to work with someone on it is useful. I would never tell someone what to wear, but I will try and encourage them down a different path to get to somewhere where they are comfortable.'

And that level of comfort can be more of a virtue than you might think. In fact, it might be eerily similar to what you wear in real life.

'If you remember in the early days of The XX, they wore black. It stood them out and wasn't necessarily a fashion thing but was a clear identity statement. People understood it; it made them interesting and made them stand out from the crowd.'

So don't be throwing out those black jeans and t-shirts just yet. In Alistair's view, having something to give you the edge is important. But if it's hard to separate the band from the audience, that might be a problem.

'If you are comfortable in jeans and a t-shirt, that's great, but it doesn't stand you out from your fans. I think you need to think about what you can wear that your fans can aspire to, rather than just look like the guy in the first row.'

But sometimes looking just like the fans can be exactly what you're after. And for Enter Shikari's Rou Reynolds, it provided a eureka moment.

'I'd be wearing a flannel shirt and sports shorts; it was a mish-mash of hardcore and emo. I get really hot on stage, so it worked for me. I need loose fitting clothing. I remember looking out over a few tours and seeing more and more people dressed like that. That was interesting.'

Enter Shikari's image allowed them to connect with their fans on an equal level, without any of the 'rock star' barriers that come with a contrived image. Which was just as well, as that wasn't something that was ever likely to be on the cards.

'Image has always been important in pop music, but for us to think about it or talk about it was a sin. Which was weird because punk is fifty percent image, as much as punks don't want to admit it. We all dressed differently and you can see that from the early press shots. Now we understand more how interlocked music and fashion are, it's just another art form.'

But understanding the importance of image isn't quite the same thing as being comfortable with it. And when it comes to getting those press shots, no amount of conceptual knowledge will prevent you from feeling like an idiot.

'I still feel awkward doing press shots, it's so unnatural and weird to stand in front of a small machine and look cool. We often try and do press shots that are us hanging out as mates and clicking at the right time having a chat. It's not something we massively thought about back in the early days.'

You can afford not to worry about it too much at the very beginning, but if it is something that you're drawn to, it can only be a benefit. And in a lot of ways, it can actually be a really rewarding and satisfying part of starting a band, just like crafting a really great song, or finding that person who is the elusive missing part of your lineup.

Annie Mac is best known as a BBC Radio 1 DJ, and she's seen plenty of artists come and go, with all manner of visual styles in vogue. But with her AMP Sounds work, she gets first-hand experience of how bands are working and what's working for them.

'You have to think about the nature of the project and what

you want to project. It's about keeping it simple – your logos, your artwork. Keep it recognisable. The good bands are the ones that you can see a font or an aesthetic, and you associate it with them. It's good to have something definitive.'

Even Annie Mac, with her distinctive shock of curly hair has a recognisable brand image. Although, she was born with that, so it's probably not the best idea to try and rip that one off. You've either got it, or you don't.

But when it comes to nailing that band identity, sometimes it's better to not overthink it.

'I think it's important to have a certain look and a feel as a band,' she explains. 'It doesn't have to be the case where everyone wears white. I like it when the whole band feel synonymous with each other, when it's cohesive. Everything Everything wear boiler suits, it's simple and a great aesthetic. You could all be wearing suits, dungarees, boiler suits, going topless like Biffy Clyro. It doesn't matter.'

Pro Tip: It's maybe not a great idea to go topless like Biffy Clyro if you aren't absolutely ripped, like Biffy Clyro. Don't get me wrong, you'll likely create a striking brand image, but it might not be one that you want to have.

But if you do get it wrong, or you find something successful but start to get bored of it, you aren't locked into it forever. Bands change their image as often as most of us change our sheets. Maybe more often than most of us change our sheets.

Of course, the annals of music history are full of bands who have unsuccessfully changed their image, and lost a host of fans in the process. But someone who consistently managed it was David Bowie. And unsurprisingly, he remains a totem for plenty of artists, like Rou of Enter Shikari.

'The only person I keep thinking of about image is David Bowie. He was able to constantly change but you still always knew "that's him." He's been very influential to us musically and visually.'

And for T of Jungle, Bowie is still the artist by which others are judged.

'People didn't know everything about David Bowie's life. He presented himself in a way that was other to his personality and his normal life. Music is an art form and if you want to be an artist then you have to amplify some parts of yourself and hide other parts. You are your own show; it's up to you how much you want to show people.'

So there you have it: just be David Bowie.

Sadly, that's not an option for all of us. But there's still hope. And for Alastair White of Machine Management, if you're looking after the music, and taking it all in, the image might just take care of itself.

'I think you will probably arrive at it by virtue of the music you create. You will see it in the bands that you like. Obviously you don't want to be completely ripping them off. How can you distinguish yourself a little bit so that you're not lost amongst all the other acts? You have to be true to who you are. Identity is a hard thing to fake.'

TOP TIPS ON GETTING PRESS SHOTS

PHOEBE FOX
PHOTOGRAPHER

Know What You Want

It's super important you know your own image, what fits your band and what doesn't. The photographer can only know as much as you tell them. This really helps create a clear style you can use with all surrounding artwork.

Know Your Photographers Style

Pick a photographer who's style matches what you want. Don't look at who they've shot but how they've shot it. The colours, the lighting, how they have portrayed the people in the photo. When you've found someone that fits the style that you're after, go with them.

Speak to the Photographer Before and Plan Together

Firstly, so you feel comfortable in front of the camera when the time comes, but also so that you're both clear on what the objectives of the shoot are. Brainstorm inspirations and shots you like, talk about why you like them and have ideas you can bounce off each other with. It makes a huge difference working as a team.

Don't Just Have One Setup

Although it can be tempting to put all your focus into one idea, it's a really good idea to have a few different set ups (background, lighting, movements). The shots you end up using may actually come from those, and if not then you have extra social media content.

Have a Banging Playlist

Having some speakers and a long playlist of music that everyone can relax and move around with creates a relaxed atmosphere that'll be reflected in the photos.

Have a Laugh in the Photos

Even if you're after dead serious portraits, just having a laugh or pulling silly faces in a few really helps get any nerves out and shows off individual personalities.

Don't Ask to See Photos After Each Shot

Although it may be tempting, your photographer is busy thinking about how to direct you, and stopping every min to show a single photo just slows down the process and takes the photographers mind away from what they're doing. You're best to have a teathered preview on a laptop on the side out of view, and stop every 15 mins to have a quick flick through.

Set a Realistic Deadline for the Photos

Next day delivery means you're not going to get the best out of your photographer. They need time to retouch and grade, a week is usually the perfect amount of time.

TOP TIPS TO MAKING ARTWORK

DEBORAH SHEEDY

ARTIST

Research

Make mood boards, either on your wall, print stuff out or make one on Pinterest/Photoshop. I always like to have something physical to work from, therefore I print out all visual references and tape them to a wall. More ideas will spark once you take a step back.

Ask for Lyrics/Listen to the Music

You really should have a good understanding how the music should be represented visually.Sit down with a clear mind, put your headphones on or play the music out loud, close your eyes, where is the music taking you? What feeling do you get when you listen to it? Is it slow and sombre or maybe it has a fast pulse. Listen to the track again and get out a notebook, write down how the music made you feel and where it took you.

Draw up Drafts

Depending on how much work is involved or how polished the idea is, drawing up drafts could take some time, going back and forth changing layouts, colour palette, etc.

Deadlines

Give yourself plenty of time. Going back and forth with drafts can take up a lot of time. Never underestimate how long a piece will take you.

Experiment

Try out different techniques, don't pigeonhole yourself into one particular style. Experimenting with other mediums can take you somewhere completely new.

Don't Rip Off Other Artists

There's no escaping being influenced by other people's work but don't directly rip off someone's work. 'Imitation is suicide' - Ralph Waldo Emerson

Don't be Afraid to Say 'No'

Well, make a compromise, a musician might have an idea, that you think won't work, don't be afraid to express your thoughts. Instead of a harsh no, give them other options, remember this is a collaboration. Working together to come up with a concept is always great, but don't forget this is your body of work too, don't be a people pleaser and sacrifice your work.

Keep a Journal

My mind is constantly racing with ideas, so I keep a notebook and write down most of my ideas. I listen to an absolute ton of music, which hugely helps me come up with concepts. Concept journals are great because if you're stuck for an idea, just flick through your wee notebook.

Listen to Advice, Don't Always Take It

What works for one person may not work for you. Enjoy creating, there's a whole world of crafting you can delve into!

TIPS FOR BUILDING A WEBSITE

DARREN MCSORLEY
WEB DEVELOPER AT REFLEXT STUDIOS

1 Get your Domain

You may, or may not be interested in getting a website right away, but still register your domain. These domains are only a few pounds a year. Once you decide on your band name, buy it. You don't want to find it's been taken six months down the line when you decide to start a website.

2 Keep it Simple

Work out what your website needs to say about you. Think about the 'KISS' principle (Keep It Simple Stupid). Don't go overboard with your content. Think about what would be important to your visitor, such as who you are and what you do. Also keep in mind your mobile audience. Make sure your website is accessible on smartphones and tablets.

3 Stay Accurate and Up to Date

Before you go live, make sure your information is accurate. Is your contact address correct and working? You'd be surprised by how often a misspelled email address shows up on a website. Also, keep your content up to date. Whenever your gig is confirmed, get it up on your website right away. You don't want your visitor to be on your site and not knowing when and where you'll be playing next.

Start a Newsletter

I know it may feel like a dated medium in the era of social media, but email newsletters are an extremely effective way of marketing. Over 25% of subscribers open and read artists newsletters and campaigns. If the right person lands on your website, make sure you capture their email address with a form on your website. Look into services such as MailChimp or Campaign Monitor to assist you in creating these and sending them out.

Get Blogging

Starting a blog is a great way to build up your audience. Write about your experiences and insights from gigging and being on the road. Don't be afraid to use humour to create the right tone as this will make your blog stand out and build up a following. You can maximise the blog to convert readers into fans of your music. It also incentivises users to keep returning to your website.

Add Audio

The most important part of any band is the music! If you are posting recordings on Sound Cloud or YouTube, make sure to get them linked up to your website as well. If the right person lands on your website make sure they can hear your songs and don't make them search social media channels. With that in mind, here's a word of caution. Don't autoplay. Never autoplay. Your user might just want to check your gig schedule at lunch time during work, if so they'll not want your music to blare over their office. If the user is in an environment where they can listen to audio, then make it easy for them to do so.

Sell Merchandise

Websites can be a great way to generate some extra income. You can easily set up an online shop on 3rd Party Services such Big Cartel or Shopify, and link it to your website. It is a fairly low cost way to flog some extra T-Shirts, CD's or Badges. Check to see what monthly costs or commission there is (if any) before choosing the service that works best for you.

Add a Press Pack

It is always useful to have a press pack available and downloadable on your site. You're going to make a journalist's job easier for them if you can direct them to your website for any information they require. It could be the difference in getting featured in a publication or not.

Get Social

Your online promotion can't just be your website. It is important to get your name out there on Social Media. Engage with users on Twitter, Facebook and Instagram (to name but a few). Entice people on social media and draw them towards your website.

10

Be Patient

A lot of what I said can seem like a big commitment with little reward at the start. So don't expect to be an overnight viral sensation. Building an audience takes time, so keep building your website over time and the right people will find you.

BAND
FUND

Funding

FEATURING ADVICE FROM:
Anna Meredith
Angela Dorgan (First Music Contact)
Hannah Peel
Lyndon Stephens
Mark Gordon (Output Belfast)
Claire Gevaux (Help Musicians UK)

When researching this book, I sent questionnaires to artists and bands all around the UK to scope out their collective knowledge and find out the key things they would like to see explored in these pages. One of the points that came up time after time was lack of money. It's a universal problem, not just one for musicians. Life would be a lot easier if money was doled out a little more fairly, an idea that is perhaps more pertinent to the Socialist Manifesto I'm working on.

The journey of the artist is expensive. It's hard to ignore the years it takes to hone your craft; how little you get paid until you reach those upper echelons; and how much equipment you need to buy, maintain, and replace. If you actually look at the trajectory and balance of the reward versus the struggle, then you might think twice about music as a career. However, these cold facts are swamped by the feeling of achievement, the buzz of a great show, and the completion of a body of work. The highs negate the lows in most cases, and that's why millions around the world struggle through the hardships that come with being a full-time musician.

Depending on which country you come from, there are different levels of investment by government into the arts. Countries such as Norway and France are very artist friendly. They see the tangible worth in developing hugely talented musicians, knowing that their investment will pay dividends when those artists achieve global success. Others aren't so visionary. The UK has had quite the rollercoaster with government funding in the arts, and it seems to my untrained eye to be a constant game of giving and taking away. But I'm no expert in fiscal policy.

It's probably important to begin by pointing out that receiving funding for your project is not your divine right. Not everyone who applies to the various funding bodies will receive it. Most will get turned down. That's just the reality of it, but it's also no reason to give up. There are many people who have received funding on their third, fourth or fiftieth attempt. Organisations such as the PRS Foundation, Help Musicians UK, UK Arts Councils and many more are there to make sure that money is being invested in the right artists at the right time, and to ensure they get the financial backing they need to bring their careers to the next level. (The Help Musicians Website has a full rundown of funding available for artists in the UK – www.helpmusicians.org.uk). This financial backing could be through additional aid for touring artists, getting enough money to make an album, paying for flights to a showcase event such as SXSW, or for additional help in many of the other and varied facets of building a career as a musician.

Realistically, however, you need to have put in quite a lot of hard yards by yourself at the beginning to stand any chance of a funding body taking your application seriously. If you've just started out and are playing covers of Metallica tracks, all plugged into the one multi-purpose amp, then it might be worth spending your time developing everything a little further before applying. It's inevitable that you will have to spend money on your project at the start, whether you have it or not.

When the members of my band were in our mid-teens, we saved up school dinner money to buy a drum kit for our drummer. To this day I don't remember that magnificent fuck ever missing a dinner (we are still friends). But that's drummers for you: loveable sociopaths who smash things for a living.

You'll go through a lot of hardship on the long and winding road to success, and equipment is often the very first hurdle to get over. Assuming that you have learned to play your instruments, can shred like an MI5 secretary, and are capable of writing pretty decent music, then the next step is to record and tour. Often that is when you start appealing to a funding body. It sounds strange to say that anyone would have to be 'appealing' to a funding body, but think about it: there are limited financial resources, and funding bodies have to make sure that their investments are helping musicians to have a career. Sadly, it's just not possible to give every nerd with a banjo a billion bucks and send them off to write a prog concept album about the great crop failure of 1834.

Being a musician can be a fairly lucrative career, enabling you to acquire enough money to keep yourself on a comfortable diet of Fabergé eggs, crashed Rolls Royces, and solid gold thrones. But, as an Old Sage (Lou Reed) once said, 'It takes money to make money, they say.'

And when you're starting out in a friend's garage, huddled around a solitary matchstick for heat, forcing your gnarled fingers to make some music come out of an instrument that would be perfectly at home on the Antiques Roadshow, it can seem like it's an uphill struggle.

Fast forward a little: you've just made a name for yourself on the local live circuit, opportunities are starting to open up, but when you examine the finances, you discover that the coffers are still empty. Your van is falling apart. You can't afford to tour. And you realise that the average fee you're getting for each gig amounts to the price of some sandwiches that are in the reduced section and sailing far beyond their expiry date.

It's around this time that you should avail of the opportunity to reach out towards a glowing orb of hope – the world of funding.

'The Arts Council and PRS Foundation have supported me over the years,' explains songwriter and performer Hannah Peel. She had been making a name for herself with her captivating and intricate brand of electronica, when she decided it was time to try something a little more ambitious.

'My last album, Mary Casio: Journey to Cassiopeia, just wouldn't have been possible without their support. Recording and taking a 30-piece colliery brass band on tour is an expensive feat! It's such a beautiful and historical musical tradition that is sadly being lost. So there was quite a lot of interest to fund that part of the music industry.'

In this case, Hannah Peel ticked all the boxes that a prospective funder might be looking for. She had already established a reputation (a good one, to be specific). She had developed an audience. She had a strong idea that she couldn't support herself. And she was reaching out in order to capture something that would be of cultural and historical interest in the UK. Boom! Funded!

But not every project is going to touch upon all those areas. And far from being the domain of the artistically inclined (although it does seem to apply to them in great numbers), funding can be secured for any kind of project: from a struggling indie band needing to arrange travel to some showcase gigs, a singer-songwriter wanting to release an album of heartfelt songs on vinyl, or some kind of madcap boffin with an idea so far out that it might just have major appeal. All comers will be entertained by the funding bodies, although many will walk away empty-handed.

When it comes to actually standing a chance of securing some funding, the process has something in common with building flat-pack furniture, or microwaving a particularly miserable 'meal for one'. It helps to read the instructions first.

'Read the guidelines. Then read them again. Then read them again.'

That is the advice of Angela Dorgan, the director at First Music Contact (FMC) and generally the main person in Irish music supporting up-and-coming artists. For her, it really comes down to knowing what the funding body is looking for, and working out whether your project is even eligible.

'Funders have to be explicit about who can and can't avail of funding; it is for the most part taxpayers' money you are being awarded. Everything you need to know is in the guidelines. Ask for advice. Ask me for advice. Ask FMC for advice and help. We do it a lot. (NB: Only applicable in Ireland).'

Once you've worked out who you are holding out your cap to, the next thing you need to work out is how much to ask for. In certain forms of business, it's often advisable to overreach when seeking funding. After all, the more you ask for, the more you get, right? In relation to music funding, however, this isn't really the case. There's not a huge pot of money to go round and you'll need to account for every penny you spend. And when it comes to getting the money in the first place, the more you can prove to the funder that you know what you're doing, the more likely they'll be to dig into their piggy bank.

'The best approach is to know what you need,' explains Angela. 'Do your budget and ask for what you need. I can't emphasise enough that it is not good practice to ask for more than you need, because, firstly, funding agencies have a pool of peer assessors they rely on who know what everything costs, and secondly, they won't trust you. A bad piece of advice got bandied around a while back, that funders always give less than you ask for, so ask for more than you need. Nope.'

So be realistic in what you're hoping to achieve, and do the research into what you think it's going to cost. If you're asking for a billion pounds to replace the wheels on your transport, you're not likely to get it (unless you travel from gig to gig in a Formula 1 racing car, a space shuttle, or The Batmobile. And even then, I'd guess your chances of getting funded are pretty slim, particularly if you're Bruce Wayne, and already have a seemingly bottomless pit of money).

As well as this, you need to know what makes up the money you're asking for. You might think this money is just to go towards hiring a studio, or a troupe of dancers, or a horse and cart (for some reason ... this is your funding bid, not mine). But then you forget to make accommodation for one of the most important people in the process – yourself.

'A bad piece of practice is artists who forget to account for their own spend. Every sandwich, string, or petrol receipt you spend is investment in your music. Don't forget to account for it in funding applications. Put a value on your time.'

If you have done your research, can manage a budget, and you have an idea that's likely to appeal to a funding group, then you're on your way. And then comes the hurdle of the application form. This can be the kiss of death – after all, many got into music to avoid having to fill in application forms. But just like getting the right sound out of your home studio, or driving the van from show to show, there's a knack to this. And it can be learned.

Anna Meredith is a composer, producer and performer. She has seen the funding merry-go-round from both the artists side and being on the panel that selects who gets funding.

'Be yourself and as human as possible in the application process. When trawling through endless identical generic phrases about impact and life-changing effects etcetera, etcetera, it's the ones where I got a sense of who the people are that are applying, that stuck with me.'

This hint of personalisation can be the first step in convincing a funder that you're not just after their money, but that you actually have a great idea, and they might want to part with some cash to help you realise it.

'Set a defined amount of time you're prepared to spend on the application, and send it off, even if there's still more you feel you could do. If you don't get it, then I think it's easier to live with.'

This might seem counter-intuitive, but it makes sense. Regardless of the kind of project you're undertaking, securing funding should only be one aspect of what you're involved with.

If you spend days and weeks labouring over funding application forms, agonising over what you should be saying, there's every likelihood that the creative spark that got you started in the first place could be extinguished. If it's making you anxious, just do your best but know when to call time on it. And also know that, even if it is a banger application, it might not be what they're looking for. And though rejection is always hard, it's something you're just going to have to learn to live with.

'Some things I got first time, other funds took two or three goes to get it right. It's always worth remembering that not getting funding doesn't mean your application wasn't good. Most funding bodies change the people judging the applications each time. It depends on that individual panel. I've put in virtually the same proposal and not got money one time but got it the next.'

So even if your perfectly crafted bid doesn't work with this application, hold onto it. It might be just what they are looking for next time. And if you can weather the bad news, the good news is always worth hanging on for, as Hannah Peel explains.

'There is a part of my life that has learnt to deal with rejection in this industry. I always try to find another way. And sometimes if an application is not successful, it's normally because there have been too many applicants at that time. I'd advise you to keep trying with these funding opportunities, as they can really change things for artists.'

This is the reality of the world you'll be up against, and it helps to be forewarned. It might seem unfair that you have been rejected for funding for your new project, leaving you sitting penniless in your parents' garage, while the local indie band down the road just got a golden pot of money to go to SXSW, even though they haven't got a record deal. But realistically, that so-called successful band might be just as up against it as you are, but they put in a more appealing application than you were able to muster.

So you can either wallow in despair, or suck it up and try again.

And in a profound way, one of the prime ways to avoid this kind of disappointment is not to expect success as a certainty. Most of us hope for the best, but it can be a real trap when you find yourself expecting a positive result to everything you're involved in, only to be met by constant disappointment.

Mark Gordon has worked in the music industry for many years, as an artist, a musician, and as one of Northern Ireland's leading industry voices with Output Belfast, and for him the worst thing you can do with funding is to see it as just a regular step on the road to your eventual success.

'It's essential that emerging music talent does not see funding as a prerequisite to moving through the early developmental stages of writing, recording, and touring. To see funding as being something that has a sense of entitlement attached to it, is to fundamentally misunderstand its nature. There is in music, as in life, no such thing as free money. And even the smallest and (perceived) softest development funds will require a great deal of thought and rigour to access and administrate.'

A grant from a funding body certainly isn't free money and, as we have seen, an extraordinary amount of thought has to be put into it in order to be successful. However, if it's free money you're after, then crowdfunding is the thing that most likely fits the bill.

There are a variety of platforms out there – Kickstarter, Patreon, etc – that allow you to come up with a plan of what you hope to achieve, and then turn to the public and ask them to give you money in order to get to that end-point. And if you hit your financial target through the kindness of strangers, you get to keep it. Otherwise, you walk away empty handed, your hopes and dreams crushed.

Crowdfunding initially looked like a crazy idea – essentially begging for money from your fans. But it has quickly established itself as a major way for artists to fund specific projects, assuming they appeal to the right people.

Crowdfunding has opened up a new way of doing things, so we're unlikely to stop relying on it in the future. Mark Gordon puts it in context.

'Crowdfunding changed the artist-fan paradigm forever. For heritage artists with large reach across socials and who can activate that fanbase and migrate it to a small-spend backing of a project, album, event, or tour, it remains a compelling disruptive area of the music industry. Where artists have struggled to make it work is when they cannot make their fans commit to this partnership, and monetise that big love.'

So, if you're a big star already, it's more likely that you can sucker people into paying for your project. But if you haven't got the reputation to begin with, why should a fan throw money at you in the vague hope that you'll deliver the goods?

For artist manager Lyndon Stephens, who looks after a crop of the finest Irish musicians, crowdfunding can seem like an easy answer, but it comes with its own set of limitations.

'Crowdfunding can be a powerful card to play if you have an engaged fanbase that is supportive, but it can really only be used once as I think as it can be tiresome for fans. Even if you hit your target every time, there's going to be a sense of fatigue from your fans who will inevitably get fed up having to fork out to you their own hard-earned cash every time you fancy doing something. Also, it doesn't look particularly enticing to the industry if you constantly have your virtual begging bowl on display.'

If the crowdfunding campaign has come up empty, and the funding body has just rejected your application, there's still another option. Frustratingly, it has nothing to do with free money, and just requires loads of hard graft. But as Lyndon Stephens suggests, the DIY avenue might be the best option for some artists, with certain considerations.

'As long as you have a sound financial plan and are willing to re-invest all of the money made by the band back into the band. Most bands start out with members in full-time employment. As the act gets busier, they can switch to part-time, and then go full-time as an artist. It can be done, but it takes a very strict DIY ethic, where everything is done as cost-effectively as possible and all income is invested back into the band.'

Ultimately, a funding body or a successful crowdfunding campaign can make all the difference to your artistic ambitions. It can take you from the mundanity of the real world to scaling the heights of your artistic ambitions. But, as with anything, it requires work. And if you go into it with the right attitude, it can be a game-changer, as Mark Gordon confirms.

'From an artist securing a SXSW showcase and being able to avail of a travel grant, to a group whose successful Momentum Fund application allowed them to self-record a record and then shop it to labels, there is no doubt that strategic funding at the right point for musicians, bands, and music stakeholders already in development and with emerging industry partnerships, can make a huge difference.'

You probably wouldn't want to rely on funding as your only option, but if you work hard and get to where you need to be, it can make things so much easier. And even if you aren't entirely successful, the process itself can be useful, if you learn the right lessons from it, as Hannah Peel clearly has.

'As much as I wanted to not learn and dedicate all my time to writing music, it's taught me how to structure budgets and follow them through to make it work. It's like an added dimension to making music these days. It feels like you have to be a 360-degree artist!'

And if you haven't been successful at all, and are at a low ebb, remember – even getting funding isn't the answer to your problems. Sometimes, throwing money at stuff isn't as much fun as it might sound. And for Anna Meredith, it's good to remember that, no matter how much or how little money you've managed to drum up, there's always going to be another hurdle in the way.

'Funny thing with funding is that it massively helps you with the issue you're facing at that moment but, like all pots of money, it runs out very quickly and then you've got a new set of problems to face!'

If all that doesn't put you off, then you're ready to look for funding. And helpfully, one of the key bodies behind music funding in the UK, Help Musicians, has put together a one-stop shop to help you to navigate your way to a financed project.

Help Musicians UK

Help Musicians UK

Help Musicians UK is the leading independent music charity. Since 1921, HMUK has provided help, support and opportunities to empower musicians and those working in the industry at all stages of their lives. The charity's evidence-led approach to make a meaningful difference to the lives of musicians across the UK combines Creative and Health Welfare services and initiatives that reflect the issues affecting musicians. The charity has a deep knowledge base and strong, trusted relationships within the music industry, wellbeing sectors and beyond. HMUK's research-led approach creates a strong evidence base from which to educate and advocate for musicians, influencing and working in partnership to help improve working conditions across the sector. Over 14,000 people working in music were impacted and benefited from the work of HMUK in 2017 through direct grants and funding to creative professionals and musicians, or indirectly through funded organisations and wider services.

There are different types of funding schemes and support

that HMUK can offer musicians and the wider music industry throughout their careers and lives.

Claire Gevaux, Director of Programme shares some of the reasons why the funding is vital and some more top tips for making successful applications.

'The life of a musician can be extremely fulfilling, often it's a calling or a passion that is fundamental to the artists self. But along with this, we appreciate that a career in music is not an easy route to take. Very few artists make a substantial or sustainable living from music and if they do, there's still a balancing act between being creative and all the other pressures that life brings such as relationships, developing a business, parenting and health challenges. Respondents to the study that we commissioned in 2016, Can Music Make You Sick, regularly referred to the uncertainty of the career, poor working conditions, a lack of recognition for their work and the fusing of music and identity as all being potential causes of anxiety and worry.

'Our approach at Help Musicians is to offer a broad programme of support to enable musicians to have long and healthy career, giving assurance that our support will have the most impact at the greatest time of need. We look at the different career paths into music from starting out at the age of 18 and the variety of opportunities there are to study or to follow a self-taught route. Our funding mirrors moments of transition and discovers gaps in support along the journey from emerging to mid career and beyond. We invest in research to identify real need to fill in gaps in support so that artists can springboard to the next point in their career, be supported back to work after illness or have longer term welfare support to manage finances when regular income becomes more difficult. All of our funding opportunities are on our website, (www.helpmusicians.org.uk) so whether an artist is in need of a mentor to help think through their next career move or someone has had a significant health problem that's preventing them from working, we might be able to help.

And if we can't help directly with funding we may be able to help through our wider services such as the Musicians Hearing Health Scheme or Music Minds Matter. The Hearing Health Scheme has been our most successful opportunity to date and offers affordable access to specialist hearing assessments and bespoke hearing protection. It's really the best £40 (£30 for MU members) you might ever spend.

Our professional team is skilled at giving advice, support and signposting to other sources of help and a lot of them are musicians themselves, so they really do understand what it's like to work on music. HMUK can be reached on 020 7239 9100 or you can also email help@helpmusicians.org.uk.

More information on the breadth of support can be found by visiting **www.helpmusicians.org.uk**.

HELP MUSICIANS TOP TIPS

First, do your Homework and Research

Spend some time sitting down and researching what funding options are available - noting when the deadlines are. This way you will find what's right for you and you can plan to make sure you hit key dates. Don't write your application in a way that you think a funder will want to hear, find the right funding for what you want to do. Check out the Help Musicians UK Funding Wizard for inspiration.

Check Guidelines and Don't Rush it

Make sure you've checked all areas of eligibility, application and decision dates. Start writing well ahead of the deadline. Put it aside for a couple of days and come back to it with fresh eyes. Ideally, get someone else to read it through. Bad spelling and grammar won't rule you out but have someone else check it first.

It's All About the Music

Put your best music examples first. Ensure your music is easy to access (with working links) and you promote what you do best. Make sure you put your best foot forward nice and early in the example – think about what information best represents you.

Update Your Socials

If you decide to include a digital link, do make sure it is up to date and relevant by showcasing your most recent gigs and current social media activity. Remember we will probably Google you!

Write it Like a Business Plan

Funders are looking for artists with credibility. If you're not yet starting to get noticed in the industry, you're probably not quite ready to apply for funding. Provide evidence that shows if you're getting radio airplay, good write-ups, prestigious gigs or a fast-growing fanbase. Funders are willing to take risks, but want to balance that risk by ensuring there is a strong plan in. Convince us that the money will be well spent. Think of the funder as an investor – it's not an X-Factor-style talent contest and funding isn't a prize to be won.

Keep it Simple and Clear

Try to find the right balance between providing too much information and too little. Avoid jargon or overly academic language. Be as clear as possible about what you want to achieve and how you would achieve it if you received a grant. Headings and bullet points can help to structure an application and makes it easier to read. It can also help you stick to word count limits. Ask yourself if the person assessing your application will understand your ideas and intentions properly? Remember who your audience is, read through and imagine you are the funder – would you back your project? Have you put forward a compelling case for someone to do so?

Make Those Budgets Balance!

Add realistic costs and make sure your budget balances – that all your actual or potential income matches your expenditure for the project. Also consider what other sources of income/match funding there are.

Ask for Feedback

Most funders will be happy to share some feedback on your application and usually they will say at which point in the process they can do this. Just remember that those who take feedback on board before re-applying are twice as likely to receive funding next time.

9

If at First You Don't Succeed, Try Again

A lot of the most successful artists have had previous funding applications rejected so don't give up! It may be that you've not quite pitched it right, or the funder just hasn't the resources left to fund any more. But receive the feedback positively and then really reflect on how you can make changes to your application before submitting it again.

Keep in Touch

Funders are more likely to help you again in the future – and to provide helpful advice – if you keep them 'warm'. Think of the support you get from any funder as if they're your biggest fan. Because they are! If you're lucky enough to receive a grant, make sure you take note of any specific conditions, and keep the funder up-to-date with any changes to your plans. There is usually some flexibility if your project develops in a slightly different way to how it was originally planned. Remember also to credit the funder appropriately, invite them to gigs, and to give them a shout-out every now and then! Independent funders will need your success stories as their fundraising pitch so you're helping to bring in more investment for other artists in the future.

TOP 10 TIPS FROM PRS FOR MUSIC

1

Honesty

Write honestly, and try to convey your message concisely.

2

Originality

Be original, copying words/melodies/harmonies from other works could land you in hot water.

3

Collaboration

Collaborate with others, get out of your comfort zone.

4

Join

Join PRS for Music and MCPS when the time is right, it's £100 each, check our website for what kind of usages will create £100 in royalties.

5

Splits

Agree your writing splits with collaborators before you commence working on a track.

Registrations

As soon as the track is finished, register it correctly on the PRS for Music system.

Live

Take a note of your set list and report this to PRS for Music.

Statements

Your PRS for Music statements can provide valuable information about the location and listening habits of your fans.

Admin

Familiarise yourself with the various tools on the PRS for Music website, don't rely on somebody else doing this for you.

Distributions

The main PRS for Music distributions happen in April, July, October and December.

TOP 10 TIPS FROM THE PPL

1

Join PPL

If you've performed on recorded music that has been broadcast or played in public, or if you control the rights for when recorded music is broadcast and played in public, PPL could be collecting money for you.

2

Performers, Tell us About Your Repertoire

Once registered with PPL, to help us pay you as accurately as possible, make sure your repertoire list is comprehensive and up-to-date in our database, covering all periods and genres of your work.

3

Record Companies, Register Your Recordings

Register the details of your recordings in the PPL Repertoire Database and populate as many of the data fields for each recording as you can.

4

Sign up for International Collections

Your recordings might be getting airplay outside the UK and, if you register your international mandate with PPL, we can collect international royalties on your behalf.

Attend your Local #PPLinSession

Our popular member events, #PPLinSession, help you to get the most out of your PPL membership and better understand the work we do on your behalf. Visit the Events section of the PPL website.

Research Funding Opportunities to Help You

PPL supports PRS Foundation, the charitable funder of new music and talent development. If you're looking for financial support for your next tour, album or campaign, check out their website.

Immerse Yourself in our Insights

PPL statements show where your recorded music is being played and receiving support from broadcasters. You can use these insights to help inform the next steps in your music career.

Register with Our friends at PRS for Music

If you are a songwriter, composer or music publisher, you might like to find out more about PRS for Music and the services they provide.

Explore the PPL website

Visit ppluk.com to find out more about the work we do and how we can help you in your music career.

If in doubt, get in touch!

If the PPL website doesn't answer all of your questions, you can contact our specialist Member Services team at memberservices@ppluk.com or call on 020 7534 1234.

OK KIDS, YOU'S WANT A RECORD DEAL? DO YA? WELL I GOT A RECORD DEAL FOR YA'S!! 25 ALBUMS AND ALL I NEED IS FOR YOU TO CHANGE YOUR IMAGE, SONGS, LOGO, AND A COUPLE OF BAND MEMBERS, OK? DEAL?
I ♡ $

Record Label

FEATURING ADVICE FROM:
Ali Tant (Senior Project Manager Polydor Records)
Connie Meade (AMF Records)
Darcus Beese (President of Island Records)
James Passmore (Head of National Anthem Records + Radio Plugger)
Matt Riley (VP of A+R at AWAL)
NAO
Simon Neil (Biffy Clyro)
Twin B (1Xtra Broadcaster + Head of A+R at Atlantic Records)

'And if you would just initial there, there, and there, and a little John Hancock there... That's you all signed up to Money Bags Records. Your dump truck of gold bullion will arrive next week, and you'll be a household name within the fortnight. It's been a pleasure signing your band.'

A pretty easy daydream for anyone who has recorded the final note of their first masterpiece demo and is pondering the future. I spent roughly 3,650 days with this particular notion in my head. That, and about 3,201 wondering what a Wotsit sandwich would taste like. It's normal to get a giddy rise after laying down a piece of music you are excited about. If you didn't get that kick after pouring hours of time and money into your recording, then what is the point? There's plenty more lucrative or listless ways to spend your time.

In my ten or so years playing in bands, the main goal for us was to sign to a record label. There was a sense that once you had the backing of one of the major record companies (Sony, Universal, Warner) or a really cool independent (Domino, Rough Trade, XL, 4AD etc.), you were set. The big comedy cheque would mean I could ditch my job on the tills at ASDA and live the life of an international playboy. Money would be no object, world tours were on the cards, and all that remained was the small matter of releasing the seminal debut album. Perfect!

It turns out that – just like waking up in terror at the thought of your teeth falling out – this is one of the most common dreams for musicians worldwide. Ask any of them to strap their collective genitals to a car battery for even a small taste of label life and there wouldn't be too much push back. It can often feel like you are banging your head against a wall trying to get noticed.

Still to this day, I don't think I told the boys in the band that I sent out a hundred EPs to record labels and other industry people around the UK and Ireland, and put the wrong stamp on the envelopes. That means all but one CD is probably lying in a bin at the Post Office. You now know, lads, we could have made it.

This was only one misadventure in the pursuit to finding our spiritual and financial record-label home. Taking a bus to Dublin with a notepad of scrawled label addresses could be viewed by many as the great opening gambit of a serial killer movie, but we just wanted the ten or so blank

CDRs in our pocket to get to the right ears. To be fair, however, we did get picked up by a scout at Universal. Nothing came of it.

However, these sorts of setbacks can actually be useful. When we started self-releasing, instead of waiting for it to come in the shape of a record label, we began to feel that the band had a real identity and purpose. That sense of owning your achievement, and knowing you did it yourself, is massively important. It's much more important than the concept of 'who the fuck is going to sign us and do all the leg work for us?'

The concept of a band being 'signed' and 'unsigned' is blurred now. Traditionally, if you were 'unsigned' you were treated like a three-legged dog: 'Awwwww, he's really trying. Someone give him a biscuit.' Whereas in 2019, holding on to the rights of your own music and having the acumen to pull off a half-decent marketing campaign can lead to more success and money in your pocket than any bottom-of-the-pile major label act.

The question I still hear a lot is, 'How do we get signed?' Yet it's being asked less and less. Artists are becoming much more savvy with self-releasing. However, it would be foolish to say labels have no part in the modern music industry. They're still massively important. It just happens to be that we're living in a time when it's never been easier to record and release music.

Releasing your own albums, EPs, singles, mixtapes, or whatever else, is possible if you have serious grit, knowledge, and determination. But what is it that makes so many yearn to be represented by a good label? It's the team, the guidance, the belief, the marketing, and sometimes the association that drives most artists to put their careers in the hands of a record label. They have history with breaking artists to a bigger audience. They'll get professionals to work on your marketing, distribution teams to make sure it's in the right places and hell of a lot more, leaving you free to concentrate on writing, rehearsing, and playing live.

However, they don't do this for the good of their health: Record labels are businesses, and businesses are set up to make money. If you are one of the lucky few to get a record deal, be prepared for quite a big chunk of your royalties to go directly to the label as they have recoup all the costs breaking you as an artist.

I've seen more than a few young and foolish musicians get a big record deal and think their advance is just a big free cheque to spend on expensive clothes, holidays, and trips to fancy restaurants. Essentially, it's the same as a bank loan; it needs to be paid back. If it doesn't look like you're going to make it back, the likelihood is the label will cut its ties with you, write off the money, and move on to the next 'darling', while leaving you back at square one.

Plenty of successful artists have gone through this cycle a few times before something sticks. Just remember the old story about The Beatles getting turned down by lots of different labels when they started. Everyone has been turned away at some point. The trick is to not let that get you down, if signing with a record deal is your goal. Resilience in music is key.

The record industry has undergone significant changes since it first willed itself into existence way back when your dad's dad was rolling a hoop with a stick down a hill. Yet the fundamental principle behind it is still the same as it always has been: you want to make music, and they want to make money out of your music.

But it's not as black and white as that, and just because the guys in suits want to make money doesn't mean you don't want the same. On a fundamental level, most music sells because it's good, on whatever criteria you want to judge that. And if encouraging you and supporting you makes you a better musician, then the record company stands to benefit from your music. Suddenly, it seems less like a bunch of corporate ogres squeezing your creativity dry, and more like a mutually supportive relationship.

Even if one only focuses on the negative aspects of the music industry, moreover, a record deal still remains an incredibly enticing prospect. And at some point, most artists will entertain the notion of entering into a business relationship with someone else.

But how do you even get to that stage?

Matt Riley is the Vice-President of Artists and Repertoire (A&R) at AWAL, an organisation geared to making the music industry more transparent. AWAL had the radical idea that the music industry wouldn't exist without musicians, so it should be geared towards them. And for Matt, it comes down to getting your hands dirty and making contacts.

'Your network is everything. The more people you know, the more attention you can get. And that goes from getting your first deal, to getting your first play at radio. It's all hustle. You might not be good at that, but maybe you need to get a manager who is.'

On the other hand, a bit of good, old-fashioned legwork can do the job. And for Biffy Clyro's Simon Neil, that meant lots of envelopes, and lots of stamp licking.

'We sent CDs to a bunch of labels. It does work. When I think back to it, that's how we got our first label (Beggars Banquet) to come to our shows. They came to watch us play at T in the Park, and we had our worst ever show. Ironically that was the show that convinced them we were the band to invest in. You need people to know you exist and unfortunately you have to force yourself on people at times.'

However, being too pushy isn't always advisable. You can put people off with incessant pestering, actively driving them away with your bright-eyed, bushy-tailed enthusiasm. On the other hand, if Biffy Clyro hadn't aimed to impress, those envelopes stuffed with CDs probably would have remained unopened.

As someone who's been sent his fair share of envelopes over the years, Twin B is well placed to know what works when it comes to getting attention. As well as his BBC 1Xtra show, he's also the co-head of Atlantic Records' A&R division. And for him, there is a whole network of people out there who already have those connections you're looking for when it comes to opening up the arterial pathway of a record label.

'Find paths towards people who can help you with your career, paths that are trusted such as lawyers, managers, scouts – people whose job it is to present new music to people. They'll be trusted, because usually they're a filter.'

And when it comes to the major labels, you better believe you're not the only person sending in your beloved music. They are inundated with the hopes and dreams of prospective artists, and it would be naivety on a level never before imagined to think that every single note of music gets listened to.

But if there's someone to filter it, then any prospective contact at a record label is more likely to trust their enthusiasm, rather than diving into the pile of unopened mail on their desk or in their inbox.

James Passmore is the founder of National Anthem Records, and he's still happy to do plenty of the work himself.

'I find music to release by trawling blogs and radio, seeing what unsigned artists are getting a bit of attention off their own bat, meeting with publishers, agents, promoters, lawyers, A&R reps, and people whose opinions I trust. Obviously going to gigs as well can help.'

So you're out there. You're playing gigs. You're building a fanbase. You're getting some good press, and you have a kick-ass demo. You're primed and ready to go, and things are good. Then, if you've done the work, you find yourself sitting down with a contract in front of you, and lots of smiling faces looking at you in expectancy of the money you're all about to make. But what happens next?

Darcus Beese is one of the key players in the music industry. As the president of Island Records, he's guided people like Amy Winehouse, Mumford & Sons, and Dizzee Rascal to phenomenal success. And that process of signing an artist is as fraught with uncertainty for him as it is for the artists themselves.

'From a business point of view, signing an act is always a gamble, but sometimes you know what you are gambling on. You've got to be prepared to come up short, and likewise, if something takes a rocket and goes massive. Nobody can, hand on heart, walk into a deal and say "This is going to happen!" I can't say that I've always done deals based on commercial success, it's mostly from how excited and how passionate we are. From the critical acclaim can come commercial success, but not always.'

History is littered with incredible artists who barely got a whiff of commercial success but continued to find themselves supported by the record labels. Artists like Nick Drake and Tom Waits had critical success without much in the way of record sales, but they were supported by their labels for their artistic merit. And over time, their records found an audience, giving extras kudos to the labels for sticking by such important artists.

But that's the kind of gamble a major label can afford to make, whereas an independent label likely won't be in a position to support such a risk. And that's just one area in which they differ.

'There's a difference in budgets,' explains Darcus. 'Being a corporate company is completely different to an independent. Sometimes you can spend a lot of money badly. Most independents spend their money wisely, they can be laser-sighted in what they are doing. There are upsides to both, and it depends on what sort of artist you want to be.'

A&R can be the key to making this relationship work. They're the people who take an active interest in you and your music. They listen to what you've got; they look at what will work with you as an artist; and they help other people make decisions that will affect your career. And if you have good A&R, these decisions that will be mutually beneficial to both parties. This could be the beginning of a beautiful relationship.

'I want to be sitting down with people five and ten years into their career. The second album is usually the hardest. I've seen people sell millions of records and win Brit Awards, and then they are nowhere on the second album. For me the job of developing is never done.'

A really well connected, clued in, and enthusiastic A&R person can be key to making all that work. Put simply, the 'artist' is you, and the 'repertoire' is the music you make.

'Everything from a song not existing to existing, and anything in between usually has a form of A&R,' explains Atlantic Records A&R supremo Twin B. 'From introducing two people who make a record, the process of a record being made, booking the studio, mixing the record, changing it in the middle of it, introducing collaborators, pointing to references to help the record, anything that helps a record exist is A&R.'

And while a great A&R person is likely to make your relationship with the label considerably better, it's not true to say that every A&R person will just fit like a jigsaw piece with you. They're on the look-out for something too.

'Essentially you're as good as the other people you are working with and what they have to offer the world. I like people who are really talented, who are really clear about what they want from their career, and who are willing to work hard as well. Those are really key ingredients to finding someone who's great to work with.'

But, of course, even the best A&R person can't help you if the label isn't right for you. It's their job to make things work as well as they can, but they're not miracle workers. And if you've thrown in your lot with an unsympathetic label whose needs are at odds with your own, then making that relationship work is always going to be an uphill struggle. That's why finding the right label is a key factor, right at the beginning. And while major labels have the money, the profile, and the industry clout, they're not always the right option.

The 'indie vs major' debate has always been framed in 'David vs Goliath' terms and while that often makes for great stories in the press, it's not always true. Indie labels have repeatedly scored big successes in the music industry, often rivalling the majors in terms of commercial success and profile. Just look at XL's success with Adele. I bet you a tenner your mum has at least one of her records in her car glove compartment right now.

So why go indie? James Passmore of National Anthem thinks we can learn from the past, while also pointing out that indie labels have changed.

'I think the days of record labels doing hideously bad deals are long gone. You just can't get away with that anymore. A good lawyer would see straight through any of that shit, and it just doesn't cut it anymore. I don't think it's fair to call labels villains. I think sometimes there's a bit of a reputation of them throwing stuff at radio and if it doesn't work, dropping that artist. That definitely does still happen but at the same time, they can only go and spend money for so long until they need to start seeing something back for it.'

Money is always going to be a big factor in whatever situation you find yourself in, indie or major. And for a young band, the promise of untold riches can be a tempting offer. But like everything in the music industry, a degree of caution is always advised.

'An advance is a sum of cash given to a band to live off while they go away and make music. I've worked with bands who've signed a record deal, quit their jobs and then had to live off less money as you have to make it stretch. Any advance is recouped by the label before you start making money.'

A major label might be able to offer you a far larger advance than an indie, but that just means you'll owe more money back to the label from any royalties received. And when it comes to being successful, it's easy to forget that a lot of the work still has to come from the artists themselves.

'If you want to really make it as an artist, you need to dedicate your life to it,' says James. 'You need to give ample time to writing, practising, rehearsing, and gigging. And it's very hard to hold down a full-time job while you do.'

And like a snake devouring itself, label money can take the pressure off holding down a full-time job, while simultaneously making you worse off in the long run if you don't do things right. But there is a third way. AWAL is a music services company. Its intention is to reinvent the model that the music industry currently operates on, as Matt Riley explains.

'Once you sign to a record label it goes one of two ways: you become a global star, but you are on a record deal which is not amazing, or you spend a lot of money on an album and it doesn't quite work out, and you get dropped.'

But for AWAL, this isn't the end of the story.

'In some ways it's a lot less risky to build it yourself on a 'label services' deal, because it builds value in you as well, and that only makes it more attractive to record labels. And it means the deal you're going to get from a record label will be a lot better. More and more artists are asking, "Why do I need them? Why do I have to sign to a record label?"'

Essentially, label services do the stuff the record company would normally do, allowing you to get on with the business of being an artist.

'Now, most artists are making the record themselves, and then they need help with the other stuff, like marketing, A&R, and distribution," explains Matt. "There's tons of artists who just go, "Hang on, why do I want to sell my art to someone else? I can look after myself, and just hire the people I need to actually become a massive star." And you're beginning to see artists such as Chance the Rapper, Skepta, and Tom Misch, starting to blow it open without having to sign their rights away to anyone else, and they're going to make a whole lot more money doing it like that.'

It sounds ideal, using the bits of the record industry you want, and leaving behind all the outdated stuff that's of no use to you. What could possibly go wrong, eh?

'Most artists know what they want to do. The best ones, in my opinion, always have a plan. They need help, but they have a direction. They're an artist, that's the whole point. The other kind of artist – the ones that wouldn't work for what we do – are the kind of manufactured artists that maybe have a fantastic voice, or a great look, but haven't got any songs, or a brand, and the major labels are really good at that.'

But it's not just 'X Factor' type artists who benefit from a major label approach, and these days, fewer and fewer people are considering them the 'bad guys'. Ali Tant is a senior project manager at Polydor records, and has worked with the likes of The 1975, Eminem, James Blake and Billie Eilish, amongst others.

'We have an in-house promo team who look after radio and streaming, a press team that looks after online, a team that looks at the TV. We have a number of marketing people, and those are the people on a day to day basis who are working with the artist and management to put together a campaign that you know they feel is going to help the artist develop over a period of time.'

But lest it sound like record companies are just a collection of shambling, monolithic organisations who just give money to idiots (who in turn throw it away or set fire to it), while indie labels are knights in shining armour protecting your interests, most companies are actually looking for people they can invest wisely in, the kind of artists who'll thrive in this environment, and who won't be afraid of making money for themselves and their business partners at the label. And when it comes to making that connection, sometimes knocking on their door and expecting an immediate answer won't yield results.

'Few and far between have been the times a band approached a label, and the label have signed the band. It's sometimes down to pot-luck, sometimes down to the management teams, or publishers that you've worked with. And sometimes it's down to recommendations by friends. It's very rare that an artist contacts a label and the label jumps straight away. In the twelve or thirteen years I've been working in the music industry, I've only ever signed one band from an unsolicited demo and that was when I worked at an indie label years ago. It happens, but very rarely.'

Biffy Clyro's Simon Neil says you have to look at what works best for you.

'You're less likely to get a response from the huge corporate labels than you are from an indie label. You need to figure out which labels exist in your world. Don't send your rock band to a reggae label and expect to get signed. Make it a more thought-out process. And don't send your music everywhere, because you'll over-saturate it. Pick five or six labels you love and send it to them.'

But, even if you do secure a deal, that's not necessarily the end of the story. And in Biffy Clyro's case, they started out as an indie band on an indie label, but their sense of ambition began to outgrow their situation.

'Our A&R guy on our second record said, "If there's no record there for the radio, I don't care: just go and make a piece of art." The liberation and confidence that gives you is second to none.

'But we started to get frustrated when Beggars Banquet didn't match our sense of ambition. We had freedom on one hand, but we didn't have the opportunities. We moved to a major label – Warner Brothers – who had more ideas, and put more money in. And we were ready for that at that point.'

Far from destroying their credibility, or limiting their freedom, the transition to a major label allowed the band to fulfil a commercial potential they might never have achieved with an indie, whilst giving them the creative freedom that success can frequently bring. But that would have been an unlikely outcome if they'd gone straight to the major label in the first place.

For singer songwriter Neo Jessica Joshua, better known as Nao, her brand of wonky funk seemed to fall between two stools, clearly possessing commercial potential, but needing some real care before being exposed to the mainstream. And like many artists at that level, she had an in-built set of fears about the business side of things.

'I had a really negative idea of what a major label was. I thought, "Oh, they want to put me in hot pants, and take me to Ibiza and sell my soul." But, I got to the point of signing and really found the whole process a really positive experience.'

When it came to the crunch, there was something in the

opportunities afforded by a major label that just seemed right for her. But that doesn't mean you just jump in head-first.

'I had the choice of being independent or going with a major. I always felt that being independent was the way I would go. And then I learned loads from being in the industry, like what it actually cost to tour, and what it cost to put out a record. I realised that perhaps a major label was right for me. However, I still have my own record label called Little Tokyo, which is independent. With Little Tokyo we put out other artists, and also my own music comes from it. It's just that it's wheeled by a bigger machine, and I think there's no wrong or right answer for which way you should go. It's different for everybody.'

In a realistic way, if you want to see this through to the end, you need to understand why you're actually doing it. And as Nao explains, understanding your goal can be crucial.

'Don't make the record label your ambition, build it by yourself as much as you can. A lot of people might feel that when they've signed a record deal, they're going to take over the world. But that's actually where the hard work usually begins. It just means that you have a bit more money behind you and a bit of a better chance of succeeding. But in reality it's where the work begins.'

Hard work is something Frank Turner has never shied away from. And while his roots might seem the antithesis of 'making it' in the record business, it certainly meant he had the work ethic required to succeed.

'My career started with the DIY hardcore scene in London. It was a very anti-industry structure. Everyone was self-releasing or releasing their friend's records. It demystified the whole process for me. Whilst I'm not technically a DIY artist any more, I still use that mental approach: don't wait for someone else to do it for you, get it done.'

Despite those DIY roots, Turner still sees the point in the industry. For the time being, at least.

'The role of record labels has changed a lot because of the internet. The idea of getting music from artist to person, has become easy. In the old days it was difficult to get a record out, but the difficult thing now is getting people to pay attention to your music. How do you get someone to click on your link, rather than the countless others that are bombarding them? There are some people who think record labels are dead now, and that's not true yet. But it might be in the future. They still have a big role of getting music into people's field of vision.'

So, whether it's major, indie, or a label services arrangement, the 'business' side of things seems to be here to stay. Ultimately, records are 'product' and it's up to you to decide how you view yourself, and what kind of 'product' you make. Once you get a handle on yourself, you can begin to explore what kind of business situation works best for you.

And if you get that right, then you'll have a better grasp of understanding who or what is going to work best for you. Making that connection work is all-important, because if they're working well for you, you'll be working well for them.

But don't lose sight of the fact that it is work, something that's always been at the forefront of Frank Turner's approach.

'You have to work hard to be in a successful band, and there are no successful bands that don't work their arses off. If you want to be in a band because you think it's an easy life, you need to step back and educate yourselves about the world you want to step into.'

TIPS ON RELEASING MUSIC

CONNIE MEADE
AMF RECORDS

1

Release an EP Yourself

I think increasingly this is something that bands can and should do themselves before they approach labels; there are great services to help you self-release your music to digital partners, you can do this without having a full team on board!

Get the Music Out Before You Gig

It's definitely a good idea to try and tie in your release with some gigs; try and get some music out before the shows so people are already connected to the new material.

Recording An Album Takes Time. Make a Plan

Writing, recording and mixing an album isn't the quickest process in the world. A good idea might be to plan out a year in advance so you can get everything you need lined up and you might find things start gravitating towards you while you do that.

Develop A Small Fan Base Before Getting Into Album territory

When you have a fanbase that are anticipating the album and you have a touring plan to help promote it. The worst thing you can do is rush it out. As Eminem said you've only got one shot.

It's Your Music. Get Involved in the Creative

I think it's very important for the artist to be involved in creative; it's their work and the creative must feel honest and true to them so if they aren't involved fans will see that from a mile off.

Release Singles As Long As It Doesn't Compromise the Album

I don't think singles should ever compromise an album BUT if you have chart ambitions and you want to get the album heard by as many people as possible it will definitely help to arm your radio plugger with some bangers! So it is definitely important but should never compromise the artistry.

Get It Out There

Then make sure the creative is as eye-catching as possible. Come up with a logical timeline based around some tour dates and, if you have the budget, put together a solid team to help you promote it. If promoting yourself you could try and get hold of contacts to send to. It's very important to use your own social networks to promote your work and depending on your budget you could look into marketing, put spend on socials etc. Come up with some interesting content to get fans attention!

WHAT IS PUBLISHING?

Publishing

FEATURING ADVICE FROM:
Charli XCX
George Ezra
Mike Smith (Managing Director at Warner/Chappell)
Simon Pursehouse (Sentric Music)
Stephen Taverner (Manager Alt-J + Wolf Alice)

Having thrown myself into the belly of the music industry from an early age, I'm astounded looking back at how little I knew about it. Nobody tells you shit... hence this book.

'Publishing' has always been a big myth to me. I'd regularly hear of artists signing their publishing deal, followed by their record deal. In these situations, I would nod politely, too frightened to let everyone know I had no clue what 'publishing' actually was, and why people were getting money for it.

I'm 100% certain that everyone in the music industry is blagging it. If you could take a journey into the average music industry drone's brain, it would be a cross-section of spreadsheets, demos, festivals, wicked bands, and a monkey sniffing its own finger.

Recently a hugely-hyped unnamed band managed by their dads (which sets the alarm bells ringing for record labels and industry alike) was offered a fist of cash to sign their publishing to a major company, to which the 'dad-ager' (dad/manager) replied, 'The boys are only young; they don't need to write a book yet.' And sadly, I'd probably put myself about one rung above old dad-ager on the publishing knowledge ladder.

Music publishing is something you really need to look into as soon as you start putting music online. I'm not talking about signing away your three-track catalogue for a billion pounds to 'Peter Piper's Publishing Co.'. I'm talking about signing up with the likes of Sentric and Tunecore, or other companies who will look after everything from collecting your royalties from radio, streaming, and sales, to pushing your music to feature on television, film, and radio.

Essentially they'll make sure you're getting every penny that's owed to you for your music, taking a commission along the way. The bigger publishers work quite similarly, but on a bigger level. Providing they are hyped enough on your act, they'll sign you up for a certain length of time or number of albums, and they'll give you an advance of money. Many artists and songwriters sign away their publishing first, as it usually gives them money to live on while they write their debut album. These companies will want the artists to write music that they can exploit and, for once, I use the term 'exploit' in a positive way. They want your music to make them – and you – as much money as possible. They'll set up writing sessions if it suits, provide money for demos, and generally facilitate the songwriter and performers to work at an optimum level, so they can create the best music possible.

'Sync' is a really useful way for you to make money from your music and gain exposure at the same time. Every song you hear on a radio/television advert, TV programme or film has been licensed from either the act or the publisher acting on behalf of the songwriter. And in the majority of cases, they've had to pay the artist for its use. My band was stung a few times by giving our music out for 'free exposure'. Learn from our mistakes.

The appropriate music on the right show at the right time can be a real career booster for an artist, specifically new artists. I've been on my fat ass watching TV and had to pause everything, rewind, and Shazam a track because I couldn't live without it. You know you've done the same.

Take a computer game like the FIFA franchise. Each year they choose a list of relatively unknown artists and open their music up to millions of players worldwide. That, in turn, creates fans, revenue, and a great sonic backdrop to throwing a games console controller through your living-room window.

When a band is starting out, the entire music industry can seem like one huge labyrinth of secrets, a puzzling world of made-up jargon and nonsense. And nowhere is this more true than in the area of publishing, with the possible exception of 'mastering'. No one knows what that means!

Essentially, a young band will look at the course their heroes followed. Generally, that follows the path of: idea, getting friends together, rehearsing in garage, getting first gig, recording demo, getting a record deal, then instant MEGASTARDOM and private plane.

There are countless rock biographies about famous musicians getting together with industry bigwigs to sign a record contract, usually in a lavish hotel suite or boardroom with caviar and champagne. And then everyone involved presumably self-destructs in an orgy of sex, drugs, and violence. It's a dance as old as time, really.

But you'd be hard-pressed to find a rock bio that features a high tension, glamourous scene involving a publishing contract. This is really the 'under-the-hood' end of the music business, the bit that does a lot of the work, but the public never really sees. And for an aspiring megastar, it can be a complete information black hole.

'When I started, I knew nothing about music publishing,' reveals Charli XCX, who has later gone on to have global success, and a series of chart smashes. But right at the beginning, the actual nuts and bolts of that success eluded her.

'When I was younger I was afraid to ask those questions, like "What is this?" But as I got older I had to ask more and more questions. For me, publishing is one of the most important parts of my business.'

But that still doesn't quite explain what it is, and for the answers, it's best to turn to one of the most respected figures in the music business, Mike Smith.

Since the late 1980s, he's been partly responsible for the success of acts like Blur, The Libertines, PJ Harvey, Arcade Fire, and Arctic Monkeys. Since 2016, he's been the managing director of Warner/Chappell Music, one of the biggest publishing companies in the world.

'A music publisher is there to represent the interests of the songwriter. Essentially we enter into a contract with a songwriter, and our role, as I see it, is to maximise the value of the songs they write, and to collect all the income that those songs generate.'

If you're the person who writes all the songs, then the publishing deal is the bit of the music industry that will relate most to you. These are the guys who take what you've done, sell it directly to companies, collect everything you've earned, and give a portion back to you.

This has less to do with the people out there going to your gigs, or buying your records. Instead, it focuses on the industry and business end of things. A record contract might make you famous, but a publishing deal will likely make you rich. If you get the right one, that is.

'A song generates royalties from the sale of that song,' says Mike Smith. 'Every time a song is digitally downloaded, every time a CD is sold, or a vinyl record is sold, it generates what is known as a mechanical royalty, which is eight and a half percent of the dealer price. The other big income that's generated for songwriters is a performance royalty. Every time a song is played on the radio, TV, or live at a venue, from the biggest stadium to the smallest club, an amount of money is generated which is paid back to the song writer of that song.'

This essentially boils down to songwriters getting paid for their work, getting a percentage of every song that is sold in some capacity, as well as getting paid when other people want to use their music. If you happen to have written a particularly good or well-liked song, then that could amount to quite a bit of money, once the publisher has taken their share of the cut. And while you're responsible for the song, the publisher does their fair share of work, too.

'The more interesting side of publishing is about what we

can do to enhance the value of a song,' Mike Smith points out. 'A hit record may come from a guy or girl that wrote the song, recorded it, and released it. Or what often needs to happen is that the song needs to be recorded by a successful artist in order to turn it into a hit song. So our job is to try and get our songwriters' material with hit artists. That's how it used to be more in the old days. These days, it's a much more collaborative effort and it's all about getting our songwriters into the studio with a successful artist and then collaborating together. We try and put those relationships together.'

Singer songwriter George Ezra has plenty of successful records under his own belt, but as a writer, publishing allows him to forge a separate life, working with other artists if he wants to.

'Say for instance, I've written a song that didn't work for me. My publishers could quite easily say, "George, if you're not going to use this song, we've got an artist in development that we think would really benefit from singing it, and you know it would be a leg up for them." That could happen.'

In practical terms for Ezra's own career, once he'd secured a publishing deal for himself, that took the pressure off some of the more difficult aspects of being a working musician.

'Publishing, to me, has always seemed like an amazing way to get bands on tour before anything else. Everyone needs to be represented by a publisher. The advances that they can offer is what young bands need to get on tour. Touring is much more expensive than I think anyone anticipates.'

A publishing deal can be used to pay for travel, accommodation, equipment, food, or whatever else the world of touring can throw at you. On a basic level, if you get a particularly good deal, it might just pay the rent while you go off to pursue your dream of being a musician. And as Mike Smith explains, publishing companies are always on the look-out for fresh blood. After all, if they can help you, you'll be helping them.

'We have talent scouts out there scouring all the blogs, Spotify, listening to the radio, talking to other talent scouts, talking to managers, and talking to lawyers. It's exactly the same for a music publisher as it is for a record company. We're just out there constantly, scouring every network going to hear about new music.'

In terms of managing your priorities, is it better to sign a billion pound recording contract first, or a billion pound publishing contract first? Personally I don't know, but I know a wise man who might – Stephen Taverner, manager of Wolf Alice and Alt-J.

'Wait till you've got a record deal and there's a career that a publisher can work alongside,' he advises. 'It's always good to start the conversations early, and then wait and do your record deal. If you're a band, then do a publishing deal as well, I always advise. Or if you are a songwriter, then you can sign earlier.'

It's important here to make that distinction between a band and a songwriter. Some artists like REM famously split songwriting credits right down the middle between all four members. But not all people make that distinction. So if you spend your hours slaving away crafting songs, only for a guitarist, bassist, and drummer to just play along with your creative vision, you might justifiably think that they haven't been part of that writing process.

In all cases, it's better to be upfront about this at the very beginning. If one person writes the songs, they should make it clear to everyone that this is the way it works and in turn, they should be prepared to shoulder more of the work themselves. By the same token, if everyone is pitching in ideas and shaping the music, maybe it's fairer to credit it to everyone.

The nightmare situation for any writer is to have your work disputed, particularly if you've scored some success. There have been plenty of cases of writers seeing their songs rake in the money, only to discover that other people felt that their contribution to the music really requires a share of that money.

That's when the lawyers become involved, and nobody wants that. Except for the lawyers. They love it when that happens, frankly.

Assuming you can divvy up the credit appropriately after you've written an awesome song, negotiated a record contract and a publishing deal, then you'll be able to sit back and marvel at how all these things take care of each other. In an ideal world, it's like a clockwork machine, as Charli XCX explains.

'When you get an advance from a record company at the beginning, it's basically like getting free money to play with. And then the more that your songs are synced, the more you get the money you have to pay the advance back.'

For anyone not following the logic of all this: you write the songs, a record label loans you loads of money to make the songs, you get a publishing deal, you become a success, and the money you make goes into paying off the money you were given at the start. Anything left over, if indeed there is anything, you can spend on your own private plane, or executive speedboat.

Sync deals, however, are another part of the publishing industry that people need to know about. Simon Pursehouse is the director of music services at Sentric Music, an independent publishing company which has handled the publishing end of things for the likes of Blossoms, Cerebral Ballzy, and many more. For Simon, sync deals are becoming an increasingly important part of the industry.

'Sync is having your music put in stuff in a very simple way of doing things. Any time you hear music used on TV, radio, movies, computer games, they've had to pay for the right to do so.'

It sounds simple, and it is. A sync deal gets your music heard in 'non-music' places. If you're watching a soap opera, and the lead character's affair with his twin brother's girlfriend's aunt is revealed, and there's music playing in the background, then that's a sync deal. Or if you're blowing away legions of aliens in a new video game, and a particularly triumphant song starts playing, then you can thank a sync deal. And far from being the old devil of 'selling out' to advertising, they've actually become a really vital part of the musical landscape, as George Ezra explains.

'Commercials are a huge way of how we hear things. There are so many songs I've heard for the first time on adverts. That's all down to publishing.'

For Charli XCX, sync is essential. But that doesn't mean you say "yes" to everything.

'I think sync made my career. I would not be in the position I am now without syncs; they broke me in as an artist. 'I Love It' was played on the TV show Girls, it was the song's first high-profile sync. It was a really extreme scene, where the girl and her flatmate go out and take loads of drugs, and my song played the whole way through. From there it started to sync everywhere. I also got a request from the U.S. Army to use my songs, and I said "Hell no!"'

Quite why the U.S. Army wanted the music of Charli XCX, we'll never know. Suffice to say, finding the right connection to your music can pay dividends. And that's where a company like Sentric come in, as Simon Pursehouse explains.

'Publishing was quite unachievable for anyone who wasn't getting a traditional publishing deal. So we offered a really artist-friendly service, where they always keep the copyright. Coming on board with us, we can make sure an artist keeps their copyright around the world, and never has to sign it away. We're looking after around half a million plus copyrights right now.'

And for Simon, cracking into the world of publishing is something young artists should absolutely be thinking of, right from the very beginning.

'As an emerging artist, you'll make more money from your

publishing copyrights earlier than any other part of your income stream, before you sell records, merch, or get paid to play gigs. You could write a song now, and play it in the pub at the end of your street, and that will generate publishing income that you can collect. As soon as you write a song you need to make sure that copyright has been protected and been registered properly.'

Publishing companies are there to help you with that, and organisations like Sentric are open for business. And if you manage to get all your ducks in the right order, so to speak, you'll end up with a paper trail of contracts, all of which somehow complement each other. And you'll be sitting on a golden throne, listening to your music on the radio, playing a game that features your new single, whilst simultaneously watching an episode of some new Netflix drama in which a vampire is dabbing/flossing (please change as zeitgeist dictates) to a particularly tender ballad you penned on a bathroom break.

Which is more or less what happened to Adele, although Simon Pursehouse explains it better.

'Adele is signed to XL Recordings. It's the record label that looks after her, but the songs on that album are looked after by the publishers. Take "Someone Like You". She co-wrote that with a guy called Dan Wilson who is published by Kobalt. Every time you hear someone do a cover of that song, the record label doesn't make any money, as they only make money from the recording they paid for. The publishers who look after the song will make money every time someone sings it on X Factor, or when someone sings it at Karaoke in your local pub.'

And all of this adds up to a whole sitting-room of golden thrones for Adele, because that song is particularly popular with X Factor wannabes, and karaoke singers.

But while getting your music on literally every platform sounds like a lucrative opportunity, as manager Stephen Taverner points out, sometimes it pays to be canny with what you're offering up.

'You wouldn't want to do a massive sync on your first single before anyone really knew who you were, because you'd only be known as the band for that TV commercial. I think it's a very important part of the puzzle, because it does help spread the word about your music to the mainstream if it's in a TV commercial or a movie.'

So when Johnny Rotten advertised butter, that wouldn't quite have worked if we didn't know who the Sex Pistols were first. And if they'd advertised butter right at the beginning of their rock and roll odyssey, perhaps the history books would be quite different.

But if all these conversations go according to plan, and you're the writer of the songs, you could be looking at a potentially life-changing revenue stream from music. And while the rest of the band is stuck in a dilapidated transit van, slogging their way to the gig, you could just meet them there in your personal helicopter.

Navigating the world of publishing might seem complicated but as with so much in life, once you get your head around it, there are plenty of opportunities to be had. And while it doesn't just apply to publishing, Mike Smith of Warner/Chappell's advice is to keep your eyes open to new opportunities, and keep talking to people.

'The more people you meet, the more situations you put yourself in where you can bump into people from the music industry – be they journalists, agents, promoters, or lawyers – the more opportunity you have to advance your career in the business.'

T-SHIRTS=£10
CDs=£5
THIS AIN'T GOIN' WELL..
NOPE...
PINTS?
I AM WEARING A T-SHIRT
CDs £5

D.I.Y

FEATURING ADVICE FROM:
Little Simz
Ray Blk
Rory Friers (And So I Watch You From Afar)
Rou Reynolds (Enter Shikari)
Run The Jewels (El-P + Killer Mike)

At the very beginning, roughly 99.9% of artists have had to walk that lonely road into the music industry by themselves. Kanye West didn't just beam onto Earth as a multi-award-winning artist, pre-Nirvana Dave Grohl had to pack up his own drum breakables and cold call venues to get shows, and Stormzy fired bars and beats to people in the early days hoping for a reaction.

What I'm getting at is, if you are reading this book then there is a high likelihood that you too are probably grafting, planning, and plotting out your musical journey right now.

I've got so much respect for artists that graft it out themselves. Nobody will ever care about the project you are undertaking as much as you will yourself. At this point, motivation, drive, and vision are your best friends, and sometimes your worst enemy. If you have a good balance of those three things and mix them with a plan that suits your music, then maybe you don't need anyone else. And perhaps the DIY route might be the right one for you.

The whole process of releasing music is a bit of a rollercoaster. From the guys on the high street haranguing innocent shoppers to listen to their music, all the way up to the major label high-rises in London's Kings Cross, it's impossible to tell how it's going to go. When you throw in the added element of self-releasing, and plunge down the DIY hole the stakes can be a lot higher.

You've created a personal vignette of yourself through your music, and now you have to set about releasing it. That means any wrong turn will feel like a personal attack, and any right turn will feel like happy hour on your birthday.

If going it alone, you're going to have develop some seriously leathery skin and a work ethic that would make Arctic husky dogs blush. It's never easy in a market that has hundreds of thousands of music makers around the globe, all doing the same thing as you. But that's not to say you can't do it. Some of the best careers have been kicked off with a DIY attitude.

Before we get further into it, let's discuss the acronym 'D.I.Y.' because it's slightly misleading. 'Do It Yourself' does not mean you have to completely 'do it yourself'. It's more of a statement against the major record label machine. It's the statement of intent that you're going to find your own path to take your songs to the music-loving public, without the aid of the corporate cheque book. However, this sexy abbreviation does not mean that you have to hack through the musical undergrowth with a machete on your lonesome. Everybody needs a team of some description and employing the right people to work alongside your vision is imperative, just as finding people with the same work ethic as you will make your life a lot easier.

There are independent companies which look after physical and online distribution, radio, artwork, PR, royalty collection, accounting, booking agents – the list goes on. It's your job as CEO of your own music to put together the perfect team for as much as your budget allows, or doesn't. But a few words of advice: even though you own 100 percent of your music (compared to the average of 20 per cent owned by a lot of acts signed to major labels), be prepared to see a lot of scary outgoings at the beginning. You are your own label, so you have to front the costs. When the music takes off, however, you own it all. So happy days, the silly pink umbrella cocktails are on you!

Meantime, it's really crucial you look after your mental and physical health. This may sound a bit dramatic, but I've seen it happen to a lot of musicians who self-release. They see this one release as their magnum opus, so it must be worked on twenty-three hours a day. There's a difference between working hard and working smart. It's easy to get obsessive and to not be able to see the woods for the trees. It happens to us all, but when you're hitting the DIY trail you need to maintain a sense of reality.

You should set realistic goals and dates and set aside days where you don't work on any music. You don't work

24/7 in your day job, so you shouldn't do the same with your music. It's best to plan, use your time wisely, and work hard; but never work at the expense of your health. No one piece of music is more important than you.

In the early days of the music industry, the idea of DIY usually came attached to the stigma of 'outsider' art. It was work that no respectable business would go near because of its inherently uncommercial nature.

Albums of religious songs, people who played weird instruments, music with no commercial potential whatsoever – they all fell under the DIY label. And for a long time, this was really all the term referred to. Until punk came along.

By that point – or so the traditional narrative goes – rock music had become too big, and too unwieldy, to really appeal to its core audience. It was simply another kind of big business, run by accountants, and played by men with bank accounts the size of a small planet. Then along came punk, and rock got taken back to street level, back to the pubs and clubs, where anyone could have a go.

And while all the major labels dabbled in punk rock, it didn't take long before some inspired amateurs decided they could circumnavigate the business end of things and make art on their own terms.

One of the first bands to try it came from Cleveland, Ohio, in the industrial heartland of America. Using their own Hearthan Records, Pere Ubu self-released their brand of dark, angular rock, which would go on to prove hugely influential. Other labels would eventually come to their door but right at the beginning, the commercial prospects for a band like Pere Ubu were literally zero, and no record label would dare to take a chance on such a risk.

Inspired by Pere Ubu, other bands such as Joy Division and Stiff Little Fingers signed up with independent record labels, while bands like Crass, Big Black, and Minor Threat formed their own record labels, and released music on their own terms. A revolution had taken place.

These days, it's significantly easier to self-release a record. You don't have to worry about record pressing plants, gluing sleeves together, or carting boxes of vinyl around in the back of your car. However, it's also never been more difficult for a self-released record to have the kind of impact that it used to. It is competing with a tidal wave of other songs, the like of which popular music has never seen before. And you've got to do an awful lot of work to make it stand out.

Ray BLK has defiantly followed her own path in her career so far, self-releasing two critically acclaimed EPs, getting a MOBO nomination, and topping the BBC's Sound of 2017 list. She's also now secured a position with Island records, on her own terms. And for her, DIY was the only way to go.

'I just wanted to develop myself and my sound, without the pressure of a label having to recoup, or make a big pop smash banger that I'd feel uncomfortable with. I just wanted to find my own lane first.'

Of course, this comes with risks, and while a major label will want money from you if you hit the big time, at least they'll have given you money in the first place. For most DIY artists, certainly at the start of their journey, they can expect their pockets to be permanently empty.

'The financial reality is that you will be broke for quite a while, and a lot of the money that you have when you start making money, ends up having to go back into investing in yourself.'

And when the money comes in, you better make sure that you invest it in the right part of yourself. For Enter Shikari's Rou

Reynolds, that decision isn't quite as clear-cut as it might first seem.

'We had to make the choice between going into the studio or buying a banged-up old van. We decided on the banged-up old van with the leaky roof. After a gig, we were in the van listening to the Radio 1 Punk Show, worried about the battery running down, and then the DJ played our song, stopped it after thirty seconds and said, "I love the song, but the quality isn't good enough." So, we immediately questioned our decision to buy the van.'

Hindsight is a wonderful thing, but at least the van got them to a gig. Every cloud ...

Leaky van or not, going DIY isn't really a choice for many people: it's just something that's in their blood. And for Rou, there was no question that he'd go down the DIY avenue, inspired by some punk rock heroes of yore.

'I think it's probably more a mindset than anything. It's being fearless and trying to be real and genuine. We didn't have a choice; nobody was interested. So, we had to do everything ourselves at the beginning. American hardcore laid the ground for us: Black Flag, Fugazi, and Minor Threat all did it themselves.'

Like the American hardcore bands, plenty of musicians have honed their craft, won over an audience, and then discovered that no label is prepared to take a punt on them, for a multitude of reasons. They could be too raw, too noisy, or too aggressive. Sadly, they just might not look right. And in these cases, you can either pack it in and feel sorry for yourself, or you can get off your backside and do it yourself. And for some bands, this is actually a far more attractive prospect than being beholden to someone else.

'We were very wary of jumping into a major label contract, as we'd seen some local bands build up hype and then plummet fast. We didn't see the long-term benefit in it. We met plenty of labels.'

Going it alone means investing in your art at a time when no one else wants to. And whatever way you look at it, it is an investment, something that might hurt in the short term, but will hopefully pay dividends further down the line. For El-P of Run the Jewels, it meant having to look at the long-term effects.

'I think focusing on craft is the main thing. There is no short-cut. Everybody has the same tools, and some people get lucky and some people don't. This means you have to make your music stand out. If you need to spend a little money, do it. Get a fucking horn player to come in and do some crazy shit on your record. Spend it on the guy you want to mix your song. Invest in your art and keep investing. Other doors will open as soon as people connect with your music.'

Connecting with that audience is the all-important part of DIY. No matter how unconventional or uncommercial your music might be, if you actually like it and care about it, there's a very good chance that other people might too. You might not be looking forward to your own private jet, mind you, but for some artists, a small and devoted audience can allow them to continue doing what they want to do – which is writing, recording, and releasing music.

MC and North London legend Little Simz has pursued the DIY option to sizeable success, cracking the UK R&B Top 20. And for her, being in control of her own destiny allowed her to treat her career with the respect she feels it deserves, something which might not have happened if she was part of the machine.

'When I was being offered deals, I didn't feel any labels were in it with me for the long run. I felt it was all hype, it was all very short term. If I'd signed a deal, there's a possibility I wouldn't be doing this in five years, and that isn't my calling. All the decisions I make now will affect that. I wasn't trying to be a rebel; I was being a realist. I'm happy I chose this path. It's taught me a lot about myself.'

The realities of this situation have allowed Little Simz to call the shots on who she thinks she is, and not to have to worry about being packaged up as someone else's idea of success. And that authenticity shines through, allowing her to connect with an audience. She's the real deal, not some manufactured version of the truth.

And when it came to making this idea work as a career, she had the business smarts to see it through.

'A good DIY artist is a risk-taker that understands not only the musical side of things, but is business savvy as well. They'll make amazing music in the studio, but they can also go to meetings with bosses of companies, and they can be assertive and know what they want. Not to blow my own trumpet, but those are some of the qualities that I possess.'

It's a cutthroat world out there, and it's safe to assume that many people are trying to rip you off and take advantage of you. And that can be tough. But just because you're DIY, doesn't mean you're alone. Little Simz says.

'I have a manager, Eddie. We have a small team. We're fortunate enough now to afford to pay people to take them on. For a long time, Eddie was manager, tour manager, DJ. He did everything, and he did that because he was thinking long term.'

This long-term thinking is something that actually appealed to El-P of Run the Jewels, who actively relished getting his hands dirty.

'I wanted to make it happen. I wanted to be part of every process, the curator, the idea dude; get the vinyl out there. I didn't want to have to bend my will or artistic ideas to anyone else's vision. I didn't want to have to wait. Thank God now you can just put music up whenever you like!'

The internet has made this whole process a lot easier, and the days of getting all your friends together to glue record sleeves together are (largely) gone. But while some of the hard work has gone, the appeal of DIY is more than just doing a lot of work. For some people, like El-P, this is a way of life.

'The whole point really is deciding if it's an ethos that applies to you artistically. For me, doing it yourself made sense because I knew that I didn't want to change my music for anybody. It was really about being happy, it was about being a champion of my own destiny. I think that's the artist's dream: get paid for what you love to do, and keep doing it forever.'

Of course, not everyone manages to achieve this dream, and for those who do, it takes an awful lot of effort. And like El-P, it can help if you have someone who actively enjoys doing the hard work. And in Enter Shakiri's case, Rou Reynolds was always keen to get stuck in.

'I remember really enjoying booking tours. It's that typical thing of you piecing it together, and slowly seeing the dates add up, and trying to fill in the days off, and then making a crappy tour poster. I really enjoyed that, and I enjoyed making the merch designs as a whole. It wasn't very good, but it was a necessity.'

DIY artists can expect to be a jack of all trades like Rou Reynolds, designing posters, selling merch, driving the van, and booking the gigs. And occasionally, you can get around to making some music. But on some level, the music is going to take a back seat to the realities of your situation. So, you need to have the music in place long before you even think of going down the DIY route, because it's going to take a lot of your time and attention to get the books balanced and keep track of your finances. The road to DIY success is paved with plenty of people who couldn't keep an eye on the many different irons that they had in the fire.

The worst-case scenario is when you start to neglect yourself in this pursuit of artistic self-reliance. For Run the Jewels' Killer Mike, this should be concern number one.

'Don't overspend, so you have to be good at budgeting. Make sure your rent is paid. If it's paid for a year, then you can tour for no money, stay creative, and work your damn ass off. You have to preserve yourself and think smart.'

If you look after yourself, then you can buy the freedom to look after your career. And for Little Simz, this means sacrificing certain things that a major label would take care of on your behalf.

'Being independent means you are the label, you have to fund everything yourself. You have to put your business hat on. Label artists don't have to worry about booking flights, making merch, and the rest, but I choose this to be hands-on in every aspect of my career.'

So, while she might have to arrange her own transport to and from a gig (which I imagine is a bit of a downer once you come offstage), Little Simz has been able to stay true to her own vision. And for plenty of artists, like Killer Mike, staying true to your own vision is something that a major label will rarely let an artist do.

'It's all the fucking shit that comes with it, some guy called Craig with a bad haircut telling you what your single should be. A guy called Dave ... Dave likes your FIFA song. Who is this guy?'

If the only advice you've gleaned from that statement is to avoid Craig and Dave, then you might need to go back and reread it.

The business side can be brutal, and whether you're going down the DIY route or the major label approach, when someone shoves a bit of paper in front of you and asks you to sign it, make sure you know what you're getting yourself into, as Rou Reynolds of Enter Shakiri succinctly explains.

'Get management and a lawyer together before you look at contracts, otherwise you are fucked.'

Ultimately, if you have the constitution for it, the drive to do it, and the organisational skills to make it work, going down the DIY route could potentially reap huge rewards for an artist.

You get to completely control every aspect of your career and if you're successful, all the money is coming back to you. You don't have to do anything you don't want to do, and the music you make is ultimately made from your own vision, rather than someone else's idea of success.

On the other hand, you spend a lot of time doing the jobs that other people are paid to do, you have to invest a lot of your own time and money into something you love, with potentially very little coming back to you, and there's no safety net for failure. Many artists have gone down the DIY route and found it to be unsustainable by taking on a financial, physical, and emotional cost which is hard to bear and can be harder to recover from.

However, enough people have proved that it can be done, and they continue to inspire other artists. For Little Simz, she saw other people making a success of their music on their own terms, and she knew that was the way she had to go.

'Chance the Rapper is a great example and inspiration of someone who has broken the barriers, and changed what it means to be independent. He goes against the grain and does everything on his terms, with his people. I love his movement and how he carries himself.'

For Ray BLK, she looked to Stormzy as an inspiration on how she could make it work.

'Stormzy was making freestyle videos and posting them on YouTube. Then I think he was posting a video a month to get noticed. He was really trying to create his own opportunity.'

Ultimately, it can be very rewarding to experiment with DIY music. And if you dip your toe in that water, you'll likely know that it's for you, as El-P explains.

'Do you believe in yourself? Me and Mike never questioned our belief, we were like "Ooh we're going to do this shit." It's really then about figuring out how I am going to do it.'

TIPS ON D.I.Y

RORY FRIERS

AND SO I WATCH YOU FROM AFAR

1 Make Art That Speaks To You

Make honest music that represents you and that stirs you, something you sincerely love. You will have to stand up for this music everyday, you'll have to walk on a stage and play to an empty room and still stand proud behind the songs. You'll have to be away from your own bed and the people you love for this music, you'll have to be skint at times for this music, you'll have to teach yourself boring skills like how to fill out tax returns and understand pages and pages of legal jargon so if it doesn't make you feel alive when you're making it then it's not going to do it when you need it most along the way.

2 Take All the Help you Can Get

DIY isn't about taking every aspect of the band onto your own shoulders, it's about being the deciding and driving force of how and where your music goes, Have a clear vision of what you want and how you present and interact with the world around you, surround yourself with people who can help you get there, you steer the ship.

3 Money Matters

Cash flow is one of the most important things to look after. If you really want to be punk rock then look after it. This is what will enable all those ideas and dreams and creative endeavours to actually happen, if you hold the cash then you're the boss.

4 Trade in other Currencies

Can you put a show on for a band in return for them doing the same, can you make posters, are you good at design work, can you use Photoshop, make videos, take photographs, can you record music for people, help mix a song, master a song, do you know how to book a tour, are you good with social media, do you own a van, have you got a space people can rehearse in, do you own some cool gear, some mics, some PA. Literally, what ever you can bring to the table, someone, somewhere can make use of it. Make connections.

Opinions are subjective

Don't presume people always know what they're talking about, most people don't, there will be people who will say they know what's best for your music, but remember, opinion is subjective. One person's idea of success differs from another and what's important is that you are fulfilled and content in your own idea of success.

Don't be Afraid to do Things Differently

Its your music, present it however speaks truest to you and however serves your vision best, things are wide open now, no one really knows what they're doing no matter how much they try and tell you they are.

Look after your Fans

After the art itself they come first no matter what. Whether there is one or one million fans

Find Ways to Connect and Interact

Keep people abreast of what you're doing. Don't depend on social media, they all have a shelf life. Utilise and use what you can when you can in the way that serves your music best, don't feel pressure to go with the latest fad.

Never Sell yourself Short

If it's important enough for you to put your time, love, passion, money and energy into then its important enough for you to speak loudly and proudly about it. This is your baby, separate the art and your ego, do it justice, speak with passion.

Enjoy Every Second

You are the master of your own destiny now, the space between you and your potential fans is smaller than ever, it's an amazing time to be a musician, enjoy every minute of it.

A BAND DEMOS #1
-HQ SOUND-
-90-
A BAND DEMOS #2
-HQ SOUND-
-90-
A BAND DEMOS #3
-HQ SOUND-
-90-
A BAND DEMOS #4
-HQ SOUND-
-90-
A BAND DEMOS #5
-HQ SOUND-
-90-
A BAND DEMOS #6
-HQ SOUND-
-90-
A BAND DEMOS #7
-HQ SOUND-
-90-
A BAND DEMOS #8
-HQ SOUND-
-90-
A BAND DEMOS #9
-HQ SOUND-
-90-
A BAND DEMOS #10
-HQ SOUND-
-90-

Recording the EP/Album

FEATURING ADVICE FROM:
Charli XCX
Julie McLarnon (Record Producer)
Jungle
Kev Baird (Two Door Cinema Club)
Ollie Hodges (A + R Polydor Records)

Getting music into the public sphere is the best way to prove that your act means business. You can spend a lifetime firing up demos and single tracks online. That's fine for a while, but for me it's when you get that piece of meat between your chops and start chewing that you really get to the core of what a band or artist is all about. This can mean releasing an EP, mini-album, playlist, mixtape, and eventually the much anticipated/dreaded debut album.

You're putting years and months of your hard work, creativity and self-discovery into one place, the album. This should be something you can stand behind with confidence as the best representation of who you are as an artist. It's important to take that plunge. Over the nine years I played bass in a band, we released a string of singles and EPs with the view that when we got snapped up for a bajillion pounds by a record label, we would release our debut album. The bajillion-pound offer never came, and the band folded without leaving an album, a decision we all regret.

Moral of the story: don't be a lazy fool; put yourself and your music out there.

If you work backwards from Noel Gallagher owning a brown Rolls Royce and not being able to drive it, you will find a person furtively strumming a guitar and humming, and writing music which millions will eventually adore. Let's take it as a formality that you've already completed the writing music stage. I'm not dishing out the songwriting tips... that would be like your Nan dishing out wisdom on how to spit fire at a rap battle. The next process is getting the song recorded.

You can set up your beat laboratory and record from home. You can pitch up to a local studio with an engineer. Or you can save up all your dinner money for a light-year and head to one of the super studios with a well-known producer. You know your financial boundaries more than anyone, and you'll know which option suits your style best. I've seen it happen before, where the excitement of the art blurs the financial reality. Living on the bread line for a week or two is part of the aspiring musician story, but please don't leave yourself with thousands of pounds of debt for a record. No musician likes to celebrate their album release with a visit from the bailiffs.

Before you plunge feet first into the album process, it's

good to sit back and take stock. Are you creatively ready? Do you have enough songs? Have you spent long enough building a fanbase to justify the record? There won't really be a concrete 'yes' to any of these questions: you can always have more songs, spend more time building your fan base, and sharpening your songwriting fangs. You have to judge it on a mixture of gut feeling and cold harsh reality, and only you and your trusty associates will know when to hit the big red 'album' plunger.

As in any other line of business, forward planning is key when putting together an EP or an album. It sounds obvious, but you would be surprised how many shirk the basics and just plough ahead without a second thought.

If it's the seminal debut album you're after, then make sure you write a lot more songs than will eventually end up on the record. I've known acts to go into the studio with anywhere between twenty and two hundred (no joke) songs. Imagine having to pick ten or fifteen tracks from that. What an A&R nightmare! On the flip side, going in with just ten songs isn't a good idea because you'll have nothing to choose from. It works for some, but I think it's better to have a bank to pick from in order to make the greatest record possible.

If your home recording isn't on point and you're keen to emulate your idols and get into the posh recording studio, then make sure you are prepared. Recording studios are generally quite expensive, and there's no time for fucking about and wasting money. The songs need to be demoed, the creative outlook for the record should be rolling around somewhere in your head, and every member of your group should have rehearsed so much that they could sing the song backwards underwater. Also, learn to play to a click track before you go in, as this will save you money and stress.

I made the mistake of not learning to record to click track on my bands first EP. It felt like I was duelling with a taunting metronome, unable to hit all the sweet spots. It was basically Guitar Hero in real life, only no fun.

If you have a vision for the record, stick to it. Always listen to the studio engineer's advice, but remember that this is your debut album. If their ideas don't fit, don't be scared to politely decline and move on.

It can be a stressful environment for everyone involved, so encourage the other people in the studio. Don't bark at someone because they flubbed a note or hit the wrong tom-drum. They might not be so kind when it's your turn to screw up.

Eventually, your creative egg will hatch into a beautiful, potentially groundbreaking debut album. You and yours are all sitting around gazing adoringly into it, unconsciously tapered together in telekinesis, thinking 'What the fuck do we do now?'

Well, you release it, don't you! If you have management or a label, this is where they step in and start spinning the plates. If you are DIY, then this is where the real hard work starts. There's not much point in you having spent as long as you will have on the songwriting process and the recording process just to drop the ball now when it comes to getting it out into the world.

Give yourself a few months to get everything together, you'll need it. Pull together your artwork, your biography, music videos, and everything else you need. Then use online release platform services such as Tunecore (others are available) to get your album up on the digital service providers (Spotify, Apple, Amazon, Deezer).

If you have any money left, look into PR by keeping an eye on campaigns you like, both regionally and nationally, and finding out who their PRs are. If you don't have the cash (PRs are incredibly expensive, but almost always negotiable) then you're going to have to go on the charm offensive and hustle your way into and onto any newspaper, magazine, radio show, and playlist you possibly can.

Never beat yourself up if it's a difficult slog or you're a little crestfallen, you can only do your best. Major record labels fuck up way more albums than are successful, and they're meant to be the professionals!

For a long time, people have been happy to declare the album a 'dead' format. And each time someone says it's deceased, it comes back, fresh and fighting fit. And then critics and audiences alike fall in love with a classic record, something that will stand the test of time for decades to come.

Yet when albums first appeared, they were generally little more than a promotional, moneymaking item, a few singles stitched together with some filler tracks thrown in for good measure. As in many things, The Beatles led the charge on pop music's love affair with the album format. (Obviously jazz had been there before; but then, what hasn't jazz done first?) But by the end of the 1960s, every band worth their salt were turning its creative efforts into perfecting the art of the long-playing 33rpm record.

Having been released from the logistical demands of physical formats, an album these days can be anything you like... really. Ten expertly chosen songs, aiming to capture where you are as an artist? Cheers, thanks. A never-ending, constantly evolving song-cycle that will continue after your death? Why not?

But while albums have changed in many respects, the way people make them hasn't. And whether you are a stadium rock band recording in the most expensive residential studio in the world, or a lo-fi die-hard, pouring your ideas onto a battered 4-track tape recorder, the principles are much the same.

That's not to say you'll understand exactly what you're doing though.

'The broad strokes of recording yourself is quite understandable, but the intricacies are all fucking physics, and it's quite hard,' explains Kev Baird, bassist of Two Door Cinema Club. 'We recorded everything ourselves at the beginning, and found a guy who would mix it for £100. We had really awesome memories of being a little gang, and nobody else was in it.'

And while those memories are no doubt priceless, a cursory listen to the early Two Door Cinema Club demos and singles show a band with charm and great ideas, but not much idea of how to record music. By the time of their debut album, Tourist History, they sounded big, full, polished, and ready. And just in case you were worried, the charm and the ideas were still intact.

That said, sometimes if you work too hard to perfect an idea, you end up nowhere.

'We've been in the studio with a demo we've been trying to replicate and after ten hours, we rethink and go back to the demo. The basis of recording is, if it sounds good, it is good.'

Not every artist comes to the studio armed with a collection of demos, however, and for some people, the studio itself is where these ideas come together, as Charli XCX explains.

'I never prepare for the studio. I like to keep it spontaneous. The best melodies are the ones that pop into your head when you hear the music. It's the most instinctive thing you want to sing. That will generally be the most hooky, or dumb-but-good-dumb thing, as it's in your brain already.'

In these situations, you might feel like you're waiting for the lightning strike of inspiration in the studio, but you can train yourself on how to view the studio, and how to get the best out of it. And for Charli XCX, that can be helped by having the right people with you.

'I love recording with my friends. I don't like working with a lot of new different people for my own project. We know each other's strengths and weaknesses, we know each other inside out. Everybody has their own skill set. When I go into the studio, I make sure I have the people I trust and love there.'

This spontaneous approach to recording is something that's shared by J, of modern soul collective Jungle.

'We develop on the fly and go bar by bar, and make it up as we go along. If you're going into a big studio and you are using other people's time and money, then it's best to be as prepared as possible. But if you're doing it on your iPhone, then it's whatever goes, really.'

That said, if you actually are in a big studio, then it helps if you can get focussed on what you're doing. So, while that app on your phone might have been instrumental in helping you get the basic idea for a song, it might be time to put it down if you're actually recording.

'Switch off all technology,' J advises. 'Focus is super important. Any distraction is bad, internet, phone, whatever – it's all bad. You need to lock into the process. It takes you ten minutes to fully get into a focus, and if a 'ping' goes off on your phone, it puts you back to square one.'

If you write the songs, it's easy to get frustrated when you hear a gulf between what you envisaged in your head, and what your pals are playing in front of you. Even if it sounds ace on stage, in front of an audience, sometimes it's still not quite right. That's where a studio and a talented producer and engineer come in. If you get the right people, and they get what you're trying to do, suddenly this ramshackle noise can start to sound like that perfect sound you've been hearing inside your head.

But you still have to get on with them, as Two Door Cinema Club's Kev Baird reveals.

'It's pointless having an engineer you don't get along with. The more they are invested in the project, the better it's going to be.'

That's not to say that everything needs to be done in a recording studio.

'You can do so much outside of the studio in advance. The main thing that you can't replicate outside of a studio is drums. Recording bass in a studio is pointless; you can do that anywhere. There's so much great software and DI's (Direct Inputs). Nothing beats cranking up your album in a studio and playing, but there is a time and a place for that.'

Deciding on the time and place, and knowing when you're ready to make a record is something that exists outside the realm of scientific enquiry. You just 'know' it. And sometimes, even when you know it, you might be wrong. As Charli XCX tells us, you just have to go with your gut.

'You are your best judge. It's important to have people who you can trust, and to trust their judgement. But at the end of it all, it should come down to what you think. There are no right or wrong ways to record an album. You will know when it's time to put it out.'

Once you're sure, then you can think about diving in and immersing yourself in what hopefully ends up as a creatively satisfying process. And for A&R man Ollie Hodges, who has helped secure the success of albums by bands such as George

Ezra, The Vaccines and Glasvegas, that process of working and writing doesn't stop when you start recording.

'When you start making an album, you should know that you've got everything that you need to finish recording it in terms of the writing. It doesn't mean you should stop writing. I like people to keep writing all the way through.'

That continuous writing process can help when you get to the studio, and you still aren't sure what songs are going to make the grade. It's a common problem: songs that sounded great in the practice room sound poor in the studio with all their deficiencies on display. And while sometimes this can catch you off-guard, as with everything, you can do a lot of useful preparation before you even enter the room, being sure of your own material.

'"Hey Ya" by OutKast was a B Side - they didn't think it was going to be a single,' says Ollie. 'It was only when everything was finished that they thought that. The great thing about making an album is that you can record fifteen songs, and then decide the singles. You should spend time studying, writing, and from that trying to make the best songs possible.'

And a big trick that can help you when you're trying to ensure your album will have the best songs possible, is to bring plenty of songs with you in the first place.

'I usually say to have twenty-five tracks ready to choose from for the album. That might mean forty tracks you have started. A band once gave me a hundred and fifty tracks, which caused me to have a breakdown.'

Ok, so too many is too many. Use your own judgement on that one.

Your judgement should tell you that, whether or not you've brought one hundred and fifty songs to the studio, you've only really got ten or so good ones. And in that case, as Kev Baird reveals, they're going to be the songs that make the grade.

'We're always horribly unprepared. We always thought we'd

love to have more songs going into to record. It would be great to have twenty songs, and then pick and choose from that. But we always only had ten or twelve and that's the album, and there's no change in it.'

Maybe Two Door Cinema Club are just really lucky (or maybe they're really good writers) but those ten or twelve songs have done them well. And while it might not work this way for everyone, if you do the work before going to the studio, there won't be too many surprises along the way.

'For our debut album, pretty much nothing changed from demo to album. We had just enough time to make the recordings sound a little bit better, and that's all. Recording an album will take as long as you've got. If you have six months, it will take six months. If you have six days, it'll take six days. Nothing is ever finished when you're making a record.'

That last statement is likely true, regardless of what kind of music you play, or what kind of approach you've taken. There will always be something more you could do, something you could change or tweak, something that can be added. And it's not always to the strength of the record. In fact, sometimes, these creative conflicts raise their heads before you even finish the process, clouding your judgement. And as T from Jungle points out, you just have to be strong, knuckle down, and work through it.

'Nobody is in a heightened state of creativity all the time. You've got to work through bad ideas. You've got to work through writer's block. As long as you are there in the right place, then you are doing the right thing.'

This urge to create is something that drives Charli XCX. And when she's in the studio, she isn't going to let a bad idea stop her.

'I hate having a song, sitting on it, then bringing it to the studio. If a song isn't done in twenty-four hours, then it's not a good song for me. I like to go into the studio and start from nothing. If you get stuck on one song, don't freak out, move on, it's not meant to be.'

Hopefully, if you stay your course, navigate all the dangers, and don't lose your head, you'll end up with something you're proud of. Or something you don't utterly despise, at the very least. And if you do end up with something awful, shelve it. There's too much bad music in the world already, without you adding to it. And while it might be crippling (emotionally and financially) to have missed the mark, if you're really serious about it, you'll try again.

Putting out an average debut record isn't quite the sin it used to be. There was a time when a dud of a first release would ensure that there'd be no more after it. Conversely, some record companies have invested in artists who have released debut records that possess none of the spark or creativity that they'd show later in their career. You'd have to be a genius to predict how big Bowie and Springsteen would become from their debut albums, but they got the formula right further down the line.

For Charli XCX, her debut didn't set the world on fire, but it got the ball rolling.

'There was huge pressure on my first album. It was a time when, if your album didn't do well, you would get dropped. That has changed with streaming. It didn't sell a lot but "I Love It" did quite well for my record label.'

And for A&R man Ollie Hodges, you shouldn't get too hung up about making a real splash with your first record.

'When I started, it was drilled into us that if it didn't break on the first album, then that was that. I think that has changed now.'

Part of that change has no doubt come from the way albums are released now. Back in the day, records cost a lot of money to make. And most of them ended up as landfill, forming the basis of new continents as we struggled to find places to bury them. But now, the physical release is not the paramount part of an album. You can afford to do things differently, like T of Jungle.

'The industry has changed so much. We're in such a track-based industry. Proper music people love albums. We love albums, but it feels like you have to be releasing music onto an infinite streaming playlist right now. People love vinyl, but we want to find the next way of releasing something.'

Things will keep on changing, that much is certain. But for the moment, we've settled on a mixture of older, physical releases, and more flexible digital formats. And the industry is still coming to terms with how to make a success of it all, as Ollie Hodge explains.

'Ten years ago, there were only a few opportunities in the UK. You could align a few different people, and suddenly have big impact with MTV2, NME, and Radio 1 jumping on board, giving you mainstream exposure very quickly. There are less people who can do that now, so it takes longer for that to happen. Which in some ways, I think, is more healthy."

So, if you slave over a debut record, and nothing happens, don't panic, these things can take time.

And for Kev Baird, when it came to the debut Two Door Cinema Club album, it was worth the wait.

'It was a slow burn with the album. It took a long time for radio and publications to pick up on it. It was happening with real people, but the taste-makers took a while to come on board. At the time it was frustrating, but afterwards it was amazing, as we knew we got there by ourselves.'

If you're talented enough – and lucky enough – gazing down from the highs of a successful album is a very sweet feeling indeed. It can be a tortuous process, and it has been the end of plenty of bands. But finally being able to drag those ideas from the back of your mind, and plant them in someone else's brain via an album is one of the most satisfying parts of being a musician. This is your statement, your opening gambit, your calling card.

Or it might just be the ten or eleven songs you whittled down in the 'Not Shit' pile.

No matter, you've made it! Top of the world, Ma!

Now, as Ollie Hodges reminds us, all you've got to do is do it again. And again. And again. And again…

'People go crazy making albums, it can take months and years. First albums are normally fun; the artists don't really think about it, and it is quite an enjoyable process. The self-reflection and doubt generally comes on the second album.'

TIPS ON GETTING INTO THE STUDIO

JULIE MCLARNON'S
PRODUCER AND ENGINEER

1

Bands Should be Tight

I never charge anything for pre-production and won't commit to recording a band until I've spent time with them rehearsing the songs, discussing sonics and arrangements. During this time I discuss my plans for the sound and feel of the record and listen to the band's ideas.

2

Keep the Partying to a Minimum

There's pretty much no partying, maybe a couple of drinks after a 12 hour day but energies need to be reserved and heads kept as clear as possible. The better the focus and stamina the better the record.

Pre-Production is Essential

Studio time in a good studio is not cheap and shouldn't be wasted trying to negotiate artistic compromise. The actual recording process should flow fast with all the niggles ironed out in advance. If it's done that way recording is an exciting high with no misunderstanding. Good communication leads to good relationships. It's an emotionally intense experience, so people need to like each other.

Get it Mastered

Mastering is your final fine sand and varnish, it should add a little sheen but don't expect miracles at mastering, the differences should be very subtle.

Home Recording For Some, Studios For Others

Some genres can easily be recorded at home with minimal gear but if real drums, guitars and other real instruments are involved a decent studio with an excellent engineer is essential. If budgets are tight spend what you have on an experienced engineer who has made records you like the sound of. A great studio will sound rubbish in the hands of an inexperienced engineer but your kitchen can sound great in the right hands.

How Long Should a Debut Album Be

As a rule bring at least 30 mins worth of your best songs. I'm not a fan of recording much more than you need, it's a waste of focus, time and budget.

WHAT IS MASTERING AND WHY IS IT IMPORTANT

ROCKY O'REILLY

1

What Is Mastering?

Mastering is the final audio process before releasing your music. It often aligns all your tracks in terms of dynamics, overall volume and frequency balance. It makes them the best sonic version possible.

2

Why Should You Get Songs Mastered?

I usually think of it as a safety net, an audio icing service and insurance policy all rolled into one. It should be a trusted set of ears in a well set up room running your mixes through some wonderful equipment. I will catch anything you may have missed.

File Delivery

The other part of mastering is systematic, reliable delivery of the correct file types. Mastering for CD, vinyl and online services usually require a variety of different audio file types, embedding of ISRC codes, text information and more. It's not the fun artistic side of releasing music, but it's so important to get it right.

Who Should I Get To Master?

Find out who mastered the records you love. Pick some-one who will "get" what you're aiming for. Build up a relationship with them. Learn to trust them and you'll have a long term golden set of ears to help finish all your mixes forever.

How Much Should I Spend?

Keep it all relative and in balance with your plans and your progression. If you've spent £1000 on your recording and £500 on the mix, it doesn't seem like a wise choice to pay £20 for mastering. Similarly if it's your very first demo and you recorded five songs in a day live, it probably doesn't make sense to spend £150 per track on mastering. Aim as high as you can reasonably justify and make sure it has a positive impact on your experience of producing and releasing your own music.

HEY, I LIKE WHAT YOU GUYS ARE DOING HERE, GOOD WORK!!
SO? HOW MUCH MONEY HAVE WE MADE?
I DON'T KNOW, I DUNNO HOW THIS WORKS...
MATT RILEY'S WORLD OF AWAL
MUSIC FOR SHITTING
MOON MEN
33⅓ R.P.M.
JUNK
BAND E.P.S
x50 CDS
REGRET FUEL

Distribution + Streaming

FEATURING ADVICE FROM:
Alistair White (Machine Management)
Charlene Hegarty (Oh Yeah Music Centre/Artist Manager)
Darcus Beese (President of Island Records)
Frank Turner
Ian Watt (Machine Management)
Jungle
Matt Riley (VP of A+R at AWAL)

You could be sitting on a record capable of ushering in a new cultural dawn; a record so important that society as we know it collapses and is reborn around this collection of twelve songs written by you. Your sonics are reimagined and tailored as a tangible utopia for humanity, nature, and life itself. Finally, world peace! The only thing is, if you don't know how to get your music out to the public, then your vision of paradise is fucked.

There's no point spending your entire creative life learning your instrument, training your voice, sacrificing financially, travelling miles to rehearse, and recording the music, only to discover that you have no way of putting it out.

That's of equal importance to everything that has gone into getting the single, EP, album, or mixtape ready in the first place. So you should spend the time getting your strategy in place. It's important to study the world around you, perhaps look at what works for similar artists in your lane, and picking and choosing aspects that you like and don't like. There are countless case studies out there for you to cherry-pick the best ideas from. I know this method is hardly the height of innovation but it has worked for many people in the past. And having sat in major label boardrooms, I know it still seems to be their go-to method for planning a release campaign.

Being ambitious and realistic are two things that are almost impossible to balance. They are the yin and yang of any creative project. Everyone wants to have their music released on red see-through vinyl, with a thousand 12-inches ready to go. But the cost of getting it there is going to be substantial, and to make back that cost means you're going to have to hustle like a madman. That combo of ambition and reality often leads to stress and mental health problems. It can be crushing for an artist to feel their vision isn't being realised.

I approach my projects from the over-optimistic angle. My best friend – who is an artist – approaches his from the cynic's base point. When we get on the phone every week, we both sound as exhausted as the other. So I still haven't found the answer to that particular balancing act just yet.

A simple Google search 'How to Distribute My Music' will throw you up tons of options on how to get your music to the Digital Service Providers (DSPs) (Spotify, Apple, Amazon, Deezer etc.). They all do the same thing, but they are different in the way they interact with your streaming sales: some will charge a fee up-front, whereas some will take a percentage of your income. Again, it's not for me to tell you who is the best or worst to work with, but it's your duty to your project to research all of these and see what suits you.

Once your music has a scheduled date for release, you can get down to the nitty-gritty of planning. How is it going to look? What's the PR strategy? Are we getting physical copies?

At this planning stage, knowing how your distribution is going to work enables you to monetise your release, recouping some of the hard-earned money you sacrificed to get this far.

Streaming has put a lot of financial power back in the hands of the independent artist. I know of musicians who haven't gone near a record deal, and they pull in over £5K a month from streaming. And that's not being split with anyone but themselves. It means that now, as opposed to seven or eight years ago, you can make good income from being relatively unknown and putting your music online.

The best way to see a spike in your streams is by getting your music featured on a playlist on one of the many DSPs (Digital Service Providers) – Apple, Amazon, Spotify, Google, Deezer. This way you're getting exposure to infinitely more people than from organic searches of your music. This isn't as easy as you might hope it would be, and you need a little skill when navigating the dark underbelly of streaming. You have to trawl through the internet, through friends of friends, through other acts on playlists, and find out the email address of the person who curates that 'Music to Listen to While Pooping on the Moon' playlist – there is now a playlist for every single moment in life – that you really want your music featured on.

There are fair arguments about the low royalty rate you get from one stream, and I agree that unless you are hitting five-million streams, it does seem rather unfair. You can always go down the traditional route, printing up some vinyl and CDs, and go DIY, shipping off to your local record shops. Or even better, you could set up your own online store and showcase your wares from the comfort of your social media page. A genuine fan will always want to own something by an artist they love, whether it's physical music or merchandise.

In terms of streaming, let's be honest. The music industry was caught completely off-guard. Rock and roll exploded into the hearts and minds of American teenagers in the 1950s, and the industry struggled to keep up with the demand. Punk was something similar, a grassroots movement that owed little to record company trends or research, and left all the major players floundering in its wake, wondering what to do.

But all that was nothing compared to the seismic impact of streaming and downloading. Formats had changed over the years, but things seemed to have settled on the CD as the medium of choice, as older formats such as vinyl and cassette receded into the background, and newer formats like Mini-Disc or DAT failing to grab an audience.

And while big record labels were attempting to launch the expensive Super Audio CD, teenagers all over the world had discovered a way to get their music in a format that arguably sounded worse than cassettes, and cost even less. Fundamentally misunderstanding the needs of the mass marketplace, the record industry looked the other way when the internet became a key factor in how people listen to music, as millions of people cottoned on to the fact that they could download mp3s for free, circumnavigating the record shops and their high prices entirely.

Bands and labels struggled. 'We used to live in a world where you could only get into the market if you were signed to a record label,' says Darcus Beese, president of Island Records, which is still going strong, despite predictions that the old world would end.

'You needed the dough to make the records. You needed the dough to make the videos. And you needed the distribution to get your records out there. But with streaming, unsigned people can get to the marketplace worldwide pretty easily.'

It took a while, but eventually the public and the music industry woke up to the concept of people not being particularly concerned about owning music, instead being prepared to subscribe to the medium through which you experience it. Streaming services like Spotify, Deezer, Tidal, and many more, gave the average music fan the opportunity to listen to the best record collection on earth, as long as they had an internet connection. Suddenly, music fans started looking at their record collections and, instead of seeing something special, they just saw clutter. And for J + T from Jungle, it was clear we were all living in a new era.

'Streaming services are like a gas; it's a commodity beamed into your house. It's art pumped into your laptop.'

While it's no doubt fabulous to consider that art is a basic human necessity that gets delivered to your house, like heating or water, the big question for any artist is how you get it on those streaming services in the first place.

'You could just put your music onto YouTube or SoundCloud. It might get found, and it could be good,' suggests Matt Riley, the vice-president of A&R at AWAL, a business that engages with the digital realm on behalf of artists, doing the kind of work traditional record companies used to do in the real world. AWAL is just one of the players out there looking to discover your music, and work out a way of helping other people discover it too. Which, no matter how democratising the internet can be, isn't always something you can do on your own.

'To get music onto the main platforms where people are listening, Spotify and Apple Music, you have to use a partner, and that's normally a distributor like us, or sign to a label. What we do is deliver the tracks to Spotify and Apple, tell them about the artist, try and get them onto playlists, and then take what happens and report back to you, paying the money to the artist. We charge a fifteen percent commission for doing that.'

It can be difficult to work out quite what the difference between a company like AWAL and a traditional record label are, but for Matt, it's pretty clear cut.

'Artists are each their own labels, and we're doing what a record label would do for them, but without owning them like a record label does.'

If the internet represents a certain kind of freedom, then people like Matt Riley consider themselves guardians of that freedom, allowing people to realise their creative ambitions, without being beholden to the world of big business. For a percentage, of course. The guy's gotta eat!

But that aspect of money is still one of the most difficult aspects of streaming music, and many artists are still justifiably sceptical about how much money they're going to see for all of their hard work. Back in the old days of physical media, records were expensive. And that money would get broken down into several smaller pots, with most of it going to the record label, and some of it going to the artist. So, if an artist sold 20,000 copies of their new single, they could expect to see a pretty decent financial return on that; assuming they weren't on some kind of punitive record contract, or had run up massive bills on their advance.

But with streaming, if an artist's new single is streamed 20,000 times, there's a very good chance that no money has exchanged hands at all, and 5% of nothing is still nothing. There have been plenty of horror stories of artists receiving almost no money for their music, and plenty of high profile people such as Thom Yorke have raised their voices about the subject, drawing attention to what they perceive as the inadequacies of this system.

But for Matt Riley, the future looks pretty good.

'I think, in simple terms, the opportunity now for any artist is bigger than ever because you can reach the world straight away. Artists can make lots of money in the development phases of their career. You can get a track that you made, stick it online through AWAL, have it picked up on some playlists, and suddenly you have a million streams. A million streams would generate roughly about $5,000 (at time of writing) in revenue. More music is being consumed than ever, meaning more revenue flowing into music. Which means more artists than ever who can make a living off being a musician, which is fantastic.'

In simple economics, in the days before streaming you'd likely make more money from sales, because you were getting a larger percentage of every copy sold. But that was completely dependent on people actually buying what you're selling. With streaming, people who wouldn't ordinarily buy your music could be checking it out on a streaming service they've already paid for. And when the numbers break down, you're getting a small percentage of lots of streams, rather than a larger percentage of smaller sales. If people are actually listening to your music, that is.

And a good way to get heard is to be on a playlist, as Ian Watt of Machine Management explains.

'Build a relationship with those companies (streaming services). Who do you know at the editorial team at Spotify and Apple Music? The people who are best placed to have these conversations are record companies and management. If you're an artist, then it's a little harder. If you have a manager who knows these people, then of course they can help you. If you don't have a manager and you're doing it yourself, then it's a little tougher.'

If you don't have a contact at a streaming service editorial team, then you have to do things the old-fashioned way.

'The only other way to do it is by creating some heat and excitement. Once you start developing significant numbers on those services, then you get noticed internally by the editorial team because the numbers have been significant. You can do that by having an active fanbase that are already sharing the music. The editorial teams at these places will start testing it on some of the smaller playlists and if they react positively, then you'll be put onto slightly larger playlists.'

Of course, you have to actually have your music online for any of this to happen, and as Ian explains, it's actually a fairly simple process.

'There are services like AWAL and Tunecore that are really straightforward. It's very easy for anyone to establish a relationship with Tunecore and upload their own music to digital service providers like Amazon, Spotify, Apple, or Deezer. You upload your music; you upload the artwork, you update the data for the day you want it to come out, and it appears. Then once consumption of that music takes place, payments come back to you via Tunecore or AWAL or whoever, in a pretty swift and efficient manner.'

Even though there are companies that will help you at every stage of the way, it's still important that you engage with the process yourself. After all, the internet has broken down the barriers between bands and artists. Music fans like to know that they're engaging with real people, rather than just some corporate entity. Alistair White, also from Machine Management knows exactly this.

'Try and engage in the other things that are available on these platforms. Try and build your own place with a bit of an identity that says something about you. If you show yourself to be engaging with them, then they're more likely to support you. Make sure you have a good image on your profile, that your page looks good. Make use of the "artist picks" section. Don't just consider it a space where you put your music up. Make sure that the space looks interesting for when someone discovers your music.'

For Matt Riley of AWAL, one of the most important parts of living online is turning those streams into fans. Streaming allows passive listeners to just browse through tracks, without the risk of having to fork out cash for something they don't like.

Before streaming, if you bought a record and it was rubbish, then – tough luck – you were stuck with it. With streaming, if you don't like a song, you just hit skip, and move on. As Matt tells us, the trick is how to make that passive listener become someone who cares.

'The eternal struggle for the artist is that you want people to discover you and hear your music, and then somehow to reach those people and convert them into actually knowing who you are and becoming a fan of yours. We're starting to see this weird thing happening where people are becoming fans of the playlists, but not necessarily acts. "I love Chill Vibes, that's like my favourite playlist. I couldn't tell you any artist that's on there. But it's always good."'

But even if people don't know who you are, it's still all heading towards something.

'Once you build fans on a streaming service and you build

plays, it doesn't ever go down to nothing. It's like you're putting a brick in the wall every time you have a success or something good happens. Then the artist starts to build this catalogue of stuff that's all streaming away, and will pay them forever.'

In order to keep your back catalogue ticking over and making you money, you have to write music that people actually want to hear. And in a world where attention spans are shorter, it's never been easier to just skip to the next thing. That's why you have to hit people hard and fast in order to get them to stick with you. Because when it comes to statistics of how much people are paying attention, the numbers don't lie.

'Once you get on a playlist, or you get some traction, the data is hardcore,' says Matt Riley. 'If people hear your track and they skip all the time, Spotify and Apple see that straight away, and you're done. Radio has found – and streaming is no different – that three or four minutes is about the right amount of time to take someone on a journey before they get bored and want to skip. This is depending on the genre.'

If you can avoid boring the average listener to sleep, you could stand to make a nice little sum with your first release if you've made the right moves, made the right connections, secured the right exposure, and played all your cards right. And as Ian Watt reveals, that can really make a difference at the start of an artist's career.

'I mean, you have to make the best possible music that you can. You have to put it in the right place. You have to try and create some excitement by getting it in the right places or getting people to share it. And if suddenly they start streaming it, you start developing an audience and some decent numbers on those streaming services. Then, you know, a million streams of your music isn't a bad look. That income comes through quite quickly, and that sort of money can then sustain the band for the next release, or the next period of touring.'

And while that's good in the short term for an unsigned

band, it can actually have a long-term impact.

'In the first part of your career, you can potentially sustain by developing a streaming fanbase," explains Ian. 'And that will either allow you to sign to a bigger label, or give you the confidence that you're going to do this on your own, earning the income that you want to earn.'

It sounds like a land of golden opportunities, and for many, it is. But that doesn't mean that record companies are completely obsolete. They tend to do almost all of the things discussed above, and have whole teams of people working to make your music successful. But, of course, they expect more back in return for doing it.

For Darcus Beese, record companies have a role to play, although they're figuring out their own way forward in a hugely changed landscape.

'People still talk about pop and dance being the strongest playlists, but I don't just sign pop and dance records. I sign acts that are left-field, that are alternative, that are a bit cooler. So I have to figure out in this world of streaming, how I get those acts across from the left-field, and cross them over. That for me is the challenge at the moment.'

And of course, the physical formats haven't died out completely, either. They might not be the dominant way in which music fans engage with artists, but they still have a role to play. However, knowing when to release them is key, as Ian Watt explains.

'You could put two or three tracks up online or on Spotify, and that's the way you're going to start the buzz and the process. Develop a fanbase. Play shows. Then, when there's a demand for your music, you could press five hundred vinyl EPs because now you'll have an audience that will buy it.'

And from a traditional record company perspective, throwing all your eggs in the streaming basket isn't necessarily the best idea, as Darcus Beese reveals.

'I don't think you can just release one song anymore, and have it do a job for you. You have to release multi-bits of music, hand in hand with building your online profile, and your live gigging. I think that streaming is a good discovery platform. But you need to get everything else lined up.'

Ultimately, the way in which people consume music has changed totally in the last fifteen years or so, and it's likely to continue evolving. YouTube still has a major role to play, because people are increasingly more interested in looking at music than listening to it. Mp3 might have opened the door to downloading and streaming, but with advances in bandwidth, fans have access to music of significantly higher quality. And with the rise of high-end audiophile streaming services, it looks like the ill-fated Super Audio CD platform might have been the right idea at the wrong time.

For artists, there is a wealth of options out there now, but you have to go with what suits you best. And for a songwriter like Frank Turner, that means being flexible. After all, if you want people to hear you these days, you have to go to them, rather than the other way round.

'It sort of doesn't fit into pre-existing categories within the music business. Because in some ways, it's a little bit like downloading because you're getting the songs on your computer on an individual basis. But you're not keeping the file so, in turn, some people argue it's like radio. As a musician, you have to go where the audience is and, at the moment, the vast majority of people listen to music on Spotify. Therefore I'm on Spotify, because I want people to hear my music, and that's the most important thing'

TIPS ON PHYSICAL (VINYL + CD'S)

CHARLENE HEGARTY
BAND MANAGER + OH YEAH BELFAST

1

Make Sure Your Designs Stand Out

The vinyl resurgence is largely due to the fact that the format is a desirable design feature.

2

Don't Throw the Bank at Something Elaborate

Charming someone's ears and eyes simultaneously is a fast track to one form of sustainable success.

3

Plan Early to Avoid Premiums and Let it Sell Out

Planning ahead, gathering quotes and print turnarounds from your manufacturer early can help you manage the costs and meet your targets – sounds boring I know but nobody will pay £25 for a basic vinyl because you forgot to get your order in on time and have to pay premiums.

Anticipate Your Quantities

There may be money to be saved in ordering 1000 units as opposed to 300 units, but unless a dust gathering stack motivates you I would avoid the debt of 'over ordering' and maintain a consistent approach to stock and restocking.

What If It Sells Out?

If your vinyl sells out and new stock is on its way, utilize a means of assuring your fans that they will be the first to know when the option to purchase becomes available again. Sounds simple, right?

FRANK TURNER
TAPE DECK HEART
SLAVES
JAKE BUGG
RADIO X
BIGGLES
THE AGE OF PLASTIC
LOYLE CARNER
...MY...
....GOD!

Radio

FEATURING ADVICE FROM:
Annie Mac (BBC Radio 1 DJ)
Chris Price (Head of Music at BBC Radio 1 + 1Xtra)
Frank Turner
James Passmore (Radio Plugger)
Loyle Carner
Slaves
Rachel Holmberg (Former Head of BBC Music Introducing)

In the age-old tradition of 'conflict of interest', I'm going to be entirely transparent with you: I may be a little biased on this chapter, because I'm a complete radio nut. I'm not going to sicken you with how important radio is to me, but rest assured it's been orbiting my fleshy football since I can remember.

This love turned into a career after I received a letter from the dole office (Always a pleasure, never a chore) while on tour with my band, Colenso Parade. We weren't even turning over enough revenue to keep us on the road, never mind having anything leftover for the exotic thrills of, you know, paying for food or heating. Going on benefits was de rigueur for bands in our position. The only problem was that the benefits office thought I'd had quite enough time on their books, and it was time to farm my services out to some other gainful employer.

I managed to get a job making tea and chasing up loose ends on BBC Radio Ulster, working on their Across The Line and BBC Introducing shows. This trained me up in the basics of radio, while also giving me an insight into how the process works for grassroots music to end up beaming out of the BBC transmitter. From there, I sent a demo to BBC Radio 1, the biggest new music station in the world. It was broadcasting demo. I had already sent tons of my band's demos and nobody was having it at the station (apart from Colin Murray). This time, however, I was invited over for a trial show that led to me getting a job on their night-time schedule. Sometimes sending a demo does work and, in this case, it brought me to London and to my dream job.

I'll save all the rest for my autobiography, which will be coming out on a 2-inch Brain Chip in 2059!

Radio has weathered many a storm since its inception: television, home taping, the early Internet, downloading, and now streaming. It's generally been quite robust in digging deep, although many will now point to streaming as the future. Personally, I think there is enough room for both, because they still provide different things when it comes to the discovery of new music.

With streaming, you have the glut of every piece of recorded music from every musician with algorithms (I just can't warm to taste-generated algorithms), and there are curated playlists to guide you. While on radio, you have bona fide tastemakers cherry-picking the best from the glut and presenting it to you contextually, factually, and with a healthy dose of hyperbole, hype and unpredictability. They are similar, but very different.

'Alright Phil, give over and just tell us how I can get my new single on the radio, you twat!'

A fair point, well made.

Depending on where you live, you're going to have varying degrees of success at getting your music on local radio. In the UK, you can simply upload your music to a tool called the BBC Music Introducing Uploader. This was designed by the BBC to support grassroots music and to give it a place, not just on its national radio stations, but also on the forty region-specific stations. It's a sweet system and it really works in developing future talent. Unfortunately, if you're outside the UK, then this isn't applicable.

I would encourage everyone to take furtive steps into getting songs broadcast on local radio. It will give you a bit of exposure, and it'll also get you used to having your song broadcast. Never underestimate a local radio play. This can be the validation you need to prove to your partner, family, band or sous chef, that your music has merit and is a pursuit worth following. However, if you are making deeply left-field music, then it most likely won't suit many local radio stations. There are still some trailblazers out there, though. Your best bet is to pick up traction online, before tracking down a tastemaker whose radio show will suit your music hand in glove.

There are people you can pay to bring your music to radio stations and hustle on your behalf. They're called radio pluggers. These are the people I get emails from every day, with new music and deeply woven tales of the success or promise of that artist/band. I've seen it work incredibly well for some, and not at all for others. They can only work with the music they get and, in a subjective industry of tastemakers, broadcasters and music teams, it's all a bit 'hit and hope,' rather than guaranteed success. Taking on one of these pluggers at a very early stage probably isn't the best spend of your budget. If you can afford it and have the rest of your ducks in a row, then by all means. They'll do a better job than you will, and you're more likely to get your music spun. But you probably can do the early hustle yourself.

'There's a myth in my career that I achieved the whole thing by word of mouth and had no help from anybody. That's not strictly true.'

So says Frank Turner, who famously played every pub, club or bedroom that advertised itself as a venue, in his quest to connect with an audience. And it was this grassroots following that made him a success, right?

'Radio 1 played a single of mine in 2008, and it blew the doors open for my career. Suddenly I was on playlists, the attendance at shows shot up, and we sold more records.'

Make no mistake however, Frank Turner was a grassroots success. But when it came down to the crunch, good old-fashioned radio still provided the killer blow.

Within the music industry, radio still has a mythic importance. When rock and roll first inspired a whole generation of teenagers to listen to their hormones, it was radio that hit the hardest. Back in the 1950s, DJs were powerful people, filling the airwaves with new sounds, taking them right into your home. And if they said something was good, you knew it was. And sometimes they knew it was good because a record company had probably paid them to say it.

But that doesn't happen anymore. So keep your old school Payola to yourself, ya jerk!

Sinc then, trends have come and gone. And while The Buggles told us that 'Video Killed the Radio Star,' reports of radio's demise were greatly exaggerated. The MTV era came and, to all intents and purposes, it went, leaving radio sitting pretty. And even now, in an age where you can listen to pretty much whatever you want, there's still a healthy audience out there.

'I think it's still really, really important,' explains Annie Mac, one of BBC Radio 1's night-time new music crew. 'I don't think it's imperative like it used to be, and I'm quite excited by that. I like the fact that the radio doesn't have all the power. We need to be out looking at artists at gigs. We need to be following bands. We need to be looking at streaming. Streaming is quite a democratic process in that people just choose what they want to listen to.'

Like many other trusted DJs, Annie Mac has a platform where she can share these discoveries with everyone, curating her own take on what's happening in the musical world, and sharing that with her loyal audience. But the beauty of radio is that it's not just her loyal audience who are listening. Radios are switched on all over the place – in cars, shops, late-night cafés, in your kitchen. It doesn't matter where you are, there's a good chance someone nearby has left on a radio, and someone in the vicinity has just upped their chances of finding their new favourite artist. Chances are you don't do this with live streaming and even then, it's just a computer picking the tracks for you.

James Passmore is a radio plugger and for him, while there may now be other platforms to explore, radio hasn't been disarmed as a vital weapon in any artist's arsenal.

'Listening figures for radio are still incredibly healthy. I don't think radio play necessarily always equates to single sales like it maybe used to. But it does help an artist sell tickets. It can help them sell an album, or could help them build their profile to a point that they can release an album to an audience. There are other important avenues as well these days that can't be ignored but radio is still hugely important.'

It's James' job to get music played on the radio, and radio pluggers have quite a few tools at their disposal.

'A radio plugger is a person who takes music to DJs or to radio stations, with the aim of trying to get that music played on the station. I could take the music direct to DJs, or it could be taking it to the production team behind a show, or a music playlist team at that station who decide what goes into rotation.'

A successful plugger will build up relationships with the people who work in radio stations, almost all of whom do what they do primarily because they love music. A plugger will get to know them, find out what makes them tick, and work out which of the artists they represent will float someone's boat. This is the key difference between simply sending your tracks into a station, and getting a plugger to do it. A DJ is bombarded with random music every day, and would likely rather listen to stuff that someone they trust has sent them.

'Radio 1 has the best specialised programming out there of any UK station, mainly because you've got genre-specific shows across the week. Anything post-7pm on Radio 1 has been picked by the DJ or the production team to play, rather than from a set playlist. Radio X is certainly a really important station. John Kennedy is an absolute legend there and has been doing The Xposure show for many years, playing brand new artists every night. If you're a young urban or dance artist, stations like 1Xtra are hugely important. DJ Target is on every night and is playing a lot of new artists.'

By building up a relationship with these DJs and stations, James Passmore is in a position where he can bring music to a production team, and they'll want to hear what he has to offer. But in order for that to work, he has to have quality artists to deal with in the first place.

'We try and find a lot of artists ourselves, looking at blogs, and looking at what's played already on radio which doesn't have representation. There's a lot of word of mouth. It can just be socialising with friends, booking agents, promoters, managers or lawyers when trying to find new acts. We also have unsolicited demos sent to us, which we always listen to and sometimes pick up artists that way.'

But while it would be true to say that every artist who becomes a success will use a radio plugger, that's not to say it's the first thing you should go looking for when you're starting out. Indeed, a young, unsigned band still finding its feet would be throwing money away if they were to hire a plugger. At this stage, if you're looking towards the BBC, it's time to think of the BBC Music Introducing Uploader, an online system that takes your music and sends it directly to the inbox of anyone who might make use of it. It's like a robotic plugger, if you will, and something the likes of Annie Mac make great use of.

'If you're a band recording songs on a regular basis, and you're at a point where you're starting to gig, then I think that's a very good point to start sending your stuff to the BBC Music Introducing Uploader. Because that's a genuine service that provides people with a chance of radio play from a very early point in their career.'

Unlike most commercial stations, BBC Music Introducing actually has a remit to seek out and discover new and emerging talent. And if you're reading this, that most likely means you.

A radio plugger can still push artists to BBC Music Introducing shows, but because of the Uploader, they don't really need to. This can often be your first port of call when dealing with a radio station, and plenty of artists like Florence + The Machine, Two Door Cinema Club, Jake Bugg and others have found themselves graduating from BBC Music Introducing to the big leagues.

Chris Price is the Head of Music for BBC Radio 1 and BBC Radio 1Xtra. He's right at the forefront of discovering new music; and he has the power to shape and craft the careers of young musicians. And in that role, he's well aware of the importance radio has to play in establishing an artist's career, particularly with regards to BBC Music Introducing.

'If you're playing to growing crowds, if you're getting good talk-back online, if you get some good plays on all the usual places where very early music might be discovered, then what you need is to get your foot in the door. Which at the BBC is BBC Music Introducing.'

Of course, once you get that foot in the door, you'll be looking at 'night-time' radio play and then from there to mainstream 'daytime' radio play. But the mainstream is a busy place to be and, unless you're already an established artist with your own profile, it can be hard to make an impact.

'There are usually between forty-two and forty-five records on Radio 1 daytime playlists, and obviously there are a lot more records than that released every single week,' Chris explains. 'We spend an awful lot of our time just working out which are the new artists that are most deserving of that exposure to up to ten million people a week.'

The Radio 1 playlist is the stuff of legend: a bunch of people get together in a room and debate what records should be played in heavy rotation on the station.

'We look at things like how the artist is performing; what their live plot is like, have they built a fan base, and which of our specialist "night-time" radio DJs at Radio 1/1Xtra are playing it, and are extremely passionate about the track. Your best bet getting on the playlist is by getting Radio 1 Specialist (all shows post-7pm) excited.'

It's cyclical logic: hone your music so that specialists and experts love it, and then maybe you'll be in a position where everyone can love you.

And if you want to get to that level, never underestimate the benefit of hard work. Or at the very least, make sure the music you're pushing is actually good, as Chris explains.

'Check your music against the competition: is it as good as what's in the marketplace already? Can it be better? Sometimes there's a rush to put music out there because you've made something amazing. Is time best invested at this point in putting your music out there, or is it better invested in making your music better.'

As well as having a good tune, it's not a bad idea to give the DJ an idea of who you are, and where you're coming from. They're a real, live human being, not a computer generated algorithm looking for keywords. As James Passmore explains, giving a DJ something to work with can go a long way to building up that relationship.

'It helps when you're going to radio to have a general sort of set of assets around you that will be visualised to give some context. You need good press shots (photos), and a radio edit of your lyrics if they are unsuitable for radio play (swearing/glamorising drug use).'

If you're aiming at mainstream success, knowing your audience is incredibly important. In the UK, almost every station will avoid songs that feature an abundance of swearing or controversial content, particularly if it's aimed at a daytime audience. There might be kids listening, you f*%king idiot!

It's rare to find an up-and-coming artist who thinks about their commercial potential right from the get-go. Most people are just trying to do what feels right. And for hip-hop artist

Loyle Carner, he was just doing what came naturally to him. Luckily enough, that seemed to dovetail with what people were looking for.

'When I was making my first tunes, I was making them for me. I wasn't going to make tunes for the radio, fuck that. Someone would say, "There should be a chorus there," or "This should come in sooner for radio," which made it really refreshing when the tracks got picked up as they are. The music that got picked up had nothing to do with it being tailor-made for radio.'

Not everyone is going to have this kind of experience, though. If someone starts telling you to change the fundamentals of your music, that's one thing. There are many polite ways to tell them to leave you alone (and several more impolite ways). On the other hand, if a radio station is telling you they love your music, but can't play it because of the lyrical content, they're generally talking about swearing, sexual content, or drug references. So if you put them in, then the song isn't likely to make much of a splash on mainstream radio.

But for artists like Loyle Carner, mainstream radio isn't always the target.

'The time will come when radio is not the be all and end all. It's a wicked thing if it can happen. It can open doors, but doors get opened in so many different ways. Be patient. We never forced anything. If you aren't getting played, you don't need to. I have friends who are incredible who don't get played on radio. Just make the tunes, and don't make them to be a big success. Make them because you want to get something off your chest.'

That said, Loyle can still see the appeal of getting on the radio.

'I remember getting super-excited when my songs did get played on the radio. As much as I was anti-establishment, I would be lying if I didn't sit in the car and wait for it to get played. It was a big deal.'

For Laurie Vincent and Isaac Holman of Slaves, radio played

a big part in getting them to where they needed to be.

'I think BBC Music Introducing is a great platform, they sorted us out big time," explains Isaac, a point taken up by bandmate Laurie. 'Especially when you listen to a lot of radio stations that mainly only play American music. It's great to have a platform for British music.'

As the broadcaster itself would no doubt state – other broadcasters are available. But the BBC is in a unique position in the UK where it can spend time, effort and money in supporting and encouraging artists, giving them the helping hand to get to where they need to be, whilst remaining free of commercial concerns. By the very definition of what they do, a commercial broadcaster is only interested in commercial success. They use already established acts as the enticement to get people to listen to their station, thereby maximising their advertising revenue. But while that sounds pretty nefarious, it's worth noting the number of commercial broadcasters that sponsor music festivals and events, many of which feature up-and-coming artists. So ultimately, in their own way, they're feeding back into the pool of prospective artists.

But, first and foremost, the BBC offers a platform for new and emerging talent that few other broadcasters could dream of, and this is a lifeline for a band like Slaves, as Isaac explains.

'Without Radio 1, there would be a whole group of our fans who wouldn't have heard us, particularly when we get played on daytime radio.'

Away from the BBC and commercial broadcasters, online radio has started to play a more significant role in the promotion of bands, and they occupy a space all of their own. As plugger James Passmore explains, they can offer a new take on how to get your music out there.

'There are online digital stations like Amazing Radio which allow you to allow you to upload music for free, and some stations you can send your demos in to. Some DJ's advertise email addresses online, and will allow you to send digital promos which can be a good option. When you start getting some serious airplay, that's the point when you come to someone like myself, and we try and work together.'

So even if the Beeb and the local chart station are ignoring you, there are still options.

But at a basic level, there's still something kind of weird about working with a radio plugger. As James Passmore pointed out, they will be looking to work with you after you have reached a particular level, which means essentially that you have to do a lot of the legwork a plugger normally would have to do, before they even notice you. While this might seem counter-intuitive, it does have a basis in practical reality, as Annie Mac points out.

'You have to be really consistent, and you have to really stick with an artist for a long period of time. For us, it's about being aware of where that is in their career, not giving them everything too early. We have to wait for them to build up a proper fan base, for that artist to have a system in place, or people around them to be able to help push them forward in the way that they need.'

Essentially, you gotta know how this stuff works, before you're really in a position to hand it over to someone else, because if you're given the keys to the Lamborghini too soon, you're gonna crash.

'You can go crazy on a band when they're unsigned and give them everything: a "Hottest Record in the World" play, a live session, but then they don't have a record label behind them that can pay for marketing and the rest. It's about having everything in place, so that when you're getting the maximum amount of exposure on radio, then you can be pushed, and you've got the kind of backing to push yourself as far as you go.'

For an artist like Frank Turner, that still means the guiding hand of radio being extended to you at a point in your career where you can actually make use of it. And once you're up and running, the endorsement of someone you respect cannot be underestimated.

'Radio has a place as a tastemaker and a path finder. If there's a gazillion bands out there online, then a DJ that you trust will be able to wade through that for you. I guarantee you, if you listen to Steve Lamacq's show (BBC 6 Music) you will find one band you've never heard before that you'll like.'

And ultimately, if you're ready for it, radio and radio pluggers will come to you. If you've already put in the graft, they'll be able to spot that spark in you, as BBC Radio 1's Head of Music Chris Price points out.

'If you've invested one, two, three years making your music as good as it can be and you think you are ready to take it to the next step, then maybe a proportion of your time is more productively invested in trying to build a team. You've got to build your audience locally, create waves, get local radio play, so that the music industry is coming to you, and not vice versa.'

Q + A WITH RACHEL HOLMBERG

FORMER HEAD OF BBC INTRODUCING
CURRENTLY DECCA RECORDS

What is BBC Music Introducing?

BBC Music Introducing is the BBC's new music initiative, which over the years has established itself as one of the most important parts of the BBC's public service. To date, over 200,000 acts have uploaded their music for support across BBC Radio, TV and Online. It was created 11 years ago to enable musicians making music to get their music directly to the BBC, without having a radio plugger. An artist can go to bbc.co.uk/introducing, create a profile and upload their music. When they do this, they put in their postcode and it sends the music to their local radio show. Each local radio show have an Introducing show that airs from 8pm on a Saturday night playing only music that has been uploaded to their local area.

From here, local shows can forward music to a number of internal inboxes including the BBC Radio 1 playlist (Introducing slot), BBC Radio 1Xtra playlist (Introducing slot), a host of network radios shows including 6Music's Steve Lamacq, Radio 1's Huw Stephens, Radio 1Xtra's DJ Target and Radio 2's Jo Whiley, through to Radio 3 for classical, world and jazz and the Asian network.

As well as this, we open up a number of inboxes throughout the year for festival submissions from our local shows including Glastonbury, Reading + Leeds, Latitude, The Great Escape as well as a host of BBC flagship events including opportunities at Radio 1's Big Weekend, 6Music Festival and 1Xtra Live. The submissions are then sent to a panel of BBC Producers, Music Team members and BBC Presenters as well as 'friends of Introducing' such as Emily Eavis for Glastonbury Festival or Jon Mac (Fetsival Booker) for Reading + Leeds Festivals. The panel's top choices form our final stage line-ups.

How does an act get the best out of BBC Music Introducing?

Make sure to only upload your very best tracks. It's quality, not quantity. Think of it as your showcase to BBC Radio and you only want to present your best work. It is also important to build a strong relationship with your local show, as ultimately they will be the ones that champion you to network radio and beyond. They are the ones that will forward you for the festival stage opportunities. It all begins at local radio and that's key to remember. Work hard and practice your craft. Gig and gig and gig, even if you are only playing to 3 people in the room. You never know who those 3 people are…

Does everyone's music get played?

No. We do however have a promise to artists' that all music will be listened to within 6 months of it being uploaded. Artists' are notified directly by email when the BBC receives their tracks, listens to their tracks and when they are going to be broadcast on local radio. It's important we have constant communication with the artists' who upload and we endeavour to always keep them informed.

What other opportunities outside of the radio plays does BBC Music Introducing have?

As well as our national festival stages, we also have stages internationally including the likes of SXSW Music Festival in Austin Texas. We have also showcased acts at CMJ in New York, Reeperbahn Festival in Hamburg, Winter Jazz Fest in New York, Montreal International Jazz Festival, Eurosonic Festival in the Netherlands, Amsterdam Dance Event and more. All of which, are recorded for broadcast across one of our national radio shows and hosted by a national radio DJ.

RETURN OF THIS GUY!
SPIN
MUSIC FOR LIFE
Q
OUR TOP 100 BANDS
NEXT MONTH:
•EXCLUSIVE PREVIEWS!
•IGGY POP!!
•BOWIE PART 2!
FREE CD
BOWIES EARLY YEARS!
MOJO
WHERE IS ELVIS HIDING!?

Online & Print Media PR

FEATURING ADVICE FROM:
Claire Coulton (Senior Entertainment Publicist at Satellite 414 PR)
Cheylene Murphy (Honeymoon PR)
Loyle Carner
Niall Byrne (Nialler 9 + Freelance Print/Online Journalist)
Roisin O'Connor (Journalist)
Ryan Bassil (Associate Editor Noisey)

I am writing this chapter while concurrently putting together an online and print strategy for a new band on my label, Hometown Records. Comfort yourself in that knowledge as you try and plot your own journey. I'm trying to do the exact same on my end, and even though I've done it countless times before, it never really gets any easier. This is simply due to the fact that no two acts are ever the same, so they can't be presented in the same way.

Unless you're at a point in your career where you are already slaying it – selling tickets, and selling or streaming music – it can be incredibly hard for you to make a breakthrough with press, online and in print. Big press companies want clicks, eyes, and sales of/on their publication. They are businesses, and they know a news story about Drake, Arctic Monkeys or Adele will drive that sweet, glorious engagement they crave. This generally means less column/screen space for breaking new artists. Which in turn means your debut single that was recorded in your mate Roger's shed, will probably not make the front page of the broadsheet culture pull-out.

Releasing music is a constant pendulum swing of emotions. One thing will work exactly as planned, a sweet surprise might rear its gorgeous face, and, more likely than not, some highways will narrow into cul-de-sacs culminating in the deafening silence of indifference. Prepare yourself for it to go any of these ways.

When talking in this chapter about getting online exposure, I'm not talking about social media, as there's a chapter earlier in the book dedicated completely to that particularly complicated Foxtrot. Instead, this is mainly looking at the world of publications, organisations, blogs, playlists and tastemakers that take up domain space online.

The last ten years saw a feverish boom for bloggers dedicating their writing to the cause of sniffing out new music. It almost seemed at one point a few years ago that if you didn't have a new music blog, then you weren't getting a job at a bigger media company. It was a rite of passage. This flourish meant more exposure to a wider range of new music, with most niches being covered in some respect. And while they didn't all have the biggest traffic coming through their domains, it was still better than a kick in the stones, right?

The number of places to premiere your new music or

videos has slimmed down recently, and it has become a bit more focused. But a healthy amount of digging and reconnaissance will unearth the perfect website to spew superlatives over the slack-jawed sludge-metal project that I'm assuming you're working on.

The process of getting your favourite tastemakers to feature your music, both online and in press, is pretty similar. You need to have the basics nailed: completely finished music, press release, press shots, links to all your online bits, and a healthy dose of luck.

The key difference between the two media is that a little hustle can work online, if done right. Aiming at musically appropriate websites is key. Also be polite, don't expect anything, and don't be a stalker.

With print media, the hustle is different, and you're less likely to succeed without having your own publicist or PR. These are the people you pay quite a lot of money to get your wares under the noses of new music writers and editors across both online and print. They are by no means cheap, and they don't guarantee results. They are very much like the radio pluggers we covered in the previous chapter. They're more likely to succeed with securing exposure for your music than most artists going it alone.

Personally, I think a good attitude, an act that knows it's ready and has all its ducks in a row can make a good bit of noise without having to pay a massive fee for PR. Making the initial noise yourself is always heartening to see, as most people love an underdog story, and music is no different. Great music will spread quicker than 100 emails to tastemakers. If you make genuinely brilliant, unique music, then it will get shared and will find a champion to give it some much-needed hype.

Tastemakers – both online and in radio – are in a perpetual pissing contest with each other as to who can find and support the next big thing first. That might be you.

On the other hand, it might not be you, but you have to take the gamble and get yourself and your tunes in the mix if you're ever going to find out. Faint heart never won the fair lady.

PS. There's flip all places in print for new music these days, bar a few of the old guard, and a few beautiful renegades willing to stick their neck out for the next big thing.

PPS. There's flip all print around.

In the late 1970s, rock music was doing just fine. Huge stadium bands like Led Zeppelin, Pink Floyd and Deep Purple were packing them in, crafting increasingly excessive light and stage shows, and allowing the drummer to have a solo in the middle of the gig, giving everyone else the chance to get a beer, go to the loo or just have a sit-down.

By the start of the Eighties, American acts like Toto, Journey, and Styx were conquering FM radio, scoring hit after hit after hit, and the largely anonymous members of the bands could drive expensive cars, presumably take loads of drugs, and still not be recognised when they went to the shops. And this continued for years, until eventually the public moved on to something else, leaving these acts selling hundreds of thousands of copies of their records, rather than millions.

But if you look at any history of rock music written in the last thirty years, it'll tell a completely different tale. It will be about stagnation and boredom, a tale of dinosaurs roaming the earth, playing dull music to disinterested punters. And then, like a bolt from the blue, punk comes along, and wipes them all out, and changing the history of rock forever.

It's a story told over and over again, in ignorance of things like sales figures for albums and concerts, or even by looking at the UK or US charts in any year between 1977 and 1985. And if it is the case that Toto sold more records and had a larger commercial impact that the Sex Pistols, then why does that story get repeated so often?

The answer is that the Sex Pistols had better PR.

Punk as a phenomenon was dreamt up in pubs by music journalists and PR people. The music itself was a grassroots movement, fuelled by a growing need for cultural change from certain sections of society. And it was seized upon by the music press, who whipped it into a frenzy, and pushed it overground, right into the homes of little Britain.

In a realistic sense, that's not quite the story of punk either, but it does give an idea of how important PR can be. You could be making the best, most important music of your generation, but if nobody hears about it, your potential will be wasted. And beyond taking to street corners with a mobile PA and belting out your future hits, one of the best ways to do this is to hire a PR person to drum up some interest in your music.

'I do print and online press for music artists,' says Claire Coulton. 'So that means securing print coverage (reviews, live reviews), and interviews and playlists. Any coverage you see online that's not advertorial or paid for, we would secure.'

Claire is senior entertainment publicist for Satellite 414

PR, which represents the likes of Adele, Dua Lipa, and Lana Del Rey. Her job is literally what she just said and for her, a good PR person is simply another essential part of the team that will help you do whatever it is you think you're supposed to be doing.

'It is a cliché, but it comes down to the music. If it's great and you have a publicist pushing it, people will listen to it. The reason you hire a publicist is for their relationships with the press, and how they're trusted by publications.'

When you see an article in which a journalist is frothing at the mouth about some new band they've just discovered, one of two things has just happened:

1. They've been doing some digging, and have found the Next Big Thing.

Or

2. They've been contacted by a PR person, who has given them a really excellently put-together press release, and they needed something to publish.

It sounds somewhat cynical but in reality, it's not. You make music, you pay a PR person to listen to your music, and if they really like it, they'll be able to exploit their connections and relationships to convince other people that your music is great, which will lead to more exposure.

Operating originally in print, but now largely confined to the online world, the music journalist is the super-fan, the person who 'gets' your music on a profoundly different level to other human beings, and who then feels compelled to share their thoughts with the world. They are the person who intellectualises your incoherent musical ramblings, and makes you out to be the era-defining artist you really are. And when they get bored, they jump onto the next thing and forget all about you, telling the world how they never really liked you in the first place.

In essence, they are your best friend and worst enemy, wrapped up in one perfect package.

Music journalists can be tastemakers, and as such, they get bombarded with an awful lot of music, more than any one human being can comfortably listen to (especially given the quality that some of these songs will inevitably be). A good PR person will be able to cut through the noise and then grab the ear of a journo. But as music writer Niall Byrne (Nialler9 to his readers) explains, they have their own things they are on the lookout for.

'It is nice if an act has a story, and I think that goes hand in hand with the press shot and all the rest of what makes up the band. Before anyone hears your song, they're going to see something that represents you, whether it's a logo or a profile pic. Everything needs to be thought out before you start. What's my look? How do I want to be perceived?'

Through his website, Niall has been at the forefront of Irish music for many years, and has been instrumental in breaking some new talent on his home shores, and further afield. For the countless artists who approach him on a daily basis, he has some useful advice as to how best to make that initial contact.

'Be personable and approach people directly, no mass emails. Keep the email really short. Don't send downloadable links. If people want to hear it, they have to do it in the least amount of clicks possible. Keep it to a simple streaming link, don't be sending half a gigabyte files for them to download.'

This idea of being personable is echoed by Ryan Bassil, associate editor of Noisey.

'Don't copy and paste emails. Think about how you would be polite to someone on the street that you don't know. Don't try and force it. Just make it simple: "Hey Ryan, I am Blah Blah Blah from Blah Blah Blah. Here's a link to our music. Hope you like it." Send the link, and that's all it needs to be. Sending videos is way better than sending a streaming link.'

It makes perfect sense. Given the sheer number of people contacting a well-respected music writer, the less chaff in the email, the better the chance they'll actually read it. It's tempting to want to tell your whole life story when you're approaching a music journalist, but the chances are, they won't want to read it. Stick to the kind of thing they might want to know, and they'll be more likely to start asking you questions. And if it comes to that, they'll know what they're looking for, far better than you ever will.

'For me to cover something, it has to have a personality side behind it. It has to have meaning; it's colourful, funny, deep. It can't be that you're just making music for the sake of making music. You need to have a real idea of why you're making the music.'

When you get talking to music journalists, the important thing to realise is that they actually want something from you. Many bands make the mistake of going into interviews with no idea of what they're doing, and end up not getting the kind of glowing coverage they wanted.

If you have nothing to say, or don't feel like talking today, it's probably better to cancel the interview. Journalists are almost always up against a deadline, and if they spend their time chatting to you, and you give sullen, unusable one-word answers to everything, they're not going to consider you to be a maverick enigma. They'll just lose interest, and move on to something else.

By the same token, consider what you're saying to the journalist. Is it something they could actually work with? After all, that is the main reason they're talking to you; they have to get an article written, and you have to give them something to write about. If the story of your latest single is that you borrowed a van, put the equipment in it, drove to a studio, and recorded the song, then be prepared for the journo to not consider this an absolute thrill-ride of a story.

As Ryan Bassil explains, something a bit meatier is going to make the cut.

'Have a reason why you are making music. Stick to that idea and don't water it down. Make something that is really honest to you and your ideals. Don't try and force anything, people will find you out.'

This is a crucial rule when it comes to dealing with the press: unless you're very, very good at it, don't make stuff up. The music world is crammed full of massive fibbers who can spin a good yarn to journalists, rather than tell the boring story behind their new music. This might make you think that you could give it a go but, in most cases at a beginner level, the artist and the journo know each other (to some extent). And when you start telling falsehoods, both parties recognise this for what it is, and just go along with it. If you start telling lies and get caught out, it won't be looked on favourably. Writers will be sceptical of you, and will likely pass you by when it comes to getting coverage, in case you say anything that will embarrass them.

As Ryan tells us, there's plenty of ways in which you can piss off a journalist.

'The worst thing you can do if your track premiere has been accepted is to email all the time. Artists will send ten emails on Saturday night at 10pm, and it kind of puts me off them. Now I don't want to do stuff with you, because you're really annoying.'

A good PR person will help you avoid the pitfalls of dealing with journalists. They'll likely already have developed some kind of relationship with the journos, and will be able to smooth out your rough edges, enabling everyone to get the best out of you. You can make the initial overtures to journalists yourself, but picking the right time to hire a PR person can be important, as Nialler9 reveals.

'Before you get PR, you have to think, what's the plan for

the next year, and how does PR help you achieve your goal? If you don't have a campaign and a strategy, PR will be pointless. You need to make the video, book the gigs, and release the music. Have those in place, and then think of PR.'

For Senior Entertainment Publicist Claire Coulton, having the assets is important, as that's the raw material that they're going to use to get you attention.

'Whether it's a press release, a great video, remixes, or behind-the-scenes shots, the more content you have the better. If you are a grungy sort of garage rock band, you want it to look like that in the press images. If you make grime, you want it to look like that. Make sure that the images match what you do. That's really the first thing people will see. Make it striking and make it relate to what you do.'

And of course, you need to make sure you're in a position to actually work with a PR person. If you're not ready, then it can be a fabulous waste of time and money.

'I don't think you need PR straight away. It's good to build a little bit of a following on your own. If you're just starting to gig, and there's no music online, then you don't need PR. We don't tend to take a band on without management or label interest, because there has to be a plan in place for us to work to with a time schedule. We need to know there is a schedule of tracks, and that we have plenty of things (remixes, videos) to keep the momentum in the press.'

The next step is working out who to actually contact, and as Claire explains, a bit of research can save you a lot of effort.

'Find the publications that are right for you. Find journalists that are into your sort of sound. Find their contact details, and send them a personal email, and you have more of a chance of being covered. Local is a good place to start for radio, print, or online press. Student media is the same; it's got a very good network.'

Getting some kind of coverage actually isn't that hard. Getting the right kind of coverage is the tricky part. Anyone can set up a blog or website and, as such, you might have a glowing review on ihavenoidewhatimtalkingabout.com. But if no-one reads that, and they give glowing reviews to simply everything they encounter, then you might as well not have bothered. Investigate the impact of websites, see who the big players are, and work out how you could fit in.

In the real world, despite how it might appear, if you get your review in certain print publications, there's a good chance more people will see it. And for plenty of people in the industry, there's something about the legitimacy of print that is appealing, a seal of approval that can't be found online. However, in practical terms, the opportunities to get written about in print are becoming fewer and fewer, as Nailler9 points out.

'There are less outlets for press and print media now. You have to be a more established artist to get yourself in the printed press. It's really more something you look into when you reach a certain level.'

This has the knock-on effect of making well-respected online media outlets a little harder to crack, too. And as Claire Coulton tells us, getting online coverage isn't quite the cop-out some people would have you believe.

'It's difficult to get print, but it's getting a lot harder for acts to get coverage online too. Blogs have died. More and more people are deactivating them. The culture around it has changed. It's moving to social takeovers with Instagram and Facebook. For example, we'll get an artist to take over the NME's social media.'

In a realistic way, this allows you as an artist to bypass the music journalist completely, and just appeal to their fans. And as musician Loyle Carner reveals, that can be quite appealing.

'The internet evolves properly every ten years, and every generation gets better at it. I thought I was a master of it, but my little brother understands it better, and he shows me things that I don't understand. If you have a younger sister or brother, they'll know where the young fans are.'

That's not to say you should throw the baby out with the bathwater, though. And Loyle is well aware that the press are an important part of the process.

'It's a necessary beast, you just have to use it and not let it use you. Which means, know as much about it before you get involved. Online press is potentially important at the start for artists to get premieres. If you have a small fanbase or small following on social media, then it will open up your music to people.'

As an artist, you have to be savvy as to how you promote yourself, and for Loyle, music blogs just don't cut it anymore.

'I don't think they're that important. Before, you could only see opinions from blogs, but now everyone has Twitter, and you build up your followers and have your own opinion.'

Social media has unquestionably changed the nature of PR, breaking down many of the barriers that previously existed between artists and their fanbase. But the music press still play an important role. And in a world where we have access to everything, sometimes putting some of those barriers back up can be a helpful thing.

When you're confronted by ultimate freedom of choice, sometimes the only helpful thing can be to seek the advice of someone who knows what they're talking about. And that role still falls to the music journalist.

And when it comes to standing out from the crowd, and showing that spark of originality, the onus is on you as an artist, rather than the music journalist. They can only do so much, as Ryan Bassil explains.

'Just do something you fucking believe in, and it will come out good. Don't try and look at someone else; just come up with your own idea and do it. It sounds so basic, but if you're good, it's going to be good. Believe in what you're doing.'

TOP TEN TIPS FOR ONLINE PR ON A BUDGET

CHEYLENE MURPHY
PR

1

Create a World Around Your Song

Photos, music videos, gigs, dance moves, costumes… whatever you feel enhances your music and you can realistically achieve to a high standard, make it (ask your friends, learn how and do it yourself!) and release it.

2

Reach out to the Music Industry

Bloggers and playlisters generally don't just stumble upon new music, they have an overflowing inbox full of new releases to choose from - be in that inbox! If you can't work with a PR company you can do a lot yourself by putting some time aside to do some heavy researching and emailing.

3

Make Friends and Be Cool

Blogs that write about your genre of music as well as local and 'new music' tastemakers will be your biggest fans. Most will have a contact email on their website, so you can put together a great contact list of tastemakers with good research. Think of it as making friends and be genuinely nice when you're chatting with them, a little nice goes a long way.

Make it Easy for People to Like Your Music

When it comes to emailing tastemakers appreciate they get A LOT of emails, so make it quick and easy for them to like your music without having heard it. Keep the email short, name drop 'impressive' things your band has done so they know you don't totally suck (we played this festival, this blog said we were cool) have all the links they need (link to the song, press photos, your social media) and personalise it to each human you email.

Be Prepared

Don't release the song the day after you get the final master - get everything in order (artwork, photos, press pack, links, live dates) and start reaching out to people weeks BEFORE the release date. This is the hardest thing to do but the most important - if you take one thing away from the list IT IS THIS!

Social Media is Your Voice

Social Media is your greatest tool for online PR, especially on a budget. It's the channels that showcase all your creative assets to a bourgeoning fanbase and an interested music industry. More importantly - it's something you can control. Have it, use it and treat your social media as part of your campaign - release teasers, behind the scenes photos, play your song on recorder on Instagram live, create a treasure hunt on twitter. Get creative, lean on your strengths and think outside the box.

Plan your Posts in Advance

Post everyday on all your channels during a release. Don't feel weird about it either - most people won't see that first post about your single, so do another one. Definitely plan your social media posts in advance so you're not stuck taking a photo of your lunch with the caption 'listen to my new single.'

Bonus Tip: Don't pay for Facebook ads, except for the big release day posts. I could do 100 more tips on how to work the algorithms, but they change all the time and there are a ton of websites that keep on top of them - Sprout Social has a great blog. All that info for businesses is useful for bands too!

Take Yourself Seriously

The hardest thing to do is promote your own music, but you have to swallow that doubtful, embarrassed little gremlin that tells you your song is not worth the time. You've worked hard on this, you want to give your release the best chance it can get - so be proud, talk yourself up and GO FOR IT.

Manage Expectatops

99% of the emails you send will get no reply, this is normal. PR comes back to you in weird ways. You'll get to play your favourite festival because the booker saw you on a tiny indie blog or you'll recognise a super fan from Instagram singing along and buying merch at your gigs. Don't beat yourself up if you're not Beyonce overnight, even Beyonce couldn't do that.

Get Creative and be Your Weird Little Self

I know so many musicians who think PR is daunting, scary and the absolute worst, but it can be super fun if you let it. It's an extension of your song, an opportunity to be creative and a way to share your music with fans and potential partners in the music industry. There are infinite ways to do PR, in the same way that there are infinite ways to write a song, so do it in a way that leans on your strengths, passions and ideas.

PRESS RELEASES DOS AND DON'TS

ROISIN O'CONNOR
JOURNALIST

At a guess, I'd say I get about 200-300 press releases a day, in between various other premiere, interview, meeting and gig requests. I delete a lot of them. Here are a few tips on how not to be deleted.

1

For the Love of God, be Concise

Consider those hundreds of emails each day and top that with the actual work I'm trying to get done: writing up features, interviews, listening to new tracks, writing reviews, commissioning, filming sessions, crying over how many emails just landed in my inbox… it goes on. So keep it short. My favourites are the ones that stick to two or three paragraphs max. Short paragraphs, not long ones. A very brief bio on the artist, what they're about, and why I – me personally – should be interested enough to want to write about them.

2

Mass Mail-Outs are the Devil

It's pretty damn clear when a PR or an artist has just hit 'send all' on a release. Don't send pop music to a journalist that specialises in heavy metal. Journalists are narcissists by default - you have to be if you want your name published again and again - so consider our massive, fragile egos and pretend you care about our work enough to look it up.

3

Music Comes First

Think about the layout of your press release. The average journalist probably spends about 10 seconds (that's generous) skimming over an email that's just dropped in their inbox, so you need to grab their attention quickly, and I don't mean by a sexy picture or a 'funny' subject line. Personally I prefer a link to the actual music at the top - YouTube, Spotify or Soundcloud, in that order - so I can click that the second the email lands and listen. Then I can decide whether I like it enough to read on - and maybe even reply. Don't bury your artist's music at the bottom of five paragraphs of boring text.

Be Clear About What You Want

Literally the worst thing you can do is send a press release where there's no clear statement of what you want for your artist. Do you want someone to premiere a track? Do you want a review? Do they have a gig coming up nearby? If I'm not sure about what you want, I sure as fuck don't have time to write back and ask.

Don't be Sad When Journalists don't Respond

The honest-to-god truth is it would be physically and mentally impossible to reply to every single one I get sent. If I don't reply to you, it's (probably) not because I don't like it. It's (probably) not because I hate you. It's very, very likely that I just don't have time to read it - let alone respond.

Jump to it When a Journalist Does Bite

Don't be left blinking in the headlights when someone - and they will - gets back to you about an artist. Anticipate what they might ask for - new material to check out, gig times, interview slots - and have that information to hand. And it's hypocritical, but reply to emails quickly. Don't let that conversation lose its momentum.

LIVE
MUSIC

Booking Agents

FEATURING ADVICE FROM:
Cal McRae (Promoter)
Loyle Carner
Matt Bates (Primary Talent)
Tara Richardson (Manager at Q Prime)
Wolf Alice

Depending on how long you have been grafting at music, you will have varying degrees of success when it comes to booking your own shows. When my band started out, we put on our own shows and invited bands we knew were likely to put us on their shows. It was the only way to get out and play live.

The conundrum of conquering our home town took a long time and a lot of mistakes but getting gigs further afield was a different story. We travelled all day to play shows to nobody: we played 'pay to play' shows, the most despicable format for any young band. If you know a promoter who puts on those sort of shows, then call them a 'fuckhead' for me, because those people are vermin leeching off impressionable young bands for money.

The main way to get around all of the pitfalls that come with booking shows and tours yourself is to get yourself a booking agent. Much like managers and labels, not everyone is entitled to one or will get one, but my God, they will make your life a lot easier, especially if you can snare a good one.

A booking agent is one of the most important facets of an act's infrastructure. They are the people who will guide you in everything you do with live music. They will book all your shows, plot your tours, speak to festival and event organisers on your behalf. They'll try and secure the most amount of money they can for you and, most importantly, they will advise you on when it's best to play certain shows. No band starts off playing their first EP launch in Wembley Stadium; there's an unwritten rite of passage you must achieve on your way to those huge venues.

It goes something like this:

[*This system probably works better for a band.*]

Supporting Local Cover Band ('Headline band has fist-fight over who plays the solo in 'Sweet Child O Mine')

Incredibly Small Shit Venue ('Stinks of piss')

Any Showcase Gigs Going ('First band on at the Farmer's Journal Magazine launch')

Small Shit Venue ('The monitors are powered by a Vauxhall Corsa')

Couple of Shows Around the Country ('A couple of

mates in the audience, and one weird bloke at three of the shows')

Less Shit Venue ('Mum and Dad show up. Inter-band punch-up over last can of Red Stripe').

[*Actual fans start showing up.*]

Independent Festival ('Someone drank your four bottles of water')

Record Shop 'In Store' ('You forgot to bring your EPs to sell').

[*Little bit of industry hype around the band.*]

BBC Maida Vale Session with Radio 1's Huw Stephens ('Conclusively prove that Huw is the "Nicest Man in Music').

Play Great Escape Festival ('All the band want to move to Brighton')

Tour Support for In Trend Hype Band ('3/5 review in the Harrogate Herald. Drummer visits first Strip Club');

Reasonable Venue in London - Sold Out ('Illusions of grandeur building')

Your Own Small Tour Around the Country - Well attended ('It's starting to kick off')

European Festival Date ('J'aime le fromage et la discotheque')

Perform on Later With Jools Holland ('Lionel Ritchie walks into your dressing room by accident. What a feeling it was for him to see you naked from the waist down!')

Bigger Venue (700 Cap.) – Sold Out ('Various radio and magazine people you don't know in your dressing-room').

[*Release Debut Album*]

Headline Tour of the Country – Medium Size Venues Sold Out ('Drummer gets rail card swiped in Derby Strip Club')

Perform First BBC Radio 1 Live Lounge ('Frantically vanity search yourselves on Twitter afterwards')

Full Festival Run Around UK + Europe ('It's 3pm, you're getting everyone going. Solid job')

First Request For Lucrative Private Commercial Gig ('Tell everyone you turn it down. Go and do it anyway. First signs of Selling Out')

First US Dates – Tour Support ('Lose all money made on previous shows')

Pointless Record Shop 'In Store' Appearances, Before They All Shut Down ('You forgot to bring your albums to sell')

Large Venue (1,500) – Sold Out ('Estranged relatives start asking for free tickets').

[*Release second album*]

Intimate Return Show in Some Weird Church ('Nobody knows where the toilets are. If, indeed, there are any');

Headline Tour of the Country – Large Venues

('Drummer gets rail card swiped in Manchester Strip Club');

Perform on BBC Chat Show ('Become friends with Graham Norton')

Full Festival Run Around UK + Europe ('It's 7pm, and you are Nailing It. You wave to one of The 1975 in Gothenburg')

First Arena Show ('The fans, they are everywhere. They're selling unofficial merch with your name spelt wrong')

Pointless Record Shop 'In Store' Appearances, Before They All Shut Down ('Why are we still doing these? Someone's getting fired')

Massive World Tour ('Drummer injures hand doing press-ups in Latvian Strip Club')

[*Release Third Album*]
[*Announce Wembley Stadium*]

Play Wembley Stadium ('Drummer marries stripper. All live happily ever after').

So yeah, that's 'exactly' how you get to Wembley Stadium.

Well, not really. The thing about every single act is that they're all completely different, and there are no guarantees that what works for one will work for the other. Good booking agents will have a good grounding in the perfect plot to fit your style, temperament and where you hope to end up. They should be confidently in your corner, and be there for you to talk to if touring is taking its toll on your physical or mental health. They are the strategy men and women who will work closely with any other part of your team, be it manager, label, or even directly with yourself.

However, they can't work miracles. If your music isn't good enough – or you're simply not reacting or building a fanbase – then their hands are tied. Every success comes from great music, and that should be foremost in the thoughts of anyone willing to undertake this lunatic journey.

In the days of yore, songwriters would strap a guitar on their backs, tie a handkerchief around some possessions, dangling it from the end of a stick, and set off into the world in search of paying gigs. Obviously, this was a difficult time for piano players, but somehow they have survived to the current age, through sheer grit and tenacity. Fair play to 'em.

In the early days of the Blues, musicians would essentially do the real world version of what is described above, travelling from place to place, cultivating relationships with the owners of venues, and working out a fee for their performance. This was the real era of 'life on the road'; many of these people literally had no roots, spending their days going from place to place in search of the next gig.

At some point, an enterprising soul thought that there was sure to be money made. If someone could engage with a network of venue owners, arrange talented performers from various places to come and play, thereby orchestrating a finely tuned balance of venues and touring performers, they could all get what they were looking for – money.

And thus, the next step was taken in the evolution of exploiting unassuming Blues musicians, or – as we like to call it – Rock and Roll!

As sure as a band plays instruments, a booking agent plays music venues, knowing the chords and scales that will produce the maximum effect. The talented booking agent knows just what band will fit what venue, what tours are happening, where the next gig is, who they can support, and how all this will benefit both band and promoter. And they'll do it for a reasonable cut of the profits.

'Our fundamental responsibility is to book bands their tours, find supports, come up with ideas, and a strategy of how a band should tour around the world,' says Matt Bates, a booking agent at Primary Talent, and he has helped orchestrate tours for the likes of Two Door Cinema Club, Metronomy, The 1975, Wolf Alice and The Libertines.

'We make sure the bands play the right festivals, and the right shows, in the right slots. We are also there to safeguard bands to make sure they get paid, they get looked after, they get the things they need on their rider. We try to take all of the pressure and worries off a band that's touring. A booking agent brings years and years of experience to a band's live career. It's about knowing what's best for a band, and what the best tactic is to take for their career.'

Regardless of what kind of act he might be dealing with, for Matt there's a Golden Rule that applies to all: 'No band, no matter how good musicians you are, no matter how hard you practice, are any good until they've done fifty gigs.'

Once you have learnt all you need to about sound-checking, setting up, and cramming everything into a 25-minute set, then you're probably ready to work out how far you can take it. And this is where the booking agent enters the story

'You need to start thinking about an agent when you're really starting to think further than your hometown. When you're just playing gigs in Sheffield, there's no real need to have an agent. But once you start thinking further afield, when you have an EP or a single to promote, that's when you need to start to put a proper team around you.'

When Loyle Carner had cut his teeth playing local gigs, he felt ready to step up to the next level, and his first port of call was a booking agent.

'When we started playing shows, we were thinking about playing shows in London every six months. When we started talking to a booking agent about what they thought we should do, they said, "You need to be getting up to this place, they'll love you. Let's get you on some tours and some support slots." Really, a booking agent is a person who facilitates your touring, but also is the one who you should be asking questions of, and making them go above and beyond for your career.'

Loyle was canny enough to build a profile of his own, so that when it came time to bring a booking agent into the picture, he could do so on his own terms.

'If you have something going that people want, a buzz, it's better not to be with someone at the start. Because you can build something up, and then go in and have better conversations. If you can go in and say you have sold this place out, played these support slots – "I'm worth X amount of tickets" – then you're in a stronger place. You should meet as many booking agents as you can, don't just meet one and say, "Yeah, that's the person".'

On the other hand, booking agents themselves are on the lookout for acts that they want to represent. So while you might have an idea of the kind of person you want steering your live career for you, when it comes to meeting the person you have in mind, they might have a different feeling about you.

As Matt Bates explains, a meeting with a booking agent is as much an opportunity for them to check you out, as it is for you to scrutinise them.

'The most important thing is the songs. I've taken on some bands that have gone on to be massive, and when I took them on they were the most shocking band I've seen play live. Sometimes you have to see through the rough and see the potential. If the songs are there, and they're good enough, then you know you can make a live band with the right guidance and opportunities.'

So, the good news is that you don't have to have a Pink Floyd-esque stage show right at the very beginning in order to impress a booking agent. They're looking for talent and potential, and not every band has both of those things at the same time. It's up to the agent to spot the hidden treasures in your raw material. And sometimes, no matter how hard you try, they might not be interested in what you're selling. That doesn't mean you should give up, and there are other avenues to go down, as Theo Ellis of Wolf Alice explains.

'A lot of DIY bands and punk bands won't have a booking agent. They will do it themselves. It's very difficult and takes a lot of energy, but it's an incredible school of thought. Nobody is going to think of you less if you don't have a booking agent. At the start you need to be hands-on, seeking the gigs yourself, getting gigs through friends or friends bands. That's the normal way most bands start.'

If you go down the DIY route, you face a few possibilities. On the one hand, you could discover that you're good at it, that you can build up the relationships and connections needed to organise a tour. And you can end up saving yourself a lot of money by doing the job you'd be paying someone else to do. Of course, that means you'll be doing a lot more work, and getting that balance between creativity and commerce is a difficult enough thing to manage at the best of times.

On the other hand, you could discover that you're terrible at it. In which case, it's time to go back to the drawing board and see if you can work with a booking agent, or at least build up enough experience so they will see taking you on as less of a risk.

Regardless of whether you're doing it yourself or have a competent booking agent to look after you, once you've got a gig booked, one of the first people you're going to encounter is the promoter. And as Matt Bates tells us, they're a pretty important part of the process.

'They're the people we would go to in each territory, in each city, each country, and say, "This is what we want our bands to be doing. Can you facilitate us? Can you get the slots and money we need?" They're on the ground making sure the shows happen and people turn up.'

Cal McCrae is a promoter, and when a booking agent comes to him with an act, he knows what he's looking for, and what he can work with.

'I watch music every single night. And if I'm watching someone standing stagnant, not doing anything and not motivating the crowd, I'm going to be so fuckin' bored. So I look for people that move around who get people going, because I think that's the most exciting thing. People are just so bored of standing around watching the same kind of music with the same kind of performance. You need to be able to do something that excites people.'

Now, before you rush off to start building up a wad of phlegm, or start practising your power slap, this technique isn't likely to work for everyone. Indeed, if you've opted for the sensitive singer-songwriter route, giving off at the audience isn't going to do you any favours. Or maybe it will? The thing to take away from this is that a promoter is looking for an act that will have some kind of impact on an audience.

As an artist, you tend to operate in your own hermetically sealed world. Booking agents tend to experience you at your best (if you've done things right), and they'll be on your side before they start speaking to anyone else.

A local promoter sees music of varying quality all the time. They see it in terms of paying customers; repeat performance value, and whether the night has been a success. And they know that if you don't make an impact – whatever your chosen medium – it's likely that an audience won't come back to see you the next time you pass through their town. So they'll be reluctant to work with you.

A key part of making an impact is knowing when to play, and how often you should do it. If you hit the stage, win over the audience, and deliver the goods, you'll be tempted to want to do it again, as soon as possible.

That isn't always the best idea, and it is something a booking agent can really help you with, as Cal McCrae explains.

'A really good agent is someone that doesn't over-saturate a band in the market, and picks shows that are better for them, as opposed to just a shit ton of shows in general to keep the band happy.'

This strategy of being more selective is something that's central to the way Matt Bates operates.

'An important part of being an agent is knowing when not to play shows. If you want to have a constructive campaign, it's good not to play every festival in the first three months, so that when your album comes out, you've got no festivals left to play.'

This is a sound strategy, and a talented booking agent will know how to orchestrate a gigging campaign that will satisfy the demand for your music, while leaving the audience begging for more. And while tours used to be booked around promoting record releases, things have changed in a way that enables booking agents to do things differently, according to Matt.

'Over the last ten years, I've seen things really evolve. As a live agent, you were led by the release schedule of a band. The touring would fit around what the label needed for an album release. As time has progressed, live gigs have become more important to bands, and it tends to be now that live shows lead the release schedule a lot more.'

For Theo Ellis of Wolf Alice, touring has become a hugely important part of a band's income, and as such, having the right booking agent can be crucial to how you actually make money.

'If you're lucky enough to have an agent who's working wonders for you, and who has great connections, foresight, and knows when to say "no" at the right time, has good relationships with promoters, and can get you support tours with bands that will help your career, then really you benefit so much. Touring, for many bands, is a big source of income, and having a good agent is important.'

Those support tours and shows can be crucial to building up your profile. And they can be a perfect way to showcase your wares to a local promoter, increasing the chances of them wanting to go the extra mile when you're coming through their town wit

'We are big into our tour supports. If we can give that band a big platform, then that's amazing. Because a support tour is for you to showcase yourselves to people who might discover you.'

And Theo and Wolf Alice still remember their roots, and how important support slots were to them.

'We did a huge tour with The 1975 last summer in America, which was super important. We were in front of thousands of people each night in different cities around the states. We wouldn't have been doing that if it wasn't for the support tour.'

Once you've got yourself established, and your name carries a little bit of weight, you'll likely want to start looking at festival shows. These are an enormous part of the UK's live scene, particularly in the summer months, where huge festivals like Glastonbury, Reading or Leeds, Park Life and many more account for a huge percentage of the live music people will experience throughout the year. Throw in the countless number of smaller, boutique festivals across the country, and the festival circuit becomes a lucrative part of any band's schedule.

And for Matt Bates, a booking agent is the one who can unlock that door for you.

'Booking Agents are the ones that have the contacts for the festivals. They are the ones that the festival booker trusts year in, year out. If the agent has headliners on that festival, while they are having those conversations, they talk about the other bands they have on their roster while the door is open and you have the ear of the promoter.'

But, of course, festivals are busy, and generally jam-packed with bands trying to make a name for themselves. Simply getting on the bill might not be as beneficial to your career as you might think, and as Wolf Alice's Theo explains, a good booking agent will know what the right choice will be for you.

'With festivals, it's good to find out if the festival is worth the band's time. Who are we clashing with? Are we going to get stung for fees and rentals?'

These are the kind of pitfalls a booking agent will be well aware of. And if you build up a good relationship with them, you'll hopefully find yourself on the main stage, winning over the crowd, without later discovering that you've been charged for stage hire, or that you've been put on at that time simply because there's someone far better on a different stage at exactly the same time.

And what do these Knights of the Road ask in return for the services? Not too much, as Matt Bates reveals.

'A booking agent takes ten percent of gross of what a band makes, and that's standard across the board. As bands become more successful and as fees get bigger, things change, but fundamentally it's ten percent at the start.'

As you grow, through the help of your booking agent, so your profits will grow, and it becomes a mutually beneficial situation to both parties. A good booking agent will believe in your music, and will push you as hard as they can, because they believe in your potential for success. And as promoter Cal McCrea tells us, ultimately, if you want to make music your business, you've got to treat is as a business.

'If you want to do music as a career and are able to use it as a sustainable way of living, then you should have a booking agent. A booking agent will help you get live shows, and live shows are the primary source of income, not records or anything else. If you want to make money in your life as a musician, then you definitely need a booking agent.'

TIPS ON GETTING A BOOKING AGENT

TARA RICHARDSON
MANAGER AT Q PRIME MANAGEMENT

Ambition

Your agent needs to see the same bigger picture as you. They need to be able to give you a realistic, but creative plan of achieving everything you can with your live shows. .

Roster

The days of worthwhile support slots are almost a thing of the past. Most fans only want to see the headliner nowadays, so the agent's roster shouldn't sway you in that respect. But it should in showing what they've achieved with other acts. Always ask which ones they've had from day one, too.

3

Relationships

They need to work well with your management.

Trust

You have to believe what they say, especially when it's not what you want to hear!

A love of music

Your agent needs to love music as much as you do. That way, you know they're in the audience because they love it, not just because that's their job. It will transcend.

SO... IS OUR MANAGER'S OLD TOUR VAN REALLY GONNA GET US TO ALL THESE PLACES?
I GUESS IF IT DOESN'T BREAK DOWN... AGAIN...
WORLD TOUR MAP
N. AMERICA
EUROPE
ASIA
AFRICA
S. AMERICA
ANTARTICA
?

Touring & Festivals

FEATURING ADVICE FROM:
Andy Smith + Emma Zillman (Kendal Calling Festival)
Blossoms
Bryony October
Lucy Rose
Martha Kinn (Machine Management)
Slaves
Soak
Steve Tilly (Kilimanjaro Promoter)

Wouldn't it be amazing if you could get your parents' old map from the 1990s, plot a tour with red tacks in a manageable little snake around your country of choice, knowing that you are guaranteed food, drink, and bank-breaking fees for your hard slog? That would be a beautiful thing.

If you are able to achieve this on one of your first tours, you my friend are either:

A. A future music industry mogul

Or

B. A big fat liar, whose pants may – or may not – be on fire.

Booking gigs locally can be hard enough, but getting your act a manageable and financially viable tour is the next level. That's not to say it's impossible. And this isn't me discouraging you from doing it: you 100 percent should. This is just a caveat for rookies to expect the unexpected and be prepared to graft.

Fortune favours the brave. If you have a killer live show, then there's no easier way of building a fan base than sharing that music in a room full of like-minded souls, stale beer, and body odour.

There are so many variables you have to consider when venturing into a tour. I mean, how hard could it be to just drive or fly some place, play a show, and move on? The answer is, 'very hard indeed'.

Booking the shows yourself is difficult, but not impossible. I've done it a few times. It was a matter of sending out a billion emails, without being a pest, and then hoping for the best. A crucial help was getting intel from other bands who had toured a lot more than we had. They knew the best numbers, emails, and venues to contact. If you are lucky enough to have a booking agent, which we covered in the previous chapter, then happy days – that's one thing off your plate.

Funding a tour is pricey, and petrol doesn't grow on trees. You'll need to save. Usually if you have a decent fan base in your locality, you can put on a fundraiser gig for the tour, and use that money to offset some of the costs. Alternatively, if you are a merchandise guru, then make sure you have plenty of sexy product to bring on the road with you. It could mean the difference between a £1 egg-and-dog-turd sandwich and a hot meal that day.

The list goes on with variables, from the toll it can have on your mental health (something we will address later in the book), your physical health, your bank balance, and your relationships, etc.

But you're travelling the country/globe, sharing your music with people in different venues, in different towns and cities every night. And when it goes well, there's no better feeling. It's your own private victory, like Vikings conquering another patch of land. You've gone in, played your heart out, won over fans (slayed villagers, if you're still on the Viking metaphor), and most likely rode out with your head held high. I know I probably scared the shit out of you and made it sound as appealing as a dinner date with your ex, but it's important to know what you're getting into, and even more important to enjoy it for what it is along the way.

If everything is ticking along nicely for you, then playing the festivals has to be the next step. Be it showcase, industry, local, or one of the mainstream festivals, getting your act onto those limited slots is pretty much the Holy Grail.

It's a huge achievement to play a music festival for any band starting out. It's the working summer holiday (at the beginning anyway), where the added pressure of opening yourselves up to a whole new audience meets the giddy feeling only a festival can provide. However, there's no set-in-stone way of getting on these lineups. The many industry festivals such as The Great Escape (Brighton), SXSW (Austin), Hard Working Class Heroes (Dublin), Output (Belfast), Liverpool Sound City (guess where that is), and many more, will have a basic submission process, and it would be very useful to do your research.

As a brief aside, after playing the Hard Working Class Heroes festival in Dublin in 2009, my band was courted by Parlophone Records for a few months, until their scout ditched us to go see a Will Smith movie when we were playing in Liverpool. True story.

A lot of the bigger festivals (Glastonbury, Reading and Leeds, European Mainstream Festivals, etc) are primarily filled through booking agents and festival bookers working together. This doesn't mean you won't end up on the bill, as many festival bookers will take notice if you are building enough hype. It's always worth trying to research who these people are and drop them a line. Don't expect an email back from all of them, though.

In the UK, we have BBC Introducing, which is the fairy godmother to new musicians. They have a presence at a lot of the bigger festivals, and will exclusively book artists who need a leg up in their career. These festival slots have been the nursery for artists such as Florence and the Machine, Two Door Cinema Club, and Jake Bugg, to name a few.

Getting out there and sharing is scary, and you'll make mistakes, but once it starts to go well and you play the perfect shows, you will never want to stop.

'The Road' holds a special place in the heart of most musicians. This is the proving ground where dreams are forged, and careers are built. It's a battlefield strewn with the bodies of thousands of unworthy competitors who didn't make the grade (not literally), and if you achieve any kind of success, it's likely the place you'll spend most of your working life.

In the early 1970s, Rolling Stones frontman Mick Jagger gave a TV interview in which he stated bluntly that he wouldn't be doing the same thing in ten years, because it would not be 'appropriate'. At the time of writing (2019), the Stones are back on the road with a combined age of 2,193 (or thereabouts), filling out stadiums, and generally appearing to be having the time of their wrinkly lives. And while they're all earning mega-bucks, that's almost certainly not the biggest motivator for these multi-million septuagenarians. For Mick and the lads, the thrill is still there from being out on the road, hitting stages, and moving from town to town like conquering heroes. You can see it written in the leathery folds of their expensively manicured faces.

Of course, when you're starting out, money isn't going to be the main lure for hitting the road. But if you can make enough to get you from show to show, and hold it together in the process, this is where you discover whether or not this is the lifestyle for you. And, if you strike the right poses along the way and hit the right notes, you'll pick up other followers, people outside your friends and family, people who owe you no allegiance. This is where the long journey to The Top really begins.

'I remember that first tour, my manager had an old van which broke down all the time,' says Lucy Rose, no stranger to the road, who has built up a solid and devoted fanbase. 'We commuted from my parents' house, because it's in the Midlands. Everything was a couple hours drive from there, so we just did that for a couple weeks, and I loved it.

It was ace. But potentially, we played in front of ten or twenty people a night, and I still thought everything was really great. Playing live has been the most important part of building my fanbase.'

You might not be packing out Madison Square Garden at the start of your career, but as Lucy tells us, if you get ten people and win them over, it's a start.

When you make that decision to spread your wings and see the world, it can be daunting. Plenty of incredible bands never leave the safety of their hometown, leaving even their local fans to decry what a tragedy it is when no-one gets to experience such talent. But the local scene is a place where you can nurture your talent, and develop the skills that will take you further. And sometimes, no matter how good it is playing to your pals and getting a rapturous reception, you end up wanting more. And that's where touring comes in.

For Blossoms, touring wasn't just something they worked towards, it was the reason to start the band in the first place, as front man Tom Ogden reveals.

'We had been in bands before Blossoms, where we'd been asked to sell tickets by a promoter, and then you end up with just your parents and mates there. It would be shit and nobody would really care. With Blossoms we had a head start, as we'd been in bands for years that had been shit. It never happened, and we were frustrated. This is why we started this band.'

They hit the road and conquered venues all over the country in a relatively short space of time. And for Tom, that was only something they could do after plenty of preparation.

'You don't want to go on tour before you're ready for it. You need time to write and evolve, and when you are on the road, you don't have that time.'

For Laurie Vincent and Isaac Holman of Slaves, that preparation was crucial to their success. But even with a bit of prep, it still came down to some good, ol' fashioned hard work, and a little bit of creative thinking, as Laurie reveals.

'Isaac's brother invested 500 quid to get us some recordings and to get 250 CDs made up, that I sent to hundreds of promoters in the UK. We did about two weeks where we played a gig every other night, and then tried to book more shows while we were on the road, trying to jump on other people's tours. It was really DIY. We played loads of places to no one, jumped on other band's shows, and just went out and bodged it together.'

'Bodging it together' isn't an option for everyone, but an indication of how Slaves were suited to the road, so they took to this lifestyle quickly. You could be an excellent bunch of songwriters, fabulously talented musicians, and lovely people, but if you can't cut it with the demands of touring, things are going to get tricky. It's not a place where politeness is necessarily a virtue, and grafting can pay dividends. Frequently, it's not a particularly glamorous existence, as Isaac is happy to point out.

'We had sandwich club. We would buy a loaf of bread that would be lunch, then sit in a car park outside the venue and declare we were playing "The Sandwich Club". We slept on a lot of people's floors, there are a lot of stories of rat-infested art studios. We came up the hard way, but it was a really beautiful thing.'

A life on the road means that you're stuck in a small space with other people, some of whom you may not know too well, and some of whom you might have thought you knew. Tensions can rise. And as Blossoms' drummer Joe Donovan tells us, sometimes you just have to confront things head on.

'When you are on tour with five people, it can get a bit mad. The best thing to do is just be honest, have a little argument, and get over it.'

Easy as that, right?

Before you get to the stage of throwing punches at each other in a cramped mini-van, you have to get out on the road in the first place. And while it's absolutely feasible for you to get a map, do some digging, and start approaching every venue in the country to see if they'll give you a gig, it's a lot easier if you team up with a promoter to help you out.

Steve Tilly is a promoter for Kilimanjaro Live, and he has worked with the likes of Ed Sheeran, The 1975, and Catfish and the Bottlemen. For him, the role of the promoter is pretty straightforward.

'The promoter puts on the show, in very simplistic terms, and holds the venue, agrees the deal with the artist, puts the tickets on sale, markets the show, makes sure everyone gets paid, and makes sure the tickets sell. We either sell out as quickly as possible, or if we're not going to sell out, we work our butts off to make sure the room is full.'

It's a lot of plates to be spinning, and crucial to it all is a band that can actually deliver on what the promoter is promising. That's where you come in.

'Put on a gig in your rehearsal space. Invite twenty of your mates to come along,' says Steve. 'Get used to the sound in the room, to generally playing live, and figuring out what it's like to put on your own little gig. Those people you invited to the first show feel special, as they got to come see your first show. After that, approach venues and tell them you can get twenty people down and ask if you can get on a local band night. My theory is, you should always under-promise and over-deliver. If you tell a promoter you're going to bring twenty people, and fifty show up, then the promoter is going to be delighted. That will probably lead to your own headline show.'

Venues and promoters alike are looking for that something special in you, and when they see it, they know they've found it. And sometimes, they can see it before anyone else can.

'When I first saw Catfish and The Bottlemen, I fell in love with them. I thought Van (lead singer) had a bit of star quality, and I liked the songs. A few of my friends were like, "Whatever, another four piece guitar band." I saw a young band making an old sound fresh again.'

For Martha Kinn of Machine Management, it's a long journey to the point where you start impressing people. And sometimes, as she discovered when working with Years & Years, it's those difficult gigs that can shape your future, rather than the good ones.

'You have to have the songs ready, and they have to be pretty good. So just play as many bad shows as you can. And when I say "bad", I mean unattended shows. I've done that with all of my acts. I've put them through the mill on the worst shows you can think of. When Years & Years were a five piece, they played some terrible shows, where I was the only one in the crowd. After one show, Olly Alexander left the stage crying, and that was the end of the five piece, and the beginning of the band becoming successful.'

It can be brutal, but if you're resilient enough, you can really reap the rewards. And while you're not likely to be taking baths in a tubful of £50 notes just yet, your income from live shows can be a vital lifeline, keeping everything ticking along in the right direction. But sometimes, you have to spend money in order to make money, as Lucy Rose tells us.

'For me, I employ my band, the sound engineer, and a tour manager, so my pay roll for each gig is a lot higher than if you're in a band. I do remember my band doing a year or so for free to help me at the start, because they were all friends, which was amazing. You need to be lucky and have good people around you who believe in the music to make it work.'

It might not be rock and roll, but being careful with money is key to your survival on the road. Lucy Rose employs musicians, but most bands operate in a different way. And for Tom Ogden of Blossoms, keeping your overheads low, and being responsible with cash is crucial.

'We did it the cheapest possible way. It probably cost us a grand to go on tour. And with any money we made, we would put it straight back into the band, until we were satisfied that the band is at a sort of level where it can sustain itself.'

When you get handed over a wad of used banknotes after

packing out a sweaty indie club, it'll be tempting to hit the bar, or the nearest takeaway, but you have to think in practical terms; do you need that money? Can you make it to the next show? Once you can understand these kind of issues, you'll be better at turning down temptation.

Something that most bands encounter at some point in their career, is a promoter or venue asking them to play a show for free. This is a real pitfall of the music business, as there can often be something hugely appealing about such an offer. In 99 percent of cases when a person asks you to play for free, the carrot they dangle in front of you is 'exposure' – and not of the indecent kind.

When someone tells a struggling band that they can get on a bill with a huge crowd built-in, and with important people in attendance who could be great for their career, but they will not get paid a penny by them, it can pose a real quandary. Is the potential benefit worth the lack of immediate income? Obviously, this will depend on the circumstances.

It's a tough decision that you'll almost certainly have to face. But not everyone deals with it in the same way. And for Laurie Vincent of Slaves, it's pretty obvious what way to play it.

'I don't think bands should play for free. There's a principle about your music, and you're worth something. Never play a show where they try and make you sell tickets. That's bullshit. They're conning you.'

These kind of 'pay to play' scenarios are the bane of the live music scene. Promoters offer you a potentially lucrative gig, but you have to sell tickets yourselves, or foot the bill. It's a win-win for promoters. And in almost all cases, it's the band which suffers, by either having to put pressure on their friends to come along, or by covering the cost themselves, leaving them out of pocket.

As Lucy Rose explains, sometimes it can be really tempting to get a support slot on a bigger gig, but who knows how you'll actually go down with the crowd?

'Sometimes you can go, "Ah, that's amazing!" because they're really well known. But if their fans don't like your music, it can just be a waste of time and money doing it. I think it's really important to make sure that it is the right fit and it places you in the right world, not just because you love that band and you know they're doing really well, and you get to play in front of loads of people.'

Playing in front of loads of people who love you is great. Playing in front of loads of people who don't care at all, is soul destroying. And it pays to be canny when you're saying 'yes' to things.

However, one way in which you can play to a huge crowd, who are likely to be pretty forgiving to you, is by hitting the festival circuit.

Music festivals happen all over the world, but are particularly ingrained in the culture of the UK. Glastonbury is the biggie, an event which has grown from a bunch of hippies in a field, dancing naked to Hawkwind, to an army of hippies in a field, surrounded by people from all walks of life, with some of the biggest names in music, and global media attention. And probably still people dancing naked to some iteration of Hawkwind.

For many bands, festivals are an essential part of their life, filling in those summer months and, in many cases, actually providing enough income and exposure to get them through some fallow points at other times of the year. But getting on the bill isn't always the easiest thing in the world.

Kendal Calling Festival has grown from modest beginnings in 2006, to become one of the UK's best-loved festivals, attracting up to 25,000 people, and sweeping the boards at awards ceremonies for 'Best Small Festival'. They've had the great and the good take to their stages. And for founder Andy Smith and booker Emma Zillman, how to crack the festival circuit is not a fiercely guarded secret.

'The most effective way by far for a band that doesn't have an agent, is finding out which town the booker lives in and emailing them to introduce themselves and keep them updated,' says Andy. 'Even if you don't get a response, email me every few months, and say, "Hey, just to let you know this is happening. Maybe you have a gig in my town, and you invite me down to see it. Then, fingers crossed I like the music and I understand what is going on with the band, and that way you have a higher chance of getting booked.'

Polite persistence can open a lot of doors for you. And if you happen to be The Real Deal, that's actually what bookers and promoters are looking for. But, as with any kind of tour, you need to do some research. And as Emma explains, you need to be realistic about when you plan out your festival strategy, even down to when you make contact.

'I generally tend to tell bands to start getting in touch from the end of November. It's the month of January when we are at the busiest, filling up the smaller slots and getting ready for festival announcement. The new band slots, if you don't have a booking agent, tend to go to local bands, because we want to appeal to the local fan base. We might book a band one year because we hear they are doing great things, and we might get an email from them the next year asking to play. What we want to see is progression, a bigger following, playing bigger venues. It's all about ticket sales for the festival promoter.'

If your persistence pays off, you might find yourself on the bill for a small festival and, as we can see with Kendal Calling, a 'small' festival can be pretty flippin' big. And while most of us have been to a festival of some kind in our lives, it's a different experience as a punter. You get to chill out, drink some booze, have a dance, fall over in the mud, experience the horror of festival toilets, and sleep in a sweaty tent, surrounded by a cacophony of snoring. Great times.

But plenty of bands have failed to realise that actually playing a festival is a completely different experience, and proceed to do everything they'd normally do as a punter, causing all manner of chaos for the behind-the-scenes crew of the event. As Andy and Emma explain, there's a real sense of etiquette when it comes to playing a festival.

'Don't get drunk before you go on stage,' says Andy. 'Don't harass the more popular artists. Turn up on time, and be very polite to the sound engineer and the lighting engineer.'

Emma concurs: 'Turn up on time, at the right place, at the right gate to get the right wristband. Like Andy said, everybody on that stage is probably working 20-hour days, so be nice.'

If you're nice to them, they'll be nice to you… hopefully. And once you've taken to the stage, rocked your socks off, and had people waving lighters during the more tender moments of your set, you can kick back, drink booze, fall in the mud, and experience the horror of festival toilets.

Although, the backstage toilets are significantly better, which is almost an enticement to play a festival, enabling you to see some great bands, without wading through a cesspool to answer nature's call. That and the songs, right?

This approach of being nice to people, being respectful, and being courteous, is a good thing, something echoed by Laurie and Isaac of Slaves.

'Basically the biggest tip is to be nice to everyone,' states Laurie. 'You have to remember that every single person there doesn't have to do you a favour. Be friendly, don't act like a freak.'

Isaac Holman adds some sage advice: 'If you're a prick on the way up, the way down will be pretty fucking hard.'

If it all goes according to plan, you'll be touring the length and breadth of the country in a fleet of air-conditioned luxury tour buses, before calling in on the big festivals to play a headlining slot that will be talked about for decades by teary-eyed music journalists. And, if you've been very good, you'll be as rich as Croesus, making money for your whole organisation, and rewarding the effort and work put in by promoters and booking agents when you were forced to cram the whole band into a Mini, holding onto each other for warmth.

But through it all, as Steve Tilly from Kilimanjaro Live reminds us, the music has to be the most important thing. Because, no matter how big it gets, if you don't stay true to the music, you might as well not be doing it at all.

'If you look at Ed Sheeran, he would play anywhere. He would play in the back of your car, if he had the chance. He just wanted to play his songs.'

TOP TEN TIPS FOR NEW ARTISTS TOURING

SOAK

Eat

It's easy to get hangry on tour! Your diet is likely to consist of bread and beer but it's important to remember to get your fill and avoid unnecessary hunger fuelled conflict.

Stay in Touch

For me one of the most trialling things about touring is being far away from friends and family. It can be hard to feel like you have a home, when each day you have a brand new temporary one. So stay in touch! Let your friends know you love and miss them. I know for me, I find great comfort in face-times and phone calls because at the end of the day I know those people are my home.

Space

It's more than likely that you will have a touring party of at LEAST one other person. You'll probably spend a lot of your time traveling and sharing hotel rooms/sleeping space. Being constantly in someone's company for a few weeks can teach you a lot, not only about the person/people you're with but also about yourself. It's important to make sure you still get enough 'me' time to avoid getting overwhelmed by the intensity of living with your travelling party, and also just to give yourself some headspace.

Stretch

If you're not spending your time in cars and splitter vans you'll be spending it in unreclining airplane seats or bus bunks. Pins and needles are inevitable. Unless you've offered free beer to your friends to act as gear carriers, you'll be sweating a few beads everyday with load ins and outs. And you can never predict a load in (sometimes, when god is on your side it may be possible to park at stage door). So make sure you stretch those limbs!

Be Nice

It's free, it's easy and there is no reason why you shouldn't! Touring is hard, everyone has more than likely made a sacrifice to be there. Everyone is missing someone back home, its stressful. You're probably eating strange food and guessing language barriers while living out of suitcases, so it can be a sensitive environment and its important be aware of that. Don't forget to be thankful to the venue staff, soundtech, promoter etc, without them your performance wouldn't be possible.

Be Open

Don't be afraid to try something new, that is the brilliance of travel! In a constantly moving environment there is the opportunity to see and hear so much, try local cuisine and meet new people.

Don't forget where you came from

There was a time when you were queuing up hours before a show just to get in to the front row. Remember what it felt like when your favourite bands guitarist shook your hand? If you have earned a fanbase don't avoid them, without them you wouldn't be anywhere. I'm not saying you have to take everyone for drinks post show and spend all the petrol money on jagermeister (I'm not saying you shouldn't either though) but sometimes it wouldn't kill you to take that photo with eager Megan and Jack by the merch table.

Have Fun

Not many people get to take such a wonderful journey. Don't take it for granted. Remember that you're there to enjoy yourself, its mutual, that's why there is an audience! You give them all you have and you'll receive it back.

TIPS FROM A TOUR MANAGER

BRYONY OCTOBER
TOUR MANAGER

1

Look after yourself

There are huge temptations in terms of drinking and eating properly is not always easy.

2

Going on Tour IS a Job

My favourite joke phrase is 'it beats working for a living' because for sure it can be enormous fun and sometimes glamorous, but it is work at the end of the day, and a lot of the time it can be boring, gruelling, lonely and feel like hard work, so it's good to have that at the back of your mind as much as possible whilst remembering it ALWAYS beats sitting at a checkout in Tesco.

3

Support Your Team

Even at the highest level the tour's success is only as good as the sum of it's parts. There isn't room for loads of egos. Yes things go wrong, yes things change (a lot), and even if you wrote, recorded and masterminded the whole operation you can't get out on the road on your own.

Prepare for boredom

Make sure you have box sets galore or a good book as the show and soundcheck are only a small proportion of the day.

Be Nice to EVERYONE You Ever Meet

The music industry is really small and you will almost certainly never be more than a few degrees of separation from everyone you meet, not least bump into them again and again and again.

Keep Some things Personal

It doesn't all have to be recorded on social media. There are huge pressures on bands and artists to publicise everything, keep some stuff personal for you and your band/crew to share.

Loyalty To Tour Companies

Being loyal to certain suppliers like van hire and rehearsal space can reap long term loyalty savings

Think About Your Gear

Thinking really carefully about how your gear is cased and keeping that weight down saves huge money especially flying to shows. Pelicases are the one for this!

You Have to Be Practical

I think keeping costs down whilst getting the best value is a tricky balance, i.e spending a bit more on a hotel to include breakfast so that everyone gets at least one proper meal a day might not save you money but it could save you cancelling a show down the line. Good value that benefits the health and comfort of the tour whilst not blowing money unnecessarily is as, if not more, important than the bottom line being as low as possible.

Factor in 'Me' Time

Make time for yourself. It can get very intense, but it's always ok to go off for some 'me time' take a walk etc.

MERCH TABLE
SLAVES
BLOSSOMS
BRY
PAY HERE
BAND PINS
VINYL X 50
BAND CDS

Merchandise

FEATURING ADVICE FROM:
Blossoms
Bry
Music Glue
Tersha + Jack (Terrible Merch)

What's your favourite piece of merchandise that you have bought at a show?

Over the years, I've acquired everything from Lucy Rose's homemade jam to a tea mug from Slaves, along with over a hundred band T-shirts, even the shit ones. I've never looked back at a piece of merch from a show and regretted buying it.

It might sound cheesy to say it, but screw it, it's true: if you have an act's logo emblazoned on your shirt then you instantly feel a closer connection to them. You become a disciple, walking around like a poorly fitted advertisement for their music and what they stand for. It becomes a talking point; Who is the band? Are they any good? I love a band called Idles, a group of manic post punk performers from Bristol, and their merchandise is visually striking at best, borderline offensive at worst. When I was by myself at a show in Austin, Texas, I managed to wangle my way into a crowd by starting a conversation with someone wearing one of their shirts. It's a fail-safe way to figure out who is into the same shit as you are.

I'm not going to get down on my knees, look to the stars and weep tears for the days when music was something people paid for. Sure, nobody pays for downloads anymore or buys CD singles, but then we also don't paint on our cave walls with sabre-tooth tiger blood either. Things change, for good and for bad, and you have to roll with it.

This means, outside of a subscription to a streaming platform, merchandise in all forms is the real monetary connection between fan and artist. It's a direct transaction process, and in those early days it can really be mutually beneficial.

I don't know if you've ever costed up a tour for a new band? The vast majority will come back from those first few tours, having lost a lot of money. It's all a learning process: petrol is expensive, cheap hotels/hostels if you can afford them mount up, even shitty meal deal sandwiches can be a penny pincher.

That means on the second/third/fourth tour, you want to find a way of making money. And the secret to that is selling merchandise – T-shirts, mugs, posters, vinyl ... everything short of your body, so long as it keeps you hovering around the break-even mark. The most important thing to do when you're on stage is to make people aware of your merch and then get down to the little table or booth to flog your wares.

[Inflammatory statement Klaxon] Bands are just travelling T-shirt salesmen! [Inflammatory Statement Klaxon Ends]

If I tweeted that without context, the hate I would get would be pretty special. I don't actually believe this: music should come from a place of wanting to create and share, not from wanting to sell merchandise. However, if I took out all personality, musical purity, and soul, and just looked at cold hard numbers and spreadsheets, everything would look very different. Priorities would change.

Popular acts have the ability to make a massive amount of money on the road and through their online shops. I've heard numbers from fairly successful musicians on what they might sell during a single night at a show, and a week on the road selling merch is potentially more lucrative than the average yearly income on minimum wage. A lot of acts make so little through their recorded music that they solely survive on what they sell from merchandise. It blew my mind when I found this out. It's like opening an ice-cream shop and surviving off the money you make selling the chocolate sprinkles. It doesn't feel right.

What happens if nobody wants to buy your wares? You're going to be lumped with a few hundred unwanted T-shirts in your house. So you have to really think about what your individual pieces of merchandise will look like. If you're a bubble-gum pop duo, then having some deep, illegible Norwegian Black Metal font on your T-shirts probably isn't going to help you shift too many. You need to think about who you are as a band: who are your fans? What do they like to wear? What sort of merch would you like to make? When you have answered those questions you will have a better idea of where to take it next.

T-shirts and hoodies are the classic staple of the merch table, and they have a reputation for being cheap, easily faded, badly fitted pieces of shit. They always pin them back on the board at the big gigs to create the illusion that they actually fit and won't be loose and baggy maternity shirts. So if you can spend a little extra on fitted shirts, then you and your fans will appreciate it down the line. If it fits nice, it gets worn twice.

I made that slogan up just now; later, guys, I'm going into advertising.

No-one ever tells you they got into it for the merch. The sex? Maybe. The drugs? Too often, sadly. The music? Occasionally. But the merchandise? Never.

At the height of their success, you could buy almost any product imaginable with a picture of The Beatles on it. People loved the music, and the merch allowed them to own a piece of the band. Admittedly, it was almost inevitably some cheaply produced bit of tat with a 'likeness' of the band that wouldn't be useful in an identity parade, but it still helped make that connection, nonetheless.

These days, you'll rarely see a touring band without a well-stocked merch table. Regardless of what level they are at, most bands have a battered cardboard box full of T-shirts, hoodies, and other inexpensively produced garments. Frequently, people who would never normally spend anything on branded merchandise will end up walking away with a T-shirt emblazoned with the support band's logo, a band whose music they'll struggle to recall one note of the following day. Such is the power of music (and alcohol).

Joe Donovan of Blossoms believes the way to sell a few T-shirts after a show, is to not get too carried away with the design.

'Keep it simple. Our best-selling T-shirt is the Blossoms logo, plain white or black. Less is more. It's not complicated.'

This approach suits the band, a slightly 'no-nonsense' approach that brings continuity to everything from the stage backdrop, to the single and album covers, to the row of fans in the front row wearing T-shirts.

And for Blossoms singer Tom Odgen, it ain't rocket science to come up with something that works.

'Go with what feels natural. If you're deliberating over it for hours, then you're not being creative, you're just trying to be creative.'

Of course, if it suits you, then you might want to let your imagination run riot. And for Irish singer songwriter Bry, a striking visual image was just part of the package.

'My brand was a happy accident. Since I was 18, I've been wearing striped T-shirts and a bowler hat, just because I'm tall and I thought it was a good look for me. When people started showing up in the same clothes as me, I decided to bring out a striped T-shirt with "Bry" embroidered on it, and it sold a few thousand in a few months. It's a bizarre thing to look out into my audience and see a few hundred people dressed like me. It's very strange.'

Obviously that's not going to work for everyone. But if you have a striking look in the first place, and people latch on to it, you'd be crazy not to take advantage of it. After all, you're not exploiting it, you came up with it in the first place, right? Which is not to say that Bry invented stripes, but pairing it with a bowler hat was all him, baby.

Part of the key to the success of Bry's merch is that it's not a massive leap from the kind of thing his audience already wear. He just makes sure it looks good.

'If you know your audience – and I think I know mine by now – then you build your merchandise around the fashion they would want. Instead of just making a badly fitting baggy shirt with a bad font for the sake of it, you have to make sure it fits in with what they would wear from day to day. It's not that much about you, but more about fashion.'

Sometimes, if you're really lucky, your merch choices can go on to have a profound impact upon fashion.

'Look at the Rolling Stones T-shirts,' says Joe from Blossoms. 'A girl at my school thought it was a brand. She didn't know anything about the band. It's just because those T-shirts were a thing in my school.'

In that case, while it might not be hugely useful in shifting records, a best-selling design could still be a lucrative money-spinner. As long as you still hold the rights to it.

So let's assume you have just come up with something as iconic as the Rolling Stones' 'tongue' logo, and you want to unleash it on the world. Without having to resort to breaking out the sewing-machine and getting to work yourself, what is the best way to get merch from your head to a folding picnic table at a venue?

Enter Terrible Merch.

Despite the name, the company specialises in all aspects of making quality merch, so you don't have to. And they don't just limit themselves to printing up a few T-shirts, either.

'We do anything and everything in a boutique package,' explains Tersha and Jack from Terrible Merch. 'We've spent a long time identifying obstacles in the merch-selling process, and we provide tools and services to overcome them. We handle everything from card readers to sturdy transportation and storage boxes, warehousing and fulfilment, to design and manufacturing. We're probably more experienced in setting up and doing this, so we help the artists by lending our experience, and aiming to provide a holistic solution to their merch problems. We also make great quality merch.'

Assuming you have got a killer design, and the merch is flying off the table at the gigs, you might want to think about opening up a shop elsewhere, and there's nowhere better than the digital frontier of the internet. And this is where a company called Music Glue come in.

'Music Glue is a direct-to-fan technology platform,' explains Joe Porn of Music Glue, one of several companies aiming to provide you with a way to shift boxes of loot from your storage space, right into the hearts of fans.

'We enable artists of any size to set up a free customisable website, where they can have a blog or a gallery, or any of the things you need on the web side of things for free. We also offer listings, ticketing, merch sales, print on demand, digital bundles, everything an artist needs to be able to set up a store online and sell directly to their fans.'

One of the benefits of doing things this way is that it allows you to have a central point of focus for your fans to soak up everything you have to offer, something that perhaps isn't as straightforward as you might think.

'A lot of artists make it really difficult for fans to buy stuff from them. When a fan comes to an artist's site, you should be able to sell them everything in one place. They've just spent a bunch of money really quickly, and then we figure out who gets paid. So we might pay the promoter for the tickets. We might pay the artist for the T-shirt. We might pay the label for the CD. But we enable that ecosystem where everything should be in one place.'

This kind of service can be good news for artists, particularly those artists who don't have good bookkeeping skills, and aren't particularly interested in juggling songwriting with accountancy.

If you get all this nailed, the merch can be the fuel that keeps the engine going. And as well as the business of making music and creating art, you have a side-line in making other stuff that fans want, which also becomes a viable part of the band's identity.

Enter Shikari are a band who have a strong presence at the merch table, and as Joe from Music Glue explains, they really know what they're doing.

'Enter Shikari fans know they produce really high quality merch, and that every four months a new range of products will be coming out. Their fan base trust that what they're going to get is quality. So they don't mind spending a bit more money on it.'

So, if you were thinking of trying to increase your profits by using the lowest quality materials you can find, forget about it. Fans will know. That's why they are fans.

By using companies like Music Glue and Terrible Merch, you could potentially have a pretty tasty business empire on your hands, assuming the demand is there for what you're selling. However, it's always good to get your hands dirty too, and a lot of bands will start out doing most things themselves. And contrary to what you've just read, this isn't always as bad as it sounds, as Joe Porn of Music Glue tells us.

'Bear's Den are a great example of how to do merch at the beginning. They would get vinyls and CDs made up online, and get cheap cardboard recyclable packaging. They would get a potato and dip it in ink, or paint a hand stamp on each one. We would stamp them at a"Stamping BBQ Party". We would make up 2,000 and they would just fly out. Their margins were quite small as a touring band starting out, and they would do really well because they were clever with their merch.'

Who said rock and roll was dead, eh?

This aesthetic worked well for a band like Bear's Den, and the idea of getting some hand-made merch really fits in with who they are as a band. And as Jack and Tersha from Terrible Merch explain, getting something that works for you as an artist is a key to making successful products.

'Artists have to view merchandise as a key component of their overall offering, and treat it with the same discipline as any other part of their business. You rehearse and write music with pride in your work, and approaching merch in the same way will reap benefits. Remember who your audience is, imagine who you want your audience to be, and you'll figure out what your merch needs to be. Take great care of the little things. Opt for quality as long as it remains affordable for your audience. Make sure you can receive payment in any way that your fans could choose to use. Always man the merch stand. And your merch trade will flourish.'

Essentially, if you make the right kind of merch, then it won't really feel like a chore when it comes to selling it. And for Joe from Blossoms, manning the merch stall is a valuable part of finding out just who is into your band.

'If you are a young band, go down to the merch stall and do it yourself. Stand by the table, and get a Sharpie in your pocket in case they want something signed. You'll end up having a chat with your new fans, which we used to do. If you've seen a band for the first time and meet them at the merch stall, then you'll probably get into that band. It's a great way to connect and meet fans.'

When the gig is over, you're back on the tour bus/van/horse and cart (or the hotel, if you're doing well enough) you might want to take stock of how the merch sales are doing. After all, touring can be a slog, and sometimes the short sharp shock of the merch sales can be just the shot you need to keep your spirits up, as Tom from Blossoms explains.

'I hear how much we sell after a show and think "That's quite good". We are at a level now where we are reinvesting everything into the band, because we are going to America and things like that. We don't want to rely on other people to fund us, we want to fund ourselves.'

What you do with the money is important, and for Bry, making some money from merch allows you a great deal of freedom. The freedom to not have to worry about bills.

'Merchandise pays for my tours. I didn't realise this until I got into the actual industry side of things, that tours aren't really profitable. It's the merchandise that makes it profitable. I'll come home with a few grand from each UK or European tour, which apparently isn't that common a thing. I wouldn't be very happy if I came home from a tour with no money as I wouldn't have rent or anything.'

Making music professionally means being part of several important ecosystems, and merchandise is just one of them. It can be a huge benefit to your career, but it also requires a bit of work and effort to get right. As with other things, if it's becoming a stress to get it right, something has gone wrong. And you might be better off focusing on something else.

After all, you're a musician, as Tom from Blossoms reminds us.

'I think merchandise is just a bonus, I don't think it's that important. The songs and being the band is more important. I don't think we have any merch that immediately identifies us as Blossoms; it's just T-shirts with a logo on it. Focus on being a good band and whatever merchandise you make people will like because you are great.'

And at the very least, you need never worry about having a clean T-shirt, ever again.

TIPS ON MERCHANDISE

JACK + TERESHA
TERRIBLE MERCH

Try to plan your first run of merchandise around gigs in your hometown or smaller tours.

Your merchandise gives your fans the opportunity to shout their support of you and become a walking billboard for you.

Take a note of what your audience wears, what your audience likes and what you wear/like. We mimic or imitate our idols.

Black t-shirts sell the most, white the second-most and colours don't sell so well.

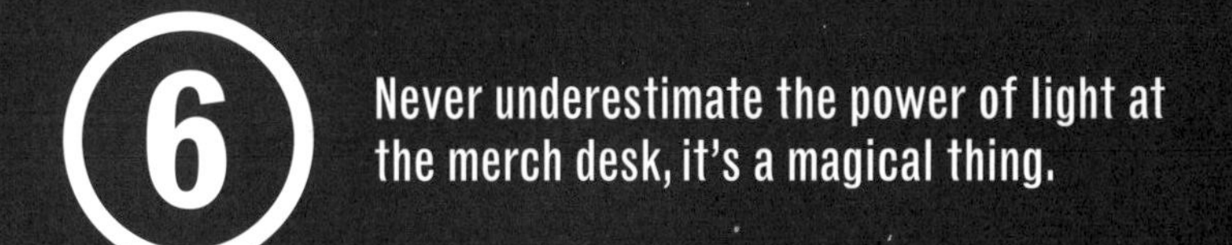

7 Presenting your products properly is something we firmly believe in.

8 Look good doing something achievable. Don't look bad doing something unachievable.

9 Keep your audience and your capabilities in mind.

BAND
FUND

How to Make Money

FEATURING ADVICE FROM:
Frank Turner
Kevin Baird (Two Door Cinema Club)
Little Simz
Joe Porn (Music Glue)
Simon Pursehouse (Sentric)

Money is one of the sure-fire triggers for anxiety. Having to dig around the back of your sofa for enough loose change to buy yourself a pot noodle in order to prevent death by starvation is a shit situation. Yet almost all of us have been in that murky financial hell-hole at one point or another.

Which leads me nicely to the band I played in. When we were really giving the future 'rock star' thing a pop, we lived together in a house in Belfast, each of us collecting benefits to pay the rent and feed our faces. However, being new to our twenties, we would spend every gathered coin on wine, rolling tobacco, and pints of piss-weak beer. I'm sure there is healthier lifestyles to follow!

Many of us at a certain point in life will try to live the bohemian life of excess. But when real life comes knocking, and the money coming in doesn't even remotely balance your needs, you know you have a problem.

Traditionally, only a small percentage of artists have been able to make enough money to live comfortably, but the times, 'they are a-changing.' At no other point in my lifetime have I heard of so many musicians making money from their work, and I'm not just talking about artists signed to major labels. There are quite a few artists I know personally who write incredible music, and it just so happens that the music they write sits quite pristinely on the playlists of Spotify and Apple Music amongst others. They might not get a lot of radio play, and their career may be building a lot slower than it would with a traditional label, but they've figured out how to make their money from streaming. And of course, they own every percent of their music.

Recently, I've been mentoring some young musicians at a music college. These students spent every penny they had on their debut releases, and without exception, they made it all back – and then some – through playlists and streaming. That concept was unheard of only a few years ago. People generally take playlists too seriously, but here you have the next generation of tech-savvy kids motivated to make their music make money, and succeeding.

It's a really satisfying thing to see. Traditionally, the knockout combo of album sales and touring would be an artist's bread and butter. If you ask anyone in the music industry today, they'll tell you that it's all about the touring. And that's fine, but only if you're selling thousands of tickets and have a mobile shop to flog your merch.

On the other hand, streaming is providing artists with a lot more money than they have been getting for a long time through recorded music, but you have to hit some serious numbers to make that money.

What do you do at the start, when you don't have any of these things? The answer is: you slog it the fuck out, and you look for any grant/funding/eccentric millionaire you can get your hands on. Nobody said it was going to be easy, and 99 percent of artists that you love have been in this position. Until you figure out how to get an audience interested in your band, you won't make much – if any – dough. I've played more gigs for no money than I have played for any money. It's all part of the start-up process.

So if you can fill out a form, have some decent music, and aren't a complete axe-wielding serial killer, then there are probably funding opportunities available to you somewhere. Places like Help Musicians (www.helpmusicians.org.uk) and the (PRS Foundation (www.prsfoundation.co.uk) are great places to start. They are full of information and aid for artists just like you. And there are other destinations for funding through government schemes, local councils, and company sponsorship.

All this means that there is money out there if you look for it hard enough and are eligible. We covered this a little more in depth in Chapter 8, so leaf back if you want to research more.

'The best things in life are free / but you can keep them for the birds and the bees / now give me money…' – The Beatles.

For all your dreams of taking on the world, and sharing your incredible artistry with your adoring public, you still need to put food on the table, and you still need a roof over your head. And while plenty of artists do everything in their power to shy away from the financial side of things, there's no ignoring the word 'business' in the term 'music business'.

So if you have what it takes, but can't take advantage of your monetary destiny, then some other opportunistic character will likely do so.

At the start, we have the romanticised image of the hungry songwriter, wearing shabby clothes, eating scraps, permanently skinny, but with an effervescent twinkle in their eye, as they crank out masterpiece after masterpiece. Then they get successful, dine on nothing but venison and caviar, whilst clad in outlandish designer clobber, and everyone starts to hate them.

It's a time-honoured image: when it comes to musicians, we seem to be hard-wired to prefer our artists to be struggling, rather than successful. And whether this is a good thing or not, the reality of the situation seems to conform to this vision of the world.

'We used to do a thing with all-you-can-eat buffets: where two people go in, one of them wears a baseball cap, while the other one talks to the waitress. And the guy with the baseball cap goes to the toilet and swaps with somebody else off the street. You can feed ten people for the price of two, that way.'

It's fair to say that Frank Turner has left his buffet-swindling days behind him, but the memory of having to sing for his supper has never quite left him.

'Starting out as a new act in music is financially very tough. If you were to add together all the hours that you spend playing music versus what you get paid, it's so far below minimum wage it's hilarious.'

Playing music costs money, there's no escaping it. From purchasing instruments and equipment, to hiring practice rooms and arranging travel to and from gigs, you're going to need some cash in the bank if you want to even think about getting to a point where you can actually make money from doing what you love. One of the first decisions you're going to have to face is whether you decide to do this as a hobby or as a career and, as Frank explains, that can be a pretty big hurdle to get over.

'There's a moment that every single person who is a freelance artist of any kind has, a tipping point where you take the jump from being part-time to full-time. And it's terrifying, because you have to do things like pack up your belongings and put them in storage, or sleep on your mum's sofa for a year.'

This can be the moment where it all becomes 'real'; where you've laid your cards on the table, and there's no going back. And, of course, it requires having a sympathetic support network of friends and family who'll put up with you being constantly broke, constantly hungry, and constantly bemoaning your lack of progress.

And if your ego can take that battering, then maybe you'll be able to commit to it, as rapper and actor Little Simz tells us.

'You need to figure out if this is something you enjoy because it's a cool hobby, or you want this to be your life. This is what separates the people that do make it, and the people that don't. Some people are willing to risk it all; people who will move to that place where they can achieve their dream. Very often it will work for them.'

For Little Simz, making music was something she believed in. And while she knew she was getting into it for all of the right reasons, it wasn't long before she had to face up to the situation it had put her in.

'You shouldn't be really doing it for the money. You should be doing it for the love and the passion, and because you can't imagine yourself doing anything else. Then the reality hits, and you think, "Cool, if this is going to take up most of my life, and I'm going to drop out of university, then this better pay off."'

In a realistic sense, the sooner you come to this revelation, the better. Like Little Simz, it can be helpful to get some perspective on where you are, by considering what you're actually giving up. If you're prepared to sacrifice your shot at higher education, or a cushy job, because you know you have got the talent and the drive to take you where you need to go, then you're probably temperamentally suited to the hardships and rewards that lie ahead. On the other hand, if you aren't comfortable with slumming it for an undetermined period of time –and this could be years – then maybe you're better treating music as a hobby, something you enjoy, but don't have to suffer to do. You're not likely to be able to become a massive success this way, but you've not lost anything in the process.

But if you can see past the risks and gambles, there can be huge treasures beyond that horizon.

'Of course it's possible to make money,' says Little Simz. 'I know people who've come from nothing and can afford to buy houses for their mums. Although just because it is possible, doesn't mean that it's going to happen. The people who made it happen put in the work.'

It didn't happen overnight for Little Simz, and she certainly put in the 'Work', but that's the kind of determination you need in order to turn this dream into a career.

For Two Door Cinema Club, years of grafting in small venues eventually translated to bigger gigs, album releases and, finally, money. And with their smart garms and jet-setting lifestyle, the three Northern Irish school friends seemed to be living the high life. But, as bassist Kev Baird explains, appearances can sometimes be deceiving.

'After a couple of years, we started to do quite well. A lot of people don't like to admit that there's still loads of money in music if you are willing to go out and get it. At the same time, a lot of people have a misconception: they think you are a billionaire because you've been on TV. Then you look at the PRS cheque for that show, and its £20.'

That amount of money doesn't split very well between three people but, right from the beginning, Kev and his two bandmates were committed to making it all work.

'We put everything into it in the first three years. I think it's a lot easier when you're younger and you have no commitments like we did, than to just do it when you get older and you have rent to pay, or a girlfriend, or responsibilities that mean you can't really put everything into it. If you believe in it, you have to put your time and money into it.'

This perseverance paid off eventually, and Two Door Cinema Club signed with their first label Kitsune Records. But while that can seem like scoring the end goal, you still have to be conscious of what you're signing up for, and how you manage your finances.

'The worst thing you can do is take loads of money from a label and commit to loads of albums. You always hear word on the street that some local band got a five-album deal from Fat Cat Records and that this is amazing. A label (advance) is just a big loan.'

At some point, the record label is going to want to see some of that money coming back in their direction and, if you've spent the whole advance on discovering what a grand piano would sound like when you play it from the deep end of a swimming pool, then there's going to be some difficult conversations between artist and label.

'No major record company will sign a new band without asking for a cut of your live shows and your merch sales. Their argument is that the album promotes the tour these days. It's daylight robbery. It takes a lot longer to turn a profit, and the size of shows you play have to be much bigger until you turn a profit.'

This kind of obligation means that you'll find yourself having to try and take your entire operation to a larger level, which will mean spending more money in order to make more money, the profits of which will likely then be filtered back into the record label to pay off the debts you drew up in the first place. Moral of the story: when the label offers you a stack of cash, spend it wisely, and only if you need to.

Frank Turner offers this cautionary tale. 'The obvious advice is to marshal your finances carefully. I have friends who've got signed, and then blown all the money in six months. Ration what you're doing. If you sign a publishing deal, that's got to keep you alive for a minimum of two years.'

Either way, regardless of how much money you owe the label, it's likely that touring is going to be one of the main sources of your cash flow. And in order to make money from touring, you'll need to graft to get to a certain level, and you'll be sorely disappointed if you expect to be rolling in dollar bills after your first mini-tour, crammed into the back of someone's van.

As Two Door's Kev Baird reveals, it takes time and money before you start seeing any of it coming back.

'The highest portion of our income comes from touring. We put the time in early on to go everywhere and lose money for years to be at the point where we can go and tour America, Europe, or Japan, and turn just as much of a profit as we can when we tour the UK.'

Album sales can contribute to this income, as can the all-important streaming revenue. It's up to you to make the most of any opportunity that presents itself. In Frank Turner's case, you take the money from wherever you make it, and you make it go as far as it can to allow you to keep doing what you love.

'I make money playing live, from radio play, and I make money from merchandise. Record sales generally break even, but I make a living and that's the important thing. It enables me to express myself and to tour and to not have another job, and that's a wonderful thing. In the early days, you're going to have to have crappy jobs in between tours. I spent years in telesales simply because they would let me walk out and go on tour for three weeks, and come back again without asking any questions.'

Who knows how many potential future music stars are engaged in telesales right now, but it's safe to imagine there are quite a few. Either way, while that might be difficult work, if it helps you stay afloat while you focus on what you love, then it's worth the pain.

And then, after all the graft, perhaps you get lucky. A song takes off, and you start seeing money come in, and suddenly your fortunes seem very different.

Simon Pursehouse, the Global Director of Music Services at Sentric Music highlights the difference one successful song can make.

'We have an artist who is on 16 or 17 million streams from one song that managed to get used on a television show. From that it picked up popularity and got put on playlists. Then it becomes a sustainable career for someone.'

Sentric's goal is to help artists get as much money as possible and, as far as Simon is concerned, artists shouldn't be picky about where that money is coming from.

'Long gone are the days of making money from selling records. It should be way down your priority list of making income. Maybe you make a couple of grand from sync, merch, tour, or your publishing income. It's about making money from a few different places. As an artist or a songwriter, you should aim to make enough money to allow you to wake up in the morning and all you have to think about is writing a song. There is no denying it's a tough old world, but it is doable.'

For Music Glue's Joe Porn, the key to all this is to never lose sight of your own business interests, and to make sure you don't cut off any potential income streams, perhaps even without knowing.

'We have acts on Music Glue that make far more on merch than they do on live performances, and there are others who make all their money live. There are some musicians who will be earning a thousand pounds a month on Spotify, but can't get any fans to come and see them live. The worst thing you can do is to have someone Google your act and it not to send them directly your page. You've got to get your online presence right, your shop, your website, the whole presence.'

It's not rocket science; if you want to make money from something, you need to work on the infrastructure that enables you to make that money, just like any other business. And if you're dealing with money, it's always advisable to hire professionals who can help keep your house in order, rather than going rogue and doing it on your own without any real experience or knowledge. For Little Simz, trusting the right people gave her the freedom to concentrate on the things she wanted to focus on.

'It's extremely important to have a good lawyer and a good accountant. As much as you think you might know about the business you're in, you actually don't know half of it. I can't understand all the terminology, so it's important to have someone versed in that area who knows that shit and is trustworthy in relaying every single detail back to you.'

That idea of 'trust' is important, and it extends to the kind of people you're going to encounter as you become more and more successful. After all, as Kev Baird reminds us, not everyone has your best interests at heart.

'People that we were never really close to you suddenly want to be your best mate. And you don't really understand why. It's really hard to trust people over time, because you're wondering how long it will be until they ask for a ticket to the show.'

On the bright side, that means – at the very least – they'd

like to see you play live, which is more than most artists can say for themselves. But not enough to pay for a ticket, obviously.

Ultimately, it's a hard slog to make music generate a decent income, but it definitely can be done. And if you have the determination, the right game plan, and the resilience to make it happen, then it might all work out fine for you. And even if you're just earning enough to scrape by, you're still getting by, and you're getting to do it by engaging in something you love.

And for an artist like Frank Turner, that's what it all comes down to – not limousines, private jets, fur coats, or crowns – just doing something you love.

'All of the costs – emotional, physical and comfort costs – of being a bottom-rung touring musician are vastly outweighed by the benefits of doing what you love, and from getting to share your music and express yourself on stage in front of an audience every night. That's worth more than all the costs put together. And if that calculus doesn't work for you, you shouldn't be doing it anyway.'

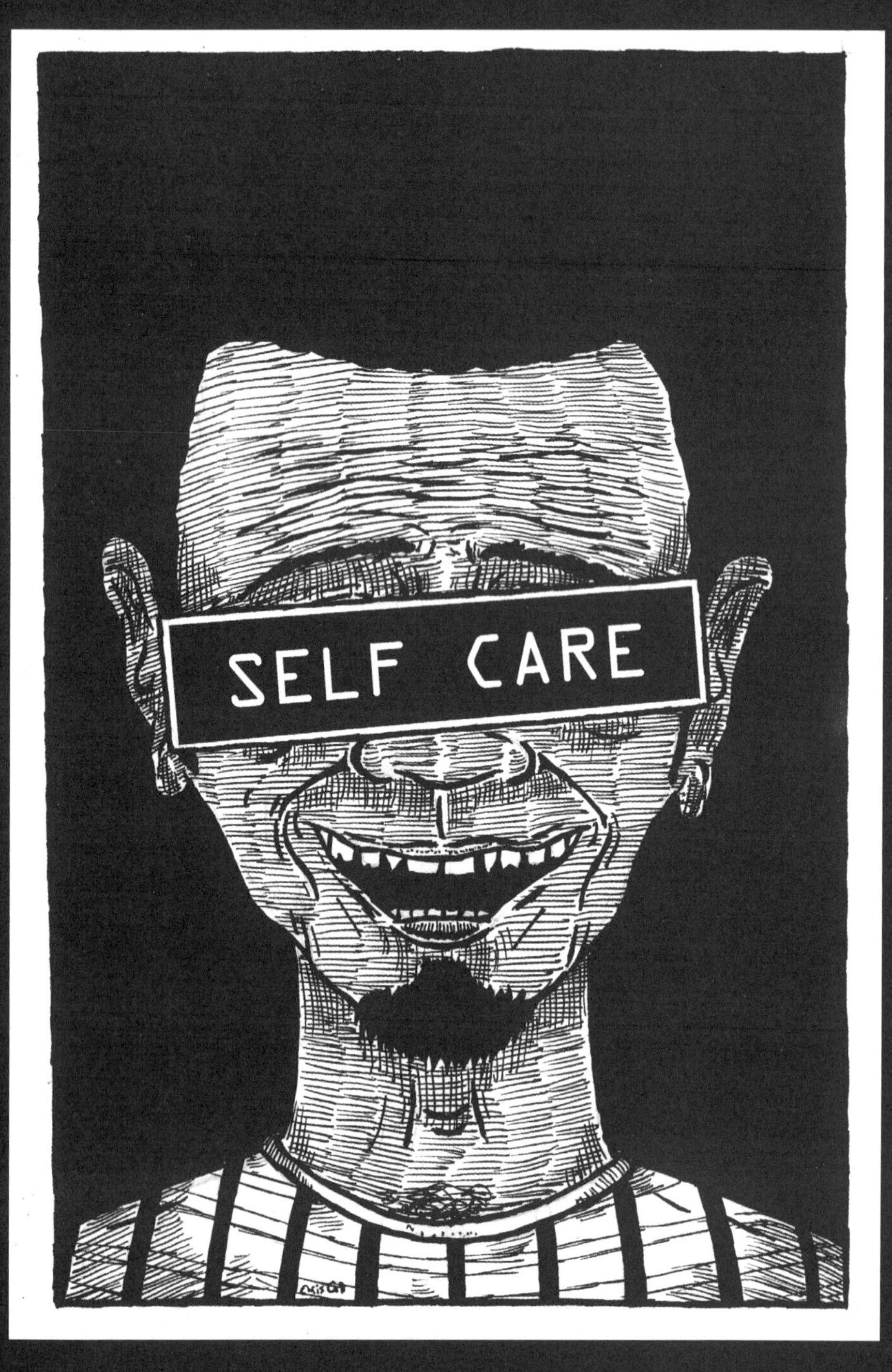
SELF CARE

Self-Care in Music

FEATURING ADVICE FROM:
Help Musicians UK
Music Support
Nadine Shah
Son of the Hound (Michael McCullagh)

If you've made it from the beginning to this final chapter, then your brain is probably like a shoal of sardines at a rave, screaming the alphabet backwards. It's hard to take in so much information, a lot of it often conflicting, and feel like you are coming out any the wiser. But trust me: there is no one-stop-shop answer on how to navigate your career. Yet there are tried and tested techniques and the advice of people who have legitimately conquered the music industry mountain and planted their little musical flag on top of it.

The many twists and turns of making your own music your career, can have a savage impact on your wallet, on relationships and, mainly and most frequently, on your mental health. Over the last few years, it's been refreshing to see artists come out and talk freely and with impunity about how they have suffered and how they recovered. It wasn't too long ago that if you showed any sign of weakness at all, it felt as if you risked losing it all. Thankfully labels, managers, and friends are starting to become a little more versed in the struggles of a musician. And, in turn, are giving artists a little more quarter. It still has some way to go, but the signs are good.

Researching this chapter on mental health, I was hit by many different statistics on how musicians and artists are more likely than most to suffer with mental health issues. This got me thinking: why is this the case? Are people who are creative and have the urge to express themselves more likely to feel the weight of the world on their shoulders? Is this constant struggle to be all things to all people (PR Guru, Social Media Wizz, Songwriting Legend, Performing Master, Studious Producer, etc) in order to get your music to the next level, a constant mind-fuck?

The answer has to be 'Yes' to all of these things, and an even louder 'YES' when you are doing everything completely on your own. This means it is very important to rationalise every step of the process, to celebrate and be kind to yourself when you attain every small goal, and not to beat yourself up when a release or a gig doesn't go as well as you hoped.

Every musician, big or small, has experienced this at some level. It's OK to not feel great, and taking the knock-backs is part of the process. Looking after yourself, and checking how you are doing, is very important.

As I mentioned many times in this book, I used to play in a band and when that stopped, I started a record label:

I'm a glutton for new project punishment. I've done all of these things with Generalised Anxiety Disorder which came on as a teenager. And when shit really hits the fan, it turns into full-on panic attacks. When I'm in the middle or towards the end of releasing a single or an EP, this usually steps up a gear as my own private expectations start to drive me to work too hard and put too much pressure on myself. I know that sometimes I work too hard, take on too much, and sometimes I lose the run of myself, becoming an introverted freak-out. But that's OK.

Personally, I've been taking steps and managing my expectations when releasing music. And to be honest, it has been working. It is a useful skill to train your brain to stop thinking that every piece of music you release into the world is a matter of life or death.

The idea of the lazy musician, or the struggling musician, is a well-worn trope. Usually it is followed by someone saying the most annoying, and utterly ridiculous, phrase that follows artists around: 'If you do something you love, you will never work a day in your life.'

What a steaming heap of crap!

If you work at something you love, you tend to get emotionally wrapped up in it. This means that the highs and lows you experience are profound. When you invest your own money, time, and creativity into something that you want to make your life and it doesn't work out, it can leave you deflated. There are countless numbers of people buying a ticket to this lottery, and only a few people will win. Which is why you should enjoy all the good sides of making music.

I was stressed to the eyeballs managing my band. Yet

with the benefit of hindsight, I wouldn't change a thing about it. The love we shared and the journey of being in a band are cherished memories I'll have forever. But, by God, did the process fuck with all of our heads. Try telling a bunch of headstrong teenagers that they won't be the biggest band in the world.

So, in this chapter we will have some personal stories from artists on how the music industry has impacted on their mental health, and also some of the processes they used to recover. We will also hear from Help Musicians UK and Music Support for some tangible tips on looking after yourself and about the services they offer.

I don't think enough people know that these organisations exist to help with musicians their mental health. So, if you know any musicians who are suffering and are in need of help, then please tell them about these organisations.

If that musician is you, then you should know that people, by their very nature, are mostly good and they want to help. So please don't suffer in silence. Speak to someone and get yourself on the road to recovery.

In the mythology of music, one thing that comes up time and time again is the idea of 'meaning it'. It's been the currency that critical reviews have thrived on for decades, and any number of 'best albums' lists are filled with music made by intense people who suffered for their art, and who poured every inch of that feeling into the grooves of the record.

And, sadly, they're also full of records made by people who didn't live to see their music feature on 'best of' lists.

Music can take a serious toll, and one of the easiest traps you can fall into is to believe that a happy, well-adjusted person can't make great music.

'Musicians are creative people and, generally speaking, creative people by nature are usually in tune with their feelings and emotions, as creativity is the artistic expression of feeling.'

Michael McCullagh is a writer and musician, also known as Son of the Hound. He previously played in a band called Colenso Parade, featuring a fantastically gifted and beautiful bassist (me). For him, it can be so easy to lose sight of the reality of the situation, in pursuit of some elusive goal of success.

'Like a lot of pursuits, you'll find yourself competing and comparing yourself to those who are working toward the same goal as yourself. What inevitably follows is a smoke-and-mirrors game that's damaging to everyone: keep a cool front on the socials, make it appear that every gig was seminal, that I have my shit together, that I am a professional who knows what they are doing. In doing that, you are unintentionally alienating yourself from others who are probably suffering the same existential crisis when it feels like everything is amounting to nothing.'

This competitive streak in musicians is pretty easy to relate to. Throughout this book, we've heard so many people talk about the uphill struggle to 'make it' in the industry. In simplistic terms, there's only so much money or attention to go around and, if someone is listening to my record, then they're not listening to yours.

So musicians struggle to make the most out of every opportunity, striving to push themselves as hard as they can. And they hope that every difficult step along the way brings them slightly closer to success, usually at someone else's expense. This is a world where someone else's downfall might well be your opportunity. It isn't pretty, but in many cases, that's the reality.

Except it doesn't have to be like that. And for Mercury Prize-nominated songwriter Nadine Shah, you can set your own terms in this race for the prize.

'Music is not a competition. You need to go at your own pace, and only you can decide what success is to you, and not be guided by someone else's definition. To me, success was accomplishing an instrument well enough so that I could finally compose my own songs, and to record and release an album. I achieved that, and have to remind myself often that I did it: I achieved what I set out to do. Now everything since is just a beautiful bonus.'

This is one of the healthiest ways to approach being a working musician. Obviously you have to put food on the table, and you're going to need money to do that. But in almost all cases, most musicians don't start making music purely for the money (although almost all musicians enjoy seeing the money come in, because they're only human, after all).

Being realistic, looking after yourself in a practical way, and setting achievable goals is one sure-fire way to keep yourself healthy, and it has the added side-effect of keeping you focussed. Take it one step at a time, and you can be sure you're doing it right.

This is easier said than done, obviously. In 2016, Help Musicians UK conducted a study into whether or not music was making people sick. The results are, quite frankly, shocking. They're also not entirely surprising.

Out of the 2,211 people who took part in the study, 71 percent believed they'd experienced panic attacks and high levels of anxiety. And 68 percent felt they were suffering from depression.

A big part of this came down to the poor working conditions that most musicians find themselves in. It's hard to sustain yourself as a jobbing musician. So when you're constantly having stress about where the next cash influx to your bank account is coming from, it has a serious impact on you. But, perhaps more worryingly, as a working musician you can expect to continually put yourself in an environment that is absolutely not conductive to a good, well-balanced mental outlook – pubs and clubs.

'For a lot of people during their formative years as a musician, it's a heinous and yet completely acceptable practice to be paid in beer,' explains Michael McCullagh. 'Break that down to its basest form: you are providing a service with a skill that you've worked incredibly hard to master, in exchange for a drug that is a depressant. There's nothing rock n'roll about it, you're poisoning your body and your mind, and it's a long descent from there. That is a broken system. If you're being paid in beer, the promoter isn't doing the job.'

We've already heard about promoters who will throw in a crate of cheap beers as your backstage rider. And when you're a struggling musician on the road, this frequently is no bad thing. Let's be honest, many people enjoy a drink. And if you're responsible, it can be managed and controlled. But if you're in a different venue every night, and you're making your way through a crate of beer every night, and you're not eating or drinking anything else, then you're on a difficult road. So it's vitally important to keep an eye on how you approach the environments you're going to find yourself in, as Nadine Shah reveals.

'I consider being a musician a proper job, but it's unlike any other job I've ever experienced. In what other professional environment would you be encouraged to drink on the job or to fulfil a task drunk? None.'

When you consider it as starkly as that, it no longer seems entirely reasonable to plough your way through a crate-load of beer every night – just because it's there. And make no mistake, it'll be tempting: waiting for soundchecks to finish, marshalling your energy as you wait to go on, sitting around doing nothing. There's plenty of opportunity to succumb to temptation. But just keep reminding yourself, this all adds up and it's part of a wider picture.

As Nadine tells us, this is your job, and whatever venue you're appearing in, that is your office.

'The hours are unpredictable and antisocial, the time spent away from home, the adrenaline highs and lows of performing, the effect of social media, and being constantly judged; all these factors contribute to a pretty unhealthy work life. And it doesn't just switch off. You don't just leave the office and forget about work. It's constant.'

On top of this, for most of us, a 'normal job' doesn't come with the added pressure of friends and family looking at you and wondering, 'When are they going to stop chasing a dream, and focus on more important things?'

Music is a career, and it has provided many with full-time employment, from the people involved in chasing up music copyright, or negotiating the minute details of record contracts, to the struggling manager trying to convince a member of an out-of-control metal band to behave themselves and make it through an airport without causing an international incident. They're all careers, and you can make a living from them.

On the other hand, if you're planning on working in a bank or on a construction site, then 'luck' doesn't play quite as much a role as it tends to in the entertainment industry. And this can be a real problem when you're working all the hours of the day on something you love and believe in, but seeing very little return on your investment, while you watch the bills start to pile up. For concerned friends and relatives, it can frequently feel like they are watching someone they care about throwing their future away in pursuit of something that doesn't seem likely to happen.

A relatively new addition to all this pressure is the world of social media. People are expected to live two lives now, and both come with their own set of problems. You might be struggling away, doing your best to just break even, but you'll still feel compelled to try convincing the world that you're living your best life, having a great time all the time, and just rolling around in your own success.

For Michael McCullagh, this illusory life has made things much more complicated.

'Social media is not real. Just remember that, because if you don't you will go demented. Be honest on it. If you're honest to who you are, potential fans will draw toward you organically. You won't have to jump through hoops and play the game to try and trick people into getting on board your hype train.'

At the same time, if you make an impact at all, other people are going to start talking about you. And that can come with its own set of particular problems.

For many musicians, the act of creating can be quite solitary, and can involve a process and meaning that is intimate and private to them. And it can be hard when the profound statement they have tentatively released into the world is utterly misunderstood by people nowhere near as invested in it as they are.

In this case, as Nadine Shah suggests, it's not always a good idea to read your own press.

'I don't constantly Google myself. That can be super damaging. I don't need to know what everybody thinks about me all of the time. If I get good reviews, my management will send them on to me to see. The negative comments are never constructive; they're just scathing and pointless. It's also worth mentioning that you need to accept that not everyone is going to like you and that's totally fine. It's personal preference, and I'm sure there's plenty artists whose music you don't like, that's just how it goes.'

But when someone is calling you out on the internet, and

you're at a low ebb, feeling the pressure from a number of different sources, it's not always that easy to just shrug it off and carry on.

Help is at hand, however. Rather than suffering in silence, and taking all this burden on your own shoulders, there are people and organisations you can reach out to. Matt Thomas is the co-founder and trustee of Music Support, a charity which has been able to help plenty of people along this journey. And for him, one of the first steps to getting help is acknowledging there's a problem, something that isn't quite as hard as it used to be.

'Mental health has become so much more recognised and validated. It's still often cloaked in "well-being," which is fine; and the buzzwords are "anxiety" and "depression" (when there's so much more to mental health, although these seem to be the cornerstones). But in general having mental health issues is more and more seen in the same light as having something like diabetes, which needs daily treatment and awareness.'

Rather than just offering general advice, Music Support is made up of people who have been through this process themselves, and they can relate to the difficulties a musician will face on a daily basis.

'Music Support is founded and run by people just like you, who have been through their own major struggles, and they understand what it's like, particularly in the context of the music industry. There's no judgment, only empathy. Please don't carry the load alone anymore.'

Music Support aren't the only organisation recognising the problems artists face. In December 2017, Help Musicians UK launched a round-the-clock mental health service and support line, 'Music Minds Matter,' for people working in music at any level, not just high-profile artists. Through extensive research, they have been able to highlight a wide spectrum of issues that are likely to affect musicians, and are working towards providing support and resources. Here is a quick link to the site for more information - https://www.musicmindsmatter.org.uk/

If you've decided to make a go of it as a full-time musician, it's likely that you're a certain kind of person. You'll be driven by a creative urge, something that burns inside you and compels you to express yourself in a particular way. You're most likely the kind of person who can't see how anyone could be satisfied behind a desk, and you'll have a restless imagination that will likely take you to some incredible places.

At the same time, there's a largely likelihood that you'll be hugely self-critical, and you will have to get used to existing in an environment of constant criticism. A lot of this criticism will come from your peers, and that'll feed into your competitive drive.

You'll almost certainly not have much in the way of cash, and will be forced to either slum it, or work several jobs at once, just to get by. And as your peers seem to sail by you on a wave of success that somehow seems elusive to you, there's every possibility you'll not feel like you're in a position to reach out for help from anyone. You won't be the first person to feel like this, and sadly, you won't be the last.

Help Musicians know this, and they're continuing to work hard to make it a thing of the past.

They launched Music Minds Matter in response to their research and, in partnership with the music industry, they have committed to long-term support for those in the music community with mental health challenges. They have trained support staff who can listen to you confidentially at any time of the day or night, and they're able to offer emotional support, advice, and information, even pointing you in the right direction for other specialist services, including debt and legal advice, as well as access to Help Musicians UK grants.

Help Musicians UK health and welfare grants offer financial support for a wide variety of circumstances, whether that's help during a crisis, disability, long-term illness or retirement. They also have specialist schemes, like the Musicians' Hearing Health Scheme, which gives people working in music affordable access to specialist hearing assessments and bespoke hearing protection. The Emerging Musicians Health scheme offers grants towards the cost of health care (psychological or physical) if a performance-related condition interrupts music studies or getting started in the music industry.

This hasn't quite eradicated mental health issues altogether, but it is a massive step in the right direction, and Help Musicians are aware that there's still plenty of work to be done. Across the industry, meanwhile, there is an immense amount of work being done by other organisations to address mental health issues among musicians. For example, the Music Managers Form (MMF) has produced a 'Music Managers Guide To Mental Health', Music Support, a charity supporting people in music with mental health and addiction issues, has launched a Safe Tents initiative at festivals, and Help Musicians UK is working with the British Association of Performing Arts Medicine (BAPAM), amongst others, to look at the pathways of support for people across the industry.

Crucially, musicians themselves have started to acknowledge that they need to change things on their own level. A few years ago, it wouldn't have been too common to hear musicians talking to each other about their own mental health struggles, but there's been a shift in recent times. People at all levels seem more open to communicating with each other, and that openness might just be the key in encouraging people who really need support to reach out for help.

What all this amounts to is a climate in which you will still face incredible hurdles, but there's a whole group of people who are in a position to give you support to reach your goal in the most painless way possible.

For Matt Thomas of Music Support, you just need to talk.

'Firstly, don't give up. You are not alone. There's so many people who have been through exactly what you're going through, and would be so happy to help. They are just a phone call away, and if you can't face that, you can send a note through the website. Sometimes even taking that first step can feel like a massive relief. Don't forget you are not committing to anything by getting in contact.'

Through it all, just remind yourself that you're not alone.

I'll leave you with the words of Michael McCullagh, who will – in turn – leave you with the words of the late, great Joe Strummer.

'You can desire to be great and still maintain a sense of solidarity. It's better for everyone's head. As Joe Strummer said, "Without people, you're nothing."'

Epilogue

OK, before you start, I know that was a lot of information to take in. So nice work, you're a determined legend for doing so! At times, reading this may have riled you up to the point of frenzy about your prospective career in the music business, and at other times made you think the whole thing is more complicated than brain surgery in space. This is a good feeling to have; it shows that you care and are willing to take your hard work to the next stage.

I can't begin to tell you how many people I pestered when my band was starting out. Anyone remotely older or borderline wiser was asked for their email address, to which they would receive a thousand questions. That's why I wrote this book. It's for all the people who are keen to learn, people who want to make something of themselves and their music, but who don't have the foggiest idea how to start. I spent years and years trying to figure it all out, and I took so many left turns I turned into a roundabout.

Personally, I think musicians should spend more time

writing songs and developing music than emailing and networking. Those things are remarkably easy when your music is good.

The harsh reality of the whole thing is, no matter if you follow this book and hustle 24/7, you won't get anywhere if your music isn't up to standard. If you feel that it's not, it's better to start again, than to try to draw attention to the sub-par tunes you plan to showcase. There's always time to rehearse and develop, it's just better sometimes to do that in private and arrive back to the world all shiny and amazing, rather than half-baked.

There's one way to make life easier for yourself, and that's to become an active and engaged member of your local music scene. There will always be like-minded souls who love to create and who are endeavouring to go down the same path as you. Even if you don't all love the same records or bands, you are all in it for the same reason – because you love what you do.

Once you get your hands mucky by getting involved, you'll quickly realise that the pool of potential people to help your project has expanded enormously. Some of the skills they possess may well be handy for your project and vice versa. It's important to help other musicians, and in turn that love will be shown back.

When you set out hell-bent down one path, it is not unusual to slipstream off along the way. If you had told me at eighteen that I wouldn't be in the world's best rock and roll band by the age of 30, I would have thought you were chatting through your back passage. Similarly, if you told me I would be a DJ on BBC Radio 1 playing new music, I would have thought the same!

I started down the route to musical stardom, but along the way I learnt a lot about myself. Several years in, it was clear that my skill in the band was less about musical craftsmanship or learning my instrument, but on the hustle and showing off. This meant that, when the opportunity arose to get into radio, I grabbed it, and everything changed for me.

What I am getting at is this: don't be surprised if you end up somewhere other than where you set out for. It's a topsy-turvy journey going it alone or with a band. It's better to be flexible and go with the flow, than to stick rigidly to a one-way plan.

Lastly, thank you for reading the book. It means a lot! I hope you get something useful from it and that it frees up a little headspace for yourself. It wasn't designed to make anyone famous or get you to the top of the charts. It was researched and written to take some of the heavy lifting and anxieties out of the question: 'Well, what do we do now?'

Good luck Slackers, I look forward to hearing your music!

Notes

Notes

Notes